PURE VEGETARIAN

SACRED AND TRADITIONAL RECIPES FROM SOUTH INDIA

PREMA SRINIVASAN

HarperCollins *Publishers* India

First published in India by Westland Books Ltd 2013
This edition published by HarperCollins *Publishers* India 2024
4th Floor, Tower A, Building No. 10, DLF Cyber City,
DLF Phase II, Gurugram, Haryana – 122002
www.harpercollins.co.in

2 4 6 8 10 9 7 5 3 1

P-ISBN: 9789354897351
E-ISBN: 9789354897368

Typeset in Baskerville URW and Forma DJR Text
Design by Haitenlo Semy

Printed and bound at
Thomson Press (India) Ltd

To

The Transcendental Essence
of the Cosmos which is No-thing

To

The Maternal and Material Forces that nourished
us as vegetarians for many generations and

For

J. Krishnamurti,
Ascetic and Aesthete at once,
who understood the Material and the Transcendental

CONTENTS

THE PURE PATH: VEGETARIAN COOKING

(Identity and Culinary Tradition)

Food is an integral part of culture. Food is about identity. It embodies beliefs that define a family's traditions. Food as a ritual is about what is appropriate for every occasion as well as what is good. A study of food is interestingly a study of the cultural anthropology of a community. Prema Srinivasan has done just that. By focusing on the vegetarian traditions of the Srīvaiṣṇavas (and more broadly Brahmins) of the southern part of India, she delves into the religious and cultural beliefs and practices embedded in the preparation and the consumption of food. She starts with 'why vegetarianism', which is an article of faith among Brahmins. As priests, the commitment to prayer, worship and the rituals associated with it defined much of a Brahmin's life. It is no surprise that the food offering in temples or at homes, as part of their prayer, is an ancient tradition. The offerings that are so 'blessed by god' through a devotee's prayer is then offered as 'prasādam'. The Vishnu temples have elaborate rituals focused on 'offerings' and prasādam. The traditional south Indian food takes a new meaning from this perspective.

Vegetarianism was not confined to temples and offerings associated with prayer. It was an integral part of daily life. Adherence to vegetarianism defined one's identity.

Mrs Srinivasan moves on to examine the changing identity of south Indian vegetarians as various ideas and tastes from other parts of India and the west permeate their culture through food. A commitment to vegetarianism may remain intact but the preferences have changed. There is now a lot more experimentation and innovation in food in India. My wife and I have had the privilege of enjoying Mrs Srinivasan's creative innovations in food while maintaining a strict vegetarian diet. This discussion provides a unique insight into how a particularly proud and somewhat insular community is changing. This is a sign of vitality. India is changing rapidly as well.

Mrs Srinivasan has done us all a great service by providing a unique cultural perspective on south Indian Brahmins through the lens of food. For those who want to experience it, she has provided easy-to-follow recipes.

C.K. PRAHALAD

(Paul and Ruth McCracken Distinguished University Professor, Ross School of Business, University of Michigan)

PREFACE

There are many cookbooks out there but the reasons for writing this one are distinctive. First, this text, along with its accompanying recipes and explanations, documents the history of a vegetarian food sensibility that was nurtured in an orthodox home, bound by traditions. Second, it records the regional cuisines of India and several international delicacies that fit more generally into a sātvik vegetarian ethos—sātvik meaning the quality of purity and goodness.

Beginning my experiences in the kitchen as a young girl of seventeen who could make only one dish, uppuma, and that too through sheer instinct and memory, I grew to delight in the amazing and unlimited variety of 'pure vegetarian' dishes from around the world, particularly influenced by the vegetarian cuisine of Italy and that of the Chinese–Buddhist temples. These non-Indian culinary traditions also assign an important place to the vegetables that form an indispensable part of the daily menu of pure vegetarians.

The use of condiments and the methods of south Indian cuisine are common to the Srivaiṣnava, Smārta and Madhwa traditions of the southern Indian states, with a few regional variations for taste and innovation. This sensibility, the belief in a pure vegetarian ethos, is not unique to these communities alone. Many families from Rājapālayam, Tondaimandalam and Kongunādu follow rigorous vegetarian principles by choice. Wealthy and cultured, the Ārya Vaiśyas who originated from Andhra and settled down in Tamil Nadu and Karnataka are strict vegetarians. What is more, their cooks are also from pure vegetarian communities. This tradition of pure vegetarianism belongs to all these groups and to others of whom one may not be aware.

Central to all these cuisines is the code of yama, moderation; and niyama, which is ahimsā or non-violence, which means not to hurt any living thing—a code laid down by Vedic seers. Another important belief, that is common not only to these groups but to the whole of India, is the vital importance of sharing one's food with others.

Given the historical importance of the Jaina religion in south India, vegetarian cuisine of the type discussed in this book was well-known and widespread in multiple communities and linguistic contexts at different points in time. Even in present-day practice, where food of this type competes for space in modern India with multiple regional and international cuisines, these recipes and their variants are familiar not just to the particular community in Tamil Nadu, Karnataka and Andhra Pradesh, but also to other communities. For this reason, we should not make the mistake of communalizing this cuisine. Rather, we should see it as a cuisine that travels across religious communities, historical periods and regions.

South Indian society, in the decades running up to Indian independence in the twentieth century, was a composite whole. The Madras Presidency—as it was known then—comprised areas of Tamil Nadu, (then) Andhra Pradesh, Kerala and two districts of Odisha. Knit by the free exchange of language, culture and cuisine, that period was a time of great understanding and harmony across this region.

Living in Madras, as it was called then, many of us were familiar with the customs of all the southern states. Friends and neighbours were from all the regions, and there was friendship and mutual love and respect amongst all of us, when state-wide divisions had not yet emerged to separate us.

Language was not a barrier for understanding stories or music. Carnatic (south Indian classical) music was appreciated all over the South. This commonality made it easy for us to enjoy the stories from the purāṇās and the epics told by the famous harikatha exponents Banni Bai and Saraswati Bai who would speak and sing in a mixture of Tamil, Marathi, Kannada and Telugu. Their powerful stories and cultural performances moulded our thoughts and influenced our conduct.

Cooks from Andhra and Mysore were brought specially to cook for weddings. Dishes from those areas were liked and accepted as one's own. The New Year's Day of these two regions, Yugādi and Kerala's Vishu, were celebrated with as much fervour as Tamil New Year's Day.

As many more began to travel to other parts of India for the sake of work, and some worked for long years in Delhi, Bombay, Calcutta or Ahmedabad, and even as far north as Kashmir, the culinary delicacies of those places became familiar in the South as they were brought back and slowly became part of our menu, appearing daily as 'tiffin' or as special dishes for various occasions.

Towards the end of the century, the pan-Indian circle of cuisine was complete. North Indian food came to dominate many wedding menus as their preparations were considered better suited to a guest list that showed a wide mix of communities and regions. It has become a pattern now to serve the standard south Indian menu for the morning (with the variations showing up only in the sweets), while the evening wedding reception has dishes from all corners of India.

Newer influences are now entering the 'authentic' cuisine that I started out knowing. Cooking methods, too, are today influenced by Euro-American and East Asian techniques and flavours. Drastically, food has come to be associated with 'fast food', a method that seems to have swept across the country, so much so that we do not seem to know—let alone understand—the subtleties of flavours and tastes within Indian regional cooking. The tongue accommodates what is given to it, and over time, all discrimination is lost. What can we expect from a society that now eats standing up?

This book is an attempt to preserve old recipes and gentler ways of cooking. The recipes represent sātvik vegetarian cooking from south India, while also spanning across communities and regions. Some recipes have had their origin in other parts of India but their popularity and usage in the South stretches back more than 150 years. These dishes now form an accepted part of the daily menu in many south Indian homes.

Many of the recipes in this book are easy to prepare and have been experimented with and enjoyed by family and friends at my home. Several recipes can be tried out successfully even by a first-time cook while others are more complex and may require more effort and practice.

I hope that my efforts will attract the attention and interest of contemporary readers as well as all those who wish to acquaint themselves with a pure but diverse vegetarian cuisine that is both traditional and personalized.

PREMA SRINIVASAN

INTRODUCTION

The first edition of *Pure Vegetarian* opened with the chapter on 'Sacred Offerings' with an extensive bouquet of recipes, twenty-two in all. The recipes ranged from the extremely esoteric Alagar Koil Dosai and Kānchipuram Idli to highly skilled preparations like Akkara Adisil and Tiruvadirai Kali to simpler dishes like Kondakadalai Sundal and Dadhiyodanam. All twenty-two dishes are linked to different temples and are considered special to the deities residing there.

I opened with 'Sacred Offerings' because for millennia, food that is not offered to a deity before consumption has been considered the equivalent of eating waste. Ancient religious traditions had the concept of sharing food with the wider community and this idea of sharing was often given a divine sanction. Thus, the Rig Veda has this to say:

> *'He who nourishes neither God nor a friend*
> *He who eats alone gathers sin.'* (X.117)

Many traditional communities in India will never partake of food at home before offering it to the deity. On ordinary days, just cooked rice with a little ghee is offered to the family deity—sadam (cooked rice) thus becomes pra-sadam, blessed by God, indeed a 'gracious gift'. Festival days and other celebrations, however, have a more elaborate and strict protocol regarding the menu to be prepared. A sweet, usually a pāyasam (whether with milk, rice or lentils), sometimes sarkarai pongal, and vadai are part of a mandatory menu for all such auspicious occasions. Besides this, specific preparations are earmarked for festivals and religious days in the calendar.

On Rāma Navami, the birthday of Sri Rāma, the special offerings are pānakam (a spiced jaggery drink) and thin buttermilk. In contrast to this simple fare, a whole array of delicacies is spread out for the baby Krishna on Krishna Jayanthi, his birthday. On Vinayaka Chathurthi day, the birthday of Lord Vinayaka, kolukattai or rice dumplings is the preferred choice (modak, a different version, is made in north India).

A secular festival like the Indian New Year is celebrated in most states of India on almost the same day in the year. The Indian New Year has distinctive names in different states: in Tamil Nadu, it is called Varushapirappu; in the Andhra region, it goes by the name of Yugadi; in Kerala, it is Vishu; Maharashtra's is Gudi Padwa; Punjab has Baisakhi; Bengalis call their new year Poila Boishakh; and in Assam and the Northeast, they celebrate Bohag Bihu. The Indian New Year that falls in the month of April coincides with the harvest season when the earth shares its bounty. The mango trees are in full bloom, and the ground is carpeted with the pale whitish-green and yellow neem flowers, with mango and neem mingling their mild distinct scents and enveloping the air around them.

A special pacchadi, a vegetable salad in a tamarind dressing, is an indispensable part of the New Year menu, at least in all the southern states. This is the veppampoo pacchadi, made with mango and fresh neem flowers, a simple dish of six ingredients representing the six different tastes: neem flowers (bitterness), jaggery (sweetness), mango (astringency), tamarind (sourness), red chillies (pungency) and salt (saltiness). This dish carries a philosophical import beyond mere taste. The shadrasa or six different tastes reminds us of the varied experiences that life can hold for us in the coming year. It also reminds us also to face every experience, whatever it may be, with equanimity.

Puran poli is the speciality for Bhogi, the day before Pongal, a preamble to the festivities and the abundance of food items to follow in the coming days. Tiruvadirai kali, a sweet made with broken rice and jaggery, is the sacred offering made to Lord Shiva on his birthday, the title bearing the name of his birth star, Tiruvadirai. So also Navaratri, the nine nights of the three goddesses of wealth, knowledge and valour, prescribes many different sundal preparations with a variety of lentils for each evening. Sundals are legume preparations high in protein, made by tempering cooked legumes with spices and grated coconut. During Navaratri, navadanyams or nine different legumes are prepared each day, offered to the goddesses and distributed to the guests.

Annam being offered to the household deity was perhaps the first sacred offering. From the home, the offering of annam became a rite in the temple. With the passage of time, the simple annam offering evolved into a great diversity of special preparations being offered in temples on festival days and special calendar days. This has now become an inevitable part of our tradition and faith. To look for and to receive the Lord's blessing in the form of food is part of our visceral consciousness.

Our memories of travels to the temples of south India are not only about the deities we beheld there but also the food that we received from each temple. We feel an intense disappointment if we are unable to receive the prasadam in a temple, for whatever reason. One such incident was when we were told that we should have reserved the previous day for the famed Ambalapuzha pāl pāyasam prasādam! A sense of deprivation engulfs us, quite out of proportion to the fact.

In contrast, when we reach the temple at Terazhundur after a long and dusty journey and find the temple under renovation, that our regret at not attaining a glimpse of the deity is greatly assuaged by the warm hospitality of the priest who offered us vattal kuḷambu (a tamarind-based kuḷambu without dal) and tayir sadam (the iconic curd-rice of Tamil Nadu). Though, in the manner of many temple offerings, both preparations had more rice than curd and kuḷambu, to this day, we feel that those simple dishes gave us more joy and satisfaction than any gourmet feast!

A natural extension to 'Sacred Offerings' in this new edition of *Pure Vegetarian* is the culinary preparations that are of particular importance for auspicious occasions or for household deities in the different regions of India.

The cuisines of the diverse regions of our country depend upon the crops and vegetables grown in those areas, or the seasonal varieties available during festivals or the microclimates of that particular region. Cultural and traditional practices over many hundreds of years also play a part in the choice of preparations to be made on each occasion.

This book is a collection of vegetarian recipes. During the research undertaken for the book, it was found that for the most part, only vegetarian preparations are offered in temples or to household deities on celebratory occasions. This is true of all communities and provinces in India. We find that elaborate sacred offerings are a feature of south Indian temples. Most north Indian temples usually offer packets of sugar crystals, sometimes a raksha (an amulet) blessed by the deity.

The home kitchen has gone through many metamorphoses. Some of us do remember the kitchen of old. The kitchen of olden times and the food prepared there shared an ambience and characteristics that are still cherished in memory. The simple appointments of the old Indian kitchen with its firewood stoves, smoked walls, the milk safe (with mesh sides and its four legs standing in bowls of water to discourage ants and other insects) and vessels and groceries at hand, lent an additional flavour to the food cooked in that atmosphere. Often, the kitchen doubled as the dining room. Everybody was seated on the floor on wooden manais (some beautifully ornamented with brass or silver at the corners, also part of a bridal dower), or woven mats.

Plantain leaves were laid out in the proper direction with the tip of the leaf on the left of the person seated. The many dishes on the celebratory menu have their particular place on the leaf: starting with half a teaspoon of sugar placed on the top right of the banana leaf, or sugar mixed in milk at the bottom right, the cooked dal below the divider of the leaf, the pickle at the top left, the vegetables cooked in different ways, in a row at the top of the leaf, with cooked rice taking its central place in the middle of the leaf. When three teaspoons of ghee have been served on the rice, it is time to start eating! It is a practice in some communities to serve the rice first as tradition forbids us from the merest taste of any other food before rice is served.

Almost all houses then had plantain trees. Catapa badam and bauhinia trees were common. The leaves of all these trees were made into plates, both for serving food and for packing, all biodegradable. Jackfruit leaves lent themselves as wrappers for cooking certain foods while the versatile plantain leaf was further dried and made into small plates for serving, siragus as they are called. It was a fine aesthetic sense that took the outer sheaths of the banana stem, flattened them, and used them as lovely silvery side plates for salads, fritters or pickles.

Now we have the most wonderful modular kitchens with state-of-the-art gadgets to make our work easier. But we have to work standing up, and bend and stretch in order to reach for our vessels, while cooks in the past, and even now in many village homes, sit on the floor or on short stools to cut vegetables and use the stove, a practice that is kind to old bones and muscles!

It is a saner option to move with the times, and modern equipment and techniques are certainly useful, yet we do yearn for the soft vibrations and calm atmosphere of olden kitchens. Perhaps it reflected the gentler cadences of a simpler life, now no longer available to us. With the alcove or altar for the household deity in the kitchen itself or just off to its side, the food prepared in that kitchen also partook of the purity and blessing of the divinity that resided there.

BEGINNINGS

I grew up in Chennai, in the heart of Mylapore, in the shadow of the gopuram of the Kapaleeswarar Temple. Ours was an orthodox middle-class Tamil household that believed in simplicity. The strong values in our home mirrored the vibrant culture outside. The temple not only nurtured our faith but also sustained our traditions with its flower decorations and lamps and the festive joy of our utsavams, when we were surrounded by fine music and dance.

Food was an integral part of our lives. Festivals meant special menus and delicacies that were different from everyday fare. Growing up in this environment, we learned important lessons about food—food as nutrition, food as an indulgence, food as worship, food as medicine.

My paternal grandfather perhaps had the earliest influence on my continuing love for food. He had strong preferences and a say in what was put on the table. Vegetables have always been the mainstay of vegetarian food, and my grandfather insisted on a minimum of four vegetable preparations at every meal. No vegetables were off-limits, except onions and garlic.

Though the everyday menu in our home was simple, (a kuḷambu, sātramudhu, two steamed and sautéed vegetables, a kūtu, a salad or kosumalli, wafers, vatral or fried pappads), there was no compromise on the quality of the ingredients used. Groceries were bought at the beginning of each month and staples like rice and dals, tamarind and condiments were bought at the beginning of the year or during harvest time. I still remember my grandfather coming home in a bullock cart hauling provisions for the month.

In addition to rice and spices, ghee (clarified butter) is an indispensable ingredient in Indian cooking and Ayurvedic practice. It also played an important role in rituals. The first serving of rice or any food was considered pure only after it was topped with a dollop of ghee. Ghee was homemade, prepared by churning butter, a daily ritual in almost every home. Sometimes the milkmaid would bring home churned butter and boil it to make ghee. When the hot ghee was taken off the fire, all of us children would hold out our palms to sample the first tasty spoonfuls. When the clear liquid is strained, a delicious sediment is left behind. This is eaten with hot rice, a combination called kasandu sādam.

Our kitchen at home was supervised by my mother and aunt. Since everything cooked at home was offered to the family deity everyday, women in Śrivaiṣṇava homes did not cook on a daily basis and children were not allowed to cook. Women, however, ran the milk and coffee counters in an ante kitchen. Here, they also prepped vegetables which were expected to be cut beautifully, kneaded dough and rolled out chapattis and puris expertly. Children participated in some of these duties. In that lively Mylapore kitchen, I learned not only about the immense variety of vegetables that were a part of the Tamil vegetarian menu but also the innumerable ways in which these could be prepared.

I also learnt the virtue of frugality. An example would be the 'natural' side plates we made with banana leaf or badam (catappa terminala) leaves. My grandfather would stitch the outer banana stems which gleamed like ivory, with sticks from coconut fronds, to make the plates.

Life in that simple Mylapore home formed the foundation of my interest in many areas—food, art, music, textiles. I learned about different kinds of cloth textures from the weavers who came home with their goods. There were some skills that were very gender specific and that every young girl was expected to know. Learning to draw rice flour designs, the auspicious kolam, was one such skill. Stringing flowers was another. Living next to the temple, the fragrance of flowers was always in the air—jasmine, lotuses and light pink roses or 'silk' roses.

Marriage brought with it new experiences. I moved into a large household in Madurai with a close extended family, many of whom were devout Gandhians. Those were the years immediately after independence. A sister-in-law who was a medical doctor had been raised in Wardha under the direct influence of Gandhiji and established Gandhigram, bringing many visitors to our house. Our home was open to everyone and became the training ground where I learned to entertain people from different backgrounds.

I learned a lot in those years. From my mother-in-law, I learnt about quality—in her old age, in spite of her failing eyesight, she was able to turn out masterly murukkus. Another sister-in-law taught me many menu combinations and the proper way in which food was to be served. An aunt-in-law taught me to make homemade collyrium, herbal oil for black locks and other cosmetic items.

My experiences are not unique. I share them with the girls who grew up during that time. It was a different world with a different value system.

My knowledge about food expanded with my move to Chennai. I was already familiar with the pure vegetarian conventions of Thanjavur and Kumbakonam, and the local food and regional favourites of Madurai and Tirunelveli. In Chennai, friends from other parts of the country taught me about their cuisines. Travel to foreign countries introduced me to mildly flavoured vegetarian foods. All this helped me see India and the world as bound together by common threads of spices, herbs, vegetables and cereals, and understand the commonality of a pure vegetarian ethos.

At the end of it all, if one were to be asked *why* a cookbook, one can only quote Dr Samuel Johnson who said that man is a cooking animal and would always be interested in food and ways of cooking it. Perhaps we should change it slightly and affirm that it is the woman who is a 'cooking animal' and who will always be curious about food in all its aspects.

VEGETARIANISM

Anthropological evidence reveals that almost all human beings were members of societies in which some particular vegetarian was considered 'good'. Because plant domestication and purposeful cultivation increased the stability of food supply and in consequence the human population itself, most of us and our ancestors during these past ten or twelve thousand years have subsisted primarily on one sort of vegetarian food.

The word 'vegetarian', coined by the founders of the British Vegetarian Society in 1842, comes from the Latin word vegetus, meaning 'whole, sound, fresh, or lively' as in homo vegetus—a mentally and physically energetic person. The British idea of vegetarianism was possibly derived from the ideal of the Indian yogi.

Yogic practice and philosophy accepts a sātvik (pure) vetegarian diet as one that promotes balance and mental clarity. This is based on the belief that a yogi is one who lives with compassion and practises ahimsā (non-violence), and therefore naturally leads a vegetarian way of life.

Having evolved over several millennia, vegetarianism is for many Indians, both a diet and a philosophy. In Europe, on the other hand, vegetarianism is a relatively recent development, despite ancient adherents like Pythagoras and Leonardo da Vinci. While there are early records of ritual vegetarian cuisine in China and other parts of East Asia, India has the longest continuous history of vegetarianism. Over the centuries, with its abundance of vegetables, varieties of spices and array of cereals, India's vegetarian cuisine has developed into a remarkable and unique tradition.

In India the idea of vegetarianism held sway as a spiritual way of life right from Vedic times. The Bhagavad Gita emphasizes the role of ahimsā in the spiritual growth of man:

> सुहृदं सर्वभूतानां ज्ञात्वा मां शान्तिमृच्छति ॥
> One who knows Me as the friend of all living things, attains peace.

There is a Western misconception that vegetarianism grew alongside the rise of Buddhism. However, Jainism, with its rigorous discipline of vegetarianism and ahimsā, predates Buddhism by at least 1,000 years. From the time of Vrishabha Deva, the first Jain Tirthankara, vegetarianism has been propagated in a systematic way in India. Vedic seers like Brahmanāndi also gave importance to sātvik food. Brahmanāndi believed that ahārasuddhi (purity of food) gave one strong focus and discriminating powers.

Tiruvalluvar, a Tamil poet and philosopher, devoted a complete chapter in the *Tirukkural*, a treatise on ethics, to the humaneness of vegetarianism. He lauded not only those who refrained from killing animals but also those who refused to eat meat. According to Tiruvalluvar, the whole world pays obeisance to ethical non-meat eaters. These teachings likely converted many in the South to vegetarianism.

With the spread of Jainism (around 400 BCE), more people in north India began to follow a vegetarian way of life. Around the first century CE, Jain ideas and influences spread across south India. Its central principle, the idea of ahimsā as a way of life, gained ascendancy in the Tamil country.

The growth of the Bhakti movement (devotion to a personal god) in south India in the fifth century CE and the surge of the movement in the North during the twelfth century helped to establish vegetarianism as a fundamental and enduring Indian tradition.

The seventh century CE witnessed the rise of Śaivism and the waning of Jainism. Śaivism gained greater momentum in the South, when the ailing Pāndya king could not be cured by his Jain physicians but was miraculously restored to health by the blessings of Lord Śiva. As a result, the king and the majority of his subjects, including the Jains, embraced śaivism. The practice of vegetarianism began to be associated śaivism and called śaivam while the eating of meat came to be called aśaivam.

In the North, however, the vaiṣṇavās were well known as vegetarians and the followers of a sātvik ahimsā tradition. Thus, vegetarian food in northern India was referred to as vaiṣṇava food and now as Jain food.

The North–South Connection

Cuisines of south India are distinctive, but we would be making a mistake if we assumed that north Indian food is never eaten in the South and vice versa. Many north Indian recipes have become part of the south Indian kitchen, including certain sacred offerings. It is therefore not incongruous if a cookbook about south Indian vegetarian food includes some recognizably north Indian recipes that have been absorbed into south Indian culinary contexts over centuries.

For instance, a mītha chaval also known as kesari bhāth, a typical Rajasthani recipe, is familiar in Tamil Nadu and rotis with ghee and sugar are offered to the Lord at Srirangam and to Sri Ramanuja at Sriperumbudur. It was common for Brahmin scholars to undertake long journeys within India in the centuries past. From as early as the seventh century CE, Kashi (Varanasi) was a centre of learning and attracted scholars versed in Sanskrit, the lingua franca of the educated. This religious travel to Kashi continued till the turn of the twentieth century.

Ādi Śankara in the ninth century CE travelled as far north as Kedar and Badri, establishing maths and temples there. In the east, he visited the Jagannath and Lingaraja temples in Orissa, and ordained that though a Śiva temple, the Lingaraja should also distribute prasādam to the devotees as the Jagannathji and Ananta Vasudeva temples did. The acharya also went to Kashmir. So did Sri Ramanuja and his chief disciple Sri Kurathāḷwan who went in search of a valuable religious manuscript. Many more maths disseminating the three vedantic philosophies, the Advaita, Visishtadvaita and Dwaita, were established in and around Badrinath and other important pilgrimage sites of the North by gurus from the South. These religious institutions had local followers who shared their local vegetarian food traditions with visiting pilgrims.

The acharyas and the people of their entourage were strict vegetarians. They associated with the priests and the pandas of the temples in the area they travelled to and learned local vegetarian recipes and brought them back to their southern towns. This is why north Indian dishes and cooking techniques are familiar in the South, like Kashmiri ways of preparing vegetables and Rajasthani recipes like rasedars or sāgus (gravied vegetables). A side dish for rotis with gravy is still called sāgu in Karnataka.

The influence of the Jains was very strong in the South and in Tamil Nadu, where they had lived from 1 CE. They wielded power in many areas till the eighth century CE in Tamil Nadu and up till the twelfth century in Karnataka. The Tathachariars of Sri Rangam were the carriers of the Visishtadvaita belief to Rajasthan and Gujarat for more than 300 years right up to 1940. Temples were established in Jodhpur, Patan, Jamnagar, and Pushkar by their disciples. The Lakshminārayana temple in Patan followed the traditions of the southern temples. This kind of mutual interest and cooperation between the North and the South continued well into the twentieth century and extended to food traditions.

The acharya took with him priests who would also be cooks for the purpose of making offerings to the deities. They were almost always from Nānguneri, Srivilliputtur and Alwar Tirunagiri, three important temple towns from the deep south.

Mītha chaval was one of the sacred offerings among the Vaiṣṇava Rajasthanis. The priests from the South learned to make mittā chaval and added the dish to the offerings made in their temples. Jagannathji ka peda is another sacred offering that is made in some south Indian homes.

It was only from the fourteenth to the seventeenth centuries due to political upheavals and new cultures that travel to holy places in the North tapered off. British rule again opened up travel to some extent but the perceived differences between North and south Indian cuisines had grown stronger. Wheat and wheat recipes became associated with the North while the southern people were thought to be passionate only about rice–a rigid and parochial view.

The Ayurvedic Basis of Indian Vegetarianism

Ayurveda or the 'science of life' is the traditional medical system of India in continuous use since the Vedic period. The *Atharva Veda* (1500 BCE) mentions more than 1,000 remedies. Other important texts of ayurveda, such as those of the physicians Charaka and Ajagara and the surgeon Suṣruta, form the basis of ayurvedic practice in India.

Ayurveda classifies the human system into three types, the vata, pitta and kapha, the three subtle energies. One's well-being depends on the balance of these three energies in the body. Vata is a combination of air and space. Pitta is mostly fire with some water, and kapha is mostly water with some earth.

Ayurveda also divides food into three categories: the sātvik (pure), the rajasic (active and passionate) or the tamasic (torpor and lassitude). By understanding one's body type, we can choose those foods that promote physiological balance and mental clarity.

Based on Ayurvedic principles, vegetarian food is considered a sātvik food. It is prepared with different herbs and spices which have medicinal properties and are used for various physiological conditions.

These ingredients are classified as heat-producing, wind-producing or phlegm-producing. Some are categorized as cooling or astringent. For example, cumin and fenugreek are cooling; chilli, pepper and cloves are heat-producing; coriander is recommended for cardiac conditions; ginger, black nightshade, neem flowers, long pepper, allspice and asafoetida for controlling wind; pomegranate seeds, amla (Indian gooseberry) and dried mango powder are for stomach disorders. These classifications lay down dos and don'ts that integrate food combinations with health considerations. For instance, ayurveda dissuades us from eating yams, green leaves and yoghurt in the evening, as this might affect digestion.

Despite this long history and tradition of vegetarianism, Indians both in the South and North are not uniformly or even largely vegetarian. But even non-vegetarians recognize the spiritually evolved nature of vegetarianism and therefore opt for this diet on religious and festive occasions.

It is important to remember that Indian vegetarianism is not the shadow cuisine of a meat-centric diet, but intrinsic and original. Indian vegetarian food does not go about simulating the taste and texture of meat dishes.

Indian vegetarian food spans a complete spectrum of taste and style. It can be an ascetic rice gruel or a simple meal of steamed rice or chapatis with accompaniments of mashed leafy greens or dal and buttermilk. Or it can reach the heights of a grand feast featuring a great assortment of regional dishes. This extraordinary variety, fine aroma and genial use of spices make Indian vegetarian cuisine unrivalled in the world.

In keeping with the idea of food as a sacred offering, the first chapter of the book is devoted to foods that are offered to the deity in temples and in homes. The subsequent chapters detail a rich variety of recipes drawn from regional and pan-Indian vegetarian cuisines. It is our sincere hope that this book will help to preserve a great yet simple sātvik vegetarian culinary tradition for generations to come.

TALKING OF VESSELS

The settled and traditional society of south India had the leisure to use its creativity in every area of life, even with respect to ordinary everyday objects such as culinary vessels. Shapes and materials were chosen according to the kind of food being prepared.

South Indians delighted in creating shapes for brass and bronze vessels, some of which can be found in stainless steel today. Thus, we find the bhogini (a low and wide-mouthed vessel used to make liquid sweets), and the chintamani, a pretty container with a rounded body and a little button-like holder on the lid. At this time, north India had fewer classic cooking vessels. Straight-sided cylindrical cooking vessels called patila made of beaten metal were the norm. Dekchis and lotas which were curvilinear were the ones in the classical style. Copper and brass coated with tin were commonly used while large aluminium vessels were used for cooking on a large scale.

Traditional Indian cooking used firewood. The earthen stove was smoothened and polished to a fine clean shine. Auspicious flour patterns were drawn on it every day to indicate the sanctity of the fire that was going to be lit. The creativity of Indian craftsmen came to the forefront in creating proper vessels to cook food on these earthen stoves. Originally, pottery of different shapes and sizes were used for cooking. These earthen vessels were used till almost the end of the twentieth century in temples, orthodox homes and in many villages all over India. To this day, the rice-dal dish pongal, on the day of Pongal or Makara Śankarānti, the south Indian harvest festival, is cooked in a new earthen pot that has been bought specially for the occasion.

The shape of each vessel was designed for the cooking of a particular dish. Thus, wide-mouthed pots were used for making kuḷambu (a thick gravy with tamarind and spices) that needed simmering even after it was pulled off the stove. Pots narrowing at the neck called eya chombu were used for rasam so that the frothing liquid would not overflow. For frying and seasoning, various sizes of vānali/woks were used. Other popular vessels were steamers and adukku (south India) and patila (north India), straight-sided round-mouthed vessels in which different liquid/vegetable preparations could be made.

Brass vessels tinned inside were the order of the day till the 1940s and '50s. Groups of metalworkers would come to the doorsteps of homes to offer their services. Many large landowning families used to own such vessels as all family functions including weddings were performed at home. These vessels came to be borrowed by other family members and friends for happy occasions in their own families.

During the 1950s, these vessels slowly disappeared from usage as they were difficult to maintain. They were replaced by the lighter and low maintenance stainless steel. Not so surprisingly, we find the old popular brass and bell metal vessels like urulis, rice pots, idli steamers and dosai kals being made in new materials today.

Urulis and Vārppus

Till as late as the 1960s, many middle-class households could afford the luxury of owning and cooking in those beautiful vessels, urulis. A product of Irinjālakuda and Mannarshala in Kerala, and Tirunelveli district in Tamil Nadu, the uruli is a heavy, shallow cooking vessel with lathed sides and a gently curving bottom, and is made of bell metal (composite of tin and non-corrosive copper with a smidgen of silver).

The vārppu is another beautiful bell metal vessel which is different from the uruli in having an ear on each side, sometimes even two. Bamboo sticks are inserted through the ears to carry this heavy vessel. This was carried by four people while two would serve directly from the vārppu from either side.

In those days, when most homes in Madurai boasted of big backyards, the artisans would come home and raise the clay and mud kiln to make the mould. Many might have watched this operation. While the metal was being poured into the mould, the householder might bring out a bagful of old silver coins and ask that they be added to the metal. This brought out silver streaks in the finished product, greatly enhancing its visual appeal. The cast uruli was then turned on a hand lathe to acquire smoothness and a soft sheen.

Some of the most beautiful examples of these ancient cooking vessels are found in many Kerala temples which use giant vārppus for the preparation of sacred offerings. These are usually set into clay ovens and are never removed. They are always cleaned *in situ*.

The weight of the uruli and its shape made it ideal for cooking on a wood fire as it helped to retain an even temperature so that the pāyasam would cook gently mostly in its own heat, intensifying its taste. Sweet rice preparations and avials were other important dishes that were cooked in urulis. Popular Kerala recipes like olan and kālan were also cooked in them.

There are urulis which are deep-bowl shaped and are used for cooking jelly-like preparations and medicinal substances over a low flame. Ayurvedic medicines that require a long period of slow evaporation would bubble in them for even forty-eight hours. Cosmetic decoctions were also boiled in them.

Changing Metals, Not Shapes

The very first vessel for boiling vegetables was made of clay. Then, as metals came into use, vessels were made of copper in different shapes for use in the kitchen. These were coated with tin to prevent acid corrosion, forming a safe barrier between the food and the metal.

Steaming pots for making idlis have been in common use for well over a century. In the early part of the twentieth century, these were made of brass or aluminium; later, stainless steel became more popular. The classic half-moon shape of the idli moulds can now be found in innovative shapes like the four suits in playing cards—clubs, spades, hearts and diamonds! Large hotels and caterers have replaced circular idli plates with square racks, ten or twelve in number, to manage the continuous stream of diners.

Dosai griddles also varied in design but were equally effective in turning out tasty dosais, as soft or as crisp as one wanted. But the iron griddle from the village of Shenkottah in the deep south is the best one to make dosais of various types. This has a smooth flat top with a heavy conical base to prevent the fire from scorching the centre. Stainless steel and non-stick griddles are available now. The Indian wok, vānali in Tamil and kadāi in Hindi, is perhaps the most versatile of vessels. Used primarily for cooking vegetables, one can sauté, stir-fry, or deep-fry equally efficiently in them.

The soapstone pot (kalchatti) has been used for centuries to make kuḷambu as well as rasam as its heaviness helps retain the heat, allowing the spices to cook slowly thus increasing flavour. Thick walled and heavy, they ensure slow and even cooking. Since they are porous, heat and moisture circulate through the pot while cooking, thereby enhancing the flavours. Kalchattis neutralize the pH balance of acidic food items and thus enhance their nutritional value. The time taken to heat the kalchatti is compensated when the slow cooking process continues even after the stove is switched off. Kalchatti (stone) is also ideal for storing pickles. Just as efficient is the iya chombu made of pure tin that is used to make rasam. Rasam requires boiling a fair amount of tamarind water and tin works well since it is not corroded by acidity.

Cooking vessels were never brought to the serving area for hygienic reasons. As much thought went into designing serving vessels as cookware. Serving vessels used in the past were as important as cooking vessels and were designed with flair. So we have the eḷu-kuḷi, seven circular containers welded to a central stem or handle where seven different dishes could be carried together and served at once. This helped to serve large numbers at weddings or special occasions. This vessel has variants with two or four vessels around a central stem, commonplace in restaurants where thalis are served today. The mookku chatti (pot with a beak) was made especially for liquid preparations like rasam as it would not splatter. The open-mouthed round bowl with a handle (thūkkuchatti) is used to serve sambar or any other thick gravy, and milk pāyasam. Another brass vessel, hexagonal in shape with a handle to serve pacchadis (raw or lightly cooked vegetables with yogurt dressing), called pachadi kinnam can be found in stainless steel today. The nei thukku (an elongated pot-shaped vessel with a round base and a long spoon) is even now used to serve ghee. Bhogini (round wide vessel) was used to serve rice and anna kori (big flat spoon) was the special type of ladle with which to serve it.

Evolution of the Indian Cooker

Before the advent of the pressure cooker that now dominates the kitchen market, India had three indigenous cookers which used steam to cook multiple dishes in one container. Bengal produced the Icmic cooker, Bombay the Santosh cooker and Tamil Nadu the well-known Rukmini cooker.

The Rukmini cooker came about in a time when women used to spend long hours in the kitchen. Firewood was the common fuel and all the dishes had to be made one after another. This set Somasundaram of Kumbakonam wanting to find a more efficient way of cooking, saving both time and fuel.

Somasundaram devised a cooker with many parts—different containers to cook rice, lentils and vegetables. All the containers which came as a set with the cooker, could be placed inside. Cooking time was pared down to 30 minutes from two hours or more. The great advantage of the Rukmini cooker is that it retains the nutritional quotient of the food cooked, along with exceptional taste.

The modern pressure cooker cut cooking time down to 10–15 minutes. This was followed by the Japanese rice cooker that also kept the cooked rice warm till it was ready to be eaten. The latest in this line is the casserole and the hot pot (one-pot cooking), which is very popular in the US.

The old coffee filter is still in use in the Indian kitchen though the heavy brass one has now made way for stainless steel. The traditional way of roasting just enough seeds in a cylindrical covered iron drum over a charcoal fire is followed by some who still have the facilities.

COOKING VESSELS

1. **Venkala pānai:** Bronze pot for cooking rice.

2. **Godavari gundu:** An oval bronze vessel with a round bottom.

3. **Vatta adukku:** These are round vessels fitting into one another in graduation—a set of six and easy to stack.

4. **Rayil adukku (kitchen in a box):** Rayil adukku (a tier of vessels) is a kitchen vessel special to India. During pre-Independence days, the rayil adukku was extensively used by government officials who travelled long distances for work. Most of them were orthodox and hence, would not partake of food prepared outside. In those days, trains used to stop for as much as an hour at many railway stations. The official's assistant or accompanying cook would set up a firewood stove on the platform, and out would come the rayil adukku. The rayil adukku had all the vessels, ladles and spoons necessary to prepare a good meal, held in a compact single vessel.

5. **Uruli:** Round flat bronze lathe-turned vessel for making pāyasam, sweet rice and vegetable preparations.

6. **Kaiya uruli:** Bronze vessel, slightly deeper than the traditional uruli, to cook for a longer time. Jellies, homemade remedies and syrups are made in these.

7. **Vārppu:** Same as uruli but with two or four 'ears' to fix bamboo poles to make it easier to carry.

8. **Iya chombu:** Tin pot to make rasam.

9. **Kal chatti:** An open-mouthed soapstone vessel for kuḷambu and sambar.

10. **Idli pātram:** Idli steamer.

11. **Dosai kal:** Iron griddle to make dosais and flatbreads.

12. **Adai madukku:** Slightly shallow concave iron griddle.

13. **Appakārai:** Cast iron pan with moulds (usually for making āppam).

14. **Vānali:** Indian wok.

KITCHEN GADGETS

1. **Akki roti press:** To press rice-flour rotis

2. **Coffee filter:** To make coffee decoction

3. **Mattu:** Churner for butter

4. **Puttu kuḷal and Chombu:** Puttu steamer

5. **Sevai naḷi:** Fresh vermicelli maker

6. **Arivāl manai:** Vegetable cutter

7. **Tengāi tiruvi:** Coconut scraper

8. **Chattuvam:** A flat round shallow ladle with a long handle to turn over things

9. **Jhārni:** Perforated ladle to slot out fried food

10. **Tuduppu:** A spatula

TRADITIONAL GRINDERS

These traditional grinders are still in use:

1. **Ammi with Kuḷavi:** A flat grinding stone with a cylindrical grinder stone used for grinding chutneys, tugaiyals, etc.

2. **Ural and ulakkai:** Pounding stone with a thick pounding stick used for pounding dry condiments into powders.

3. **Yantiram:** Grinding stone for flours. Used for dry grinding cereals and dals into flours.

4. **Āttu-kal and Kuḷavi:** Grinding stone with depression in the middle and stone grinder used for grinding rice and dals for idli, dosais, etc.

5. **Coffee grinder:** Made of iron. Used for grinding roasted coffee seeds.

SHARING AND CARING, VILLAGE STYLE—THE ELU KULI VESSEL OF TIRUNELVELI

A few villages in the Tirunelveli region (Kallidaikuruchi, Karaikurichi, Brahmadesam and Alwarkurichi), inhabited by tightly knit families, exude a regard for community ties that remain strong and meaningful. Native memory recalls how an event in one family became a common celebration.

Celebrations meant feasts to which the entire community was invited. All functions were held at home but the houses in the village were too small to accommodate all the neighbours for the feast. This is where the traditional elu kuli vessel with seven containers welded to a central handle, and owned almost by every household, came into its own. The elu kuli is made of brass with a stannum coating.

All the families would bring their collection of vessels to the celebrant's home: the vengala paanai (bronze pot), a mooku chatti (a container with a spout) and the elu kuli. The vengala paanai would be filled with the cooked rice, the mooku chatti with rasam, and all the delectable side dishes prepared for the feast would be filled in the elu kuli vessel. The mooku chatti would fit snugly on the vengala paanai and be covered with a mandara (bauhinia) leaf. After attending the function—a wedding, a birth, an engagement—the guests would return to their own homes with their vessels and dine in comfort.

We find a contemporary parallel in these pandemic times when wedding feasts were delivered to guests in their homes in the name of social distancing!

WEIGHTS AND MEASUREMENTS

Cookbooks lay a great deal of stress on correct measurements. But there was a time when teaspoons or tablespoons were rarely used as measuring tools. The most delicious food or the most complicated recipes were once prepared without the aid of measuring cups.

The supreme example of this is the grand old lady of Srirangam, Champakalakshmi Ammal (1878–1970).

She was an authority regarding the dos and don'ts of a Śrivaiṣṇava household, its observances, rites and rituals. She was also well-versed in Sanskrit and wrote many hymns and poems in the language. She was an expert in the culinary arts of the times, especially those of her community. She wrote a cookbook mostly on the offerings that were made in the household shrine.

In the cookbook, the measurements of the ingredients were given in pinches, or one up to four finger-lengthsful or fistfuls. She never needed anything else to measure ingredients except when cooking for a large feast.

This should be contrasted with modern recipes and how day after day, the same measured rasams or curries do not taste the same. Perhaps following Smt. Champakalakshmi Ammal's method may make our daily food a little more interesting!

Grains

Grains	**In Kilograms**	**Cups (British measurement = 8 oz)**
Rice	1 kg	= 5 cups
Red gram dal	1 kg	= 5 cups
Black gram dal	1 kg	= 5 cups
Bengal gram dal	1 kg	= 5 cups
Green gram dal	1 kg	= 5 cups
Grains	**Weight in Grams**	**Tablespoon (British)**
Rice	10 gm	= ¾ tbsp
Red gram dal	10 gm	= ¾ tbsp
Black gram dal	10 gm	= ¾ tbsp
Bengal gram dal	10 gm	= ¾ tbsp
Green gram dal	10 gm	= ¾ tbsp

Spices

Spices	Weight in Grams	Tablespoon (British)
Coriander seeds	10 gm	= 2 tbsp
Mustard seeds	10 gm	= 1¾ tbsp
Fenugreek seeds	10 gm	= 1 tbsp
Cumin seeds	10 gm	= 1 tbsp
Pepper	10 gm	= 1 tbsp

Cereal and Pulse Flours

Flours	Weight in Grams	Teaspoon
Rice flour	= 4 gm	1 tsp
Wheat flour	= 4½ gm	1 tsp
Black gram flour	= 2½ gm	1 tsp
Bengal gram flour	= 2½ gm	1 tsp
Ravā	= 5 gm	1 tsp
White flour	= 5 gm	1 tsp
Flours	**Weight in Grams**	**Cups (British measurement = 8oz)**
Rice flour	= 126 gm	1 cup
Wheat flour	= 128 gm	1 cup
Bengal gram flour	= 100 gm	1 cup
Ravā	= 166 gm	1 cup
White flour	= 128 gm	1 cup
Powders	**Weight in Grams**	**Teaspoon**
Turmeric powder	= 3 gm	1 tsp
Chilli powder	= 3 gm	1 tsp
Dried ginger	= 3 gm	1 tsp

Liquid measurements

	In Litres	Cups (British measurement = 8oz)
All liquids	1 litre	= 5 cups

Measurement Abbreviations

tsp = teaspoon
tbsp = tablespoon
kg = kilogram
gm = grams
l = litre
ml = millilitre

Metric Dry Measurements

Spoons	Tbsp/Cups	Grams	Nearest Grams
1½ tsp	½ tbsp	7 gm	7 gm
3 tsp	1 tbsp	14 gm	15 gm
2 tbsp	⅛ cup	28 gm	30 gm
4 tbsp	¼ cup	56 gm	60 gm
8 tbsp	½ cup	112 gm	115 gm
10⅔ tbsp	⅔ cup	149.33 gm	150 gm
12 tbsp	¾ cup	168 gm	170 gm
16 tbsp	1 cup	224 gm	225 gm
32 tbsp	2 cups	448 gm	450 gm
1 katori			**150 gm**

Metric Liquid Measures

Spoons	Tbsp	Cups	Nearest Ml
½ tsp			2.50 ml
1 tsp			5.00 ml
2 tsp			10.00 ml
3 tsp	1 tbsp		15.00 ml
6 tsp	2 tbsp	⅛ cup	30.00 ml
12 tsp	4 tbsp	¼ cup	60.00 ml
24 tsp	8 tbsp	½ cup	125.00 ml
48 tsp	16 tbsp	1 cup	250.00 ml
96 tsp	32 tbsp	2 cups	500.00 ml
1 katori			**125 ml**

PRE-COOKING PROCESSES

Asafoetida Water

1. Combine 1 tsp of asafoetida powder with 1 tbsp of water. Mix well and store in a small bottle. Or, soak ½ tsp of solid asafoetida in ½ cup of water and store.
2. Use as required, but do not keep it for more than five to six days.
3. In south Indian homes, it is made fresh every morning and normally used up by the evening.

Batter for Idli

1. Rice and black gram dal/urad dal must be soaked separately. Rice must be soaked for 3–4 hours, urad dal should be soaked only for 30 minutes.
2. Grind the urad dal with very little water (the proportion is usually one part dal with half part water) till it is light and fluffy. (A teaspoonful of the batter should float when dropped into a bowl of cold water.)
3. Rice should be ground well but remain slightly grainy to the touch. The amount of water for rice will vary according to the variety of rice used.
4. Combine both batters in a large vessel and mix well.
5. Add salt and beat well. Cover vessel and allow to ferment overnight.

Blanching Tomatoes

1. Boil water in a vessel. When the water comes to a rolling boil, drop the tomatoes and count to seven. Slot out and put into cold water.
2. Peel the tomatoes, cut into two, remove seeds, and chop.

Blanching Vegetables

1. Boil water in a vessel with 2 pinches of salt. When the water comes to a rolling boil, drop in the vegetables.
2. When the water comes to a boil again (after approximately 10–15 seconds), drain and remove the vegetables.

Coconut Milk

1. Break a coconut into two halves.
2. Grate the white portion or meat of the coconut.
3. Mix the grated coconut meat with ½ cup of warm water and grind.
4. Press through a fine-meshed strainer lined with muslin into a bowl. This is the thick milk or first extract.
5. Add ½ cup of warm water to the residue, grind once again and strain. This is the thin milk or second extract.

Hung Curd

1. Place a large strainer over a bowl and line it with muslin cloth.
2. Pour the curd into the strainer.
3. Gather the sides of the cloth and hang for about 30 minutes over the bowl to drain the liquid.
4. From 1 cup of curd, you will get ¾ cup of hung curd.

Cooking with Mustard Oil

Sri Shivram Raina, a chef of the 1950s and household name in Kashmiri cuisine, describes the preparation of mustard oil for cooking:

1. Heat mustard oil in a vānali/wok, till it smokes.
2. Sprinkle asafoetida water immediately, 10 times. The oil becomes clear.
3. Add ½ tsp of salt to the oil. Also add a small piece of lime or a piece of dried mango and let it remain in the oil, till it turns brown. Remove the lime or mango from the oil.
4. Remove the vānali/wok from heat and let the oil cool.
5. The oil is now ready for use. Store it in a container.

Chena/Paneer (Cottage Cheese)

1. Bring 1 litre of milk to boil in a vessel over high heat.
2. Add 1 tbsp of lime juice and stir. When the milk splits, turn off the heat. Cool.
3. Line a colander with a clean cheese cloth and pour the split milk into it to drain the whey. The milk solid is called paneer.
4. Gather the paneer in the cloth into a bundle and let it hang to drain out excess whey. When the whey has drained completely, untie the bundle.
5. Remove the paneer and wash it in cold water.
6. Knead it to make a smooth ball. This soft paneer can be used to make sweets such as sandesh and rasagulla.
7. To make paneer that can be cut into pieces, place the washed and kneaded paneer under a heavy weight for at least an hour. Remove and cut into desired shapes.

Note: Naturally broken milk is better than lime juice for making paneer.

Peeling Almonds

1. Place the required quantity of almonds in a bowl.
2. Boil enough water to cover the almonds and soak them.
3. After 30 minutes, drain and peel.

Preparing Banana Flowers

1. Separate banana flower combs inside the thick red sepal. Two rows of small flowers make up a comb.
2. There are many sepals arranged in a whorl in a whole banana flower. Take out the innermost flowers.
3. Remove the central pistils—hard, stringy protrusions—from each flower.

4. Chop the white flowers. As you chop, drop them in water mixed with buttermilk or curd. This prevents the flowers from oxidizing and turning brown.

Pressure-cooking Dal

All dals can be pressure-cooked. Tuvar dal is cooked with turmeric, ghee/castor oil and water in a pressure cooker for different durations.

1. 2 whistles = 2 to 3 minutes after the cooker reaches full pressure.
2. 3 whistles = 3 to 5 minutes after the cooker reaches full pressure (for tuvar dal) and 2 whistles (for mung dal).
3. 4 whistles = 4 to 6 minutes after cooker reaches full pressure.

Rice Powder

1. Wash raw rice, drain thoroughly, and spread it on a clean cloth to dry in the shade for a few hours.
2. Do not let it dry completely. Grind to make a fine powder. Sieve it.
3. Alternatively, it can be ground in a mill.

Sugar Syrup

Indian sweets require different concentrations of sugar syrup.

1. *One-thread consistency:* After boiling sugar in water, test by taking a tsp of the syrup between your thumb and index finger and pull apart gently—the syrup should be like a thin thread.
2. *Two-thread consistency:* Take a tsp of the syrup between the thumb and index finger and pull apart gently; it should be very sticky and form a thick thread.
3. *For a tougher consistency:* When a little syrup is dropped into a bowl of cold water, it forms a ball.

Jaggery Syrup

1. In a vessel, add 1 cup of water and jaggery and keep stirring till jaggery dissolves completely. Bring it to boil.
2. When it boils, remove it from the heat and strain to remove all the impurities.
3. Boil again till either one-string, two-string consistency or full maturity is reached.
   - **One-string consistency:** When jaggery syrup is taken between two fingers, it has to stretch like a string.
   - **Two-string consistency:** The string between the two fingers should be thick.
   - **Full maturity:** For making sweets with a jaggery base like kadalai urundai (groundnut balls) the syrup should have the consistency of a ball. It should make a sound when dropped on to a plate.

Tamarind Juice

1. Soak 1 packed tbsp of tamarind in ½ cup of hot water in a bowl for about 10 minutes.
2. Squeeze by hand to loosen the pulp. Add another ½ cup water to the pulp, squeeze and strain.
3. Add the second extraction to the first.

SACRED OFFERINGS

SACRED OFFERINGS–FOOD AND TEMPLES

aham annam aham annam aham annam
aham annādo aham annādo aham annādaha

I am food, I am food, I am food,
I am the eater of food, I am the eater of food,
I am the eater of food

This Upanaishadic avowal finds its tangible affirmation in the sacred offering of food at temples and homes.

The sacred offering of food to the deity either at home or in the temple occupies a central place in the Hindu ritual tradition. In most Hindu homes, the morning meal is not partaken of before it is offered to the family deities. Even in homes that do not practise this on ordinary days, it is a time-honoured custom to offer all the delicacies made on festival days to the family deity. The food that is thus blessed is the *prasādam* (the food offering to propitiate the deity, also the deity bestowing his grace/ blessings on the devotee).

The practice of sacred food offerings and its distribution is common to all the states of India. These sacred offerings are distributed to the devotees as 'prasādam'. Epigraphs on temple walls speak of the many endowments that were made by kings and wealthy devotees for feeding pilgrims and devotees. In Vishnu temples an extensive menu of food is offered to the deity as part of the rituals of daily worship. During temple festivals, important ritual occasions and religious festivals, more elaborate menus are prepared as offerings. Thus blessed, the prasādam is greatly enjoyed by the devotees, as the embodiment of His grace. Even in small village temples in Karnataka, the food offering is distributed at noon to village schoolchildren who eagerly partake of this.

The well-known temples of the South—Alagarkovil, Kānchipuram, Srirangam, Srivilliputtur, Tirumalai, to name a few, have evolved their own special foods as sacred offerings. These are considered beloved of that particular deity and there are intriguing tales that tell us why this is so.

Daily offerings of food are also made in Siva temples, usually cooked rice with vegetables. But in accordance with the customs of Siva temples, this prasādam is distributed only to the sthanedārs, the officers of the temple administration, and not to the general public. At the Avudayar (avi udayar) Siva temple near Arantangi, heaps of cooked rice are spread out on a large rock for the deity. This is distributed to the devotees along with a bitter gourd gojju and is a much sought after prasādam both for its taste and for the Lord's grace.

Some of the well-known food offerings in Vishnu temples are:

Srirangam – śelvarappam
Tirumalai – laddu and vadai
Srivilliputtur – kadambasādam, akkāradisil
Alagarkovil – dosai

Kānchipuram – idli (basket idli)
Tiruvallikeni – tenklal and śarkarai pongal
Tirupullani and Ambalapuzha – pāl pāyasam
Thiruvananthapuram – meni tulā pāyasam and dadhiyōdanam
Melkote – puliyōdarai
Appakudathan temple – appams
Tiruchanur – milagodarai

Stone inscriptions found in these temples from 850 CE onwards record the various types of food that are prepared for the deity, including the ingredients, the measurements and the special earthen pots that were used to cook the dishes. They also record the spices used like pepper, cumin, ginger, cardamom, cloves, and the different kinds of cooked vegetables. Today, many of these specialties are still prepared for the utsavams connected to the particular deities.

The sacred offerings in Vishnu temples are prepared by cooks whose forefathers had worked in the same temple kitchens, wherein each new generation of cooks naturally assimilated the subtle intricacies of taste and skill.

All the foods offered in the temple are prepared in the madaipalli/matapalli or kitchen, which forms an essential part of every temple. The etymology of the term madaipalli might refer to the cleansing and canalizing function of a sluice. In some temples of Kerala where the sluice follows from the well to the madaipalli, one is prohibited from crossing it. In Tamil, the word 'madai' means a barrier. A second interpretation of the word could be from 'matam' and 'palli' referring to the big cooking halls of the maths as maths in several places oversaw the temple rituals and the food offerings made at intervals during the day.

The madaipallis are as ancient as the temples and are usually located in the southeast corner of the temple. To maintain purity and hygiene, only the cooks were allowed to enter the madaipalli. Further, the water for cooking was obtained from a special well located within the madaipalli. The food was prepared in earthen pots on a wood fire and these pots were broken after use, preventing any bacterial contamination. These earthen pots have today given place to tin-coated bell metal vessels, yet, little else in the madaipalli has changed: the same rituals and cooking traditions endure, the same wood fires still burn but not in all the madaipallis, as some use gas stoves for cooking.

Despite the many changes that have taken place in the temple community, the temple, the rituals, the customs and the food traditions live on sustained by the unshaken faith of the devotees. The recipes outlined in the following pages will bring into your kitchen the flavours and aromas of timeless temple offerings conjuring up images of festivities and celebrations.

AKKĀRA ADISIL

Sweet Rice with Green Gram Dal

Makes: 10 servings
Serving size: 75 gms
Calories per serving: 257

INGREDIENTS

Milk 4 cups
Water 1 cup
Green gram dal/Mung dal ⅓ cup
Rice ½ cup
Grated jaggery 2½ cups
Water ½ cup
Ghee 1 tsp + 2 tbsp + 1 tbsp
Cashewnuts 6
Almonds[1] 10
Nutmeg 2 gratings
Cardamoms 6
Mace 1 small flake, coarsely pounded
Raisins ¼ cup
Saffron strands ¼ tsp dissolved in ½ tsp water

Akkāra Adisil is a sweet dish which became very popular due to its connection with the woman saint Āndal, who was devoted to the deity at Srirangam.

Many charming tales are told about Godā/Āndal. The story of the young girl who would take none other than Sri Ranganatha of Srirangam as her bridegroom is too deeply etched in the hearts and minds of Tamils to bear repetition. Her triumphant procession to Srirangam from southern Srivilliputur is memorable for the edict of the king that the villages that she passed through should offer her neermor and pānakam for the hot journey lest the young girl wilt and faint with her fasting.

Āndal expressed in her devotional poetry her deep desire to offer a hundred tadās (vessels the size of ponds), now called varpus, of Akkāra Adisil, the quintessential sweet dish of the community to the handsome god of Alagar temple near Madurai. This sacred pledge was later fulfilled by the religious preceptor Sri Ramanuja, many centuries later, so moved was he by the bhakti of this young girl.

Naru nārum polil Māliruncholai nambiku nān
Nooru tadāvil vennai Vai nerndu paravi vaithen;
Nooru tadā nirainda Akkāra adisil chonnen
Eru thiruvudaiyan Indru vandu ivai kollungolo?

To the lord of Māliruncholai surrounded by fragrant groves,
I give my word to offer a hundred large containers
of butter today,
And a hundred containers of sweet rice filled to the brim.
Will the lord deign to accept them?

METHOD

1. Break cashewnuts into small bits.
2. Take 2 cups of milk in a heavy-bottomed vessel/uruli[2] and bring to a boil. Stir till the milk thickens. Remove and set aside.
3. Toast mung dal in a vānali/wok lightly over low heat, tossing all the while; it should not change colour or turn brown.
4. Dissolve jaggery in ½ cup of water and strain.
5. Heat 1 tsp of ghee in a vānali/wok[3]. Fry cashewnuts over medium heat, till golden. Use a slotted spoon to take them out of the wok, set aside.
6. Soak almonds in boiling water and cover. Set aside for 15 minutes. Drain the water and peel the almonds. Once dry, slice into fine slivers.
7. Boil remaining 2 cups of milk with 1 cup of water in an uruli.
8. Using a grater, scrape nutmeg twice over the milk and add cardamoms and coarsely pounded mace.
9. Wash rice and mung dal and add to the boiling milk. Cook over medium heat.
10. When the rice is cooked, add strained jaggery and cook for 2–3 minutes.
11. Stir now and then, adding 2 tbsp of ghee to prevent mixture from sticking to vessel.
12. Add fried cashewnuts, sliced almonds, raisins and thickened milk to vessel.
13. Lower heat, add 1 tbsp of ghee and saffron. Stir a couple of times.
14. Remove from heat and serve.

[1]*Almonds are used only in recent times*

[2]*Varpus and urulis are heavy-bottomed bell metal vessels usually used for reducing milk for pāyasams or to cook sweets, dal and vegetable preparations. Uruli was called tadā meaning a small pond.*

[3]*For vānali, see section on 'Cooking Vessels'*

VEN PONGAL

Green Gram Dal and Rice

Makes: 5 servings
Serving size: 150 gms
Calories per serving: 452

INGREDIENTS

Green gram dal/Mung dal ¼ cup
Rice 1 cup
Water 3 cups
Ghee 2 tsp + 5 tbsp
Whole cashewnuts 12
Salt 1 tsp
Asafoetida powder 1 tsp dissolved in 2 tbsp of water

Seasoning
Jeera/Cumin seeds 1 tsp
Whole black pepper ½ tsp
Broken black pepper ½ tsp
Grated ginger 1 tsp
Curry leaves 2 sprigs

The eponymous festival dish pongal, a popular breakfast dish in south India, might have been named thus because it boils up—pongudal—as pongal.

This is an example of Tamil adjectives that become nouns based on the action, such as:

- **varuppadu turns into varuval, that which is fried**
- **kuḷambudal becomes kuḷambuthat, which is mixed and churned**
- **tugaippadu is converted to tugaiyal, that which is ground finely**
- **masippadu changes to masiyal, that which is mashed**

METHOD

1. Toast mung dal lightly in a vānali/wok over low heat, tossing all the while; it should not change colour or turn brown.
2. Wash the toasted mung dal and rice under running water. Steam-cook with 3 cups of water and set aside, covered.
3. Heat 2 tsp of ghee in a wok. Fry cashewnuts till golden. Use a slotted spoon to take them out of the wok, set aside.
4. Add cumin seeds and pepper to the wok and sauté. Add grated ginger and curry leaves and toss once.
5. Add this tempering to the cooked mung dal-rice mixture and stir gently.
6. Sprinkle salt and the asafoetida powder dissolved in water. Mix well.
7. Add 5 tbsp of ghee and mix. The rice should not be over cooked.
8. Add fried cashewnuts.
9. Serve hot with tomato, brinjal, or bitter gourd gojju or any chutney.

TIRUVĀDIRAI KALI Broken Rice with Jaggery

Makes: 10 servings
Serving size: 75 gms
Calories per serving: 212

INGREDIENTS

Rice 1 cup
Grated jaggery 1¼ cups
Water 2 cups

Garnish
Ghee 1 tbsp
Cashewnuts 10
Cardamoms 10, powdered

METHOD

1. Break cashewnuts into bits.
2. Wash rice, drain well and roast over medium heat in a vānali/wok till very light brown. Remove. Cool and pound to a coarse semolina/ravā consistency and sieve. Remove fine flour droppings from the sieve.
3. Boil jaggery in 2 cups of water till it dissolves. Strain.
4. Place strained jaggery in a vessel over high heat. When it boils, add rice. Lower heat to a simmer and keep on stirring till the syrup is absorbed.
5. Heat ghee in a wok. Fry cashewnuts over medium heat till golden. Slot out.
6. Garnish the jaggery and rice pudding with fried cashewnuts and powdered cardamom.

AMBALAPUḶA PĀL PĀYASAM

Rice and Milk Pāyasam

The word pāyasam is derived from the Sanskrit word pāyas meaning milk, and pāyasam means that which has been derived from milk. Sri Krishna Temple in Ambalapuḷa in Kerala is famous for its pāl pāyasam.

Makes: 10 servings
Serving size: 100 gms
Calories per serving: 131

INGREDIENTS

Long-grained rice ½ cup
Cow's milk 4 cups
Sugar ¾ cup
Water 2 cups

(Recipe courtesy Sri Padmanabha Sarma of Thrissur)

METHOD

1. Wash rice several times to remove bran and excess starch. Drain and set aside.
2. Place an uruli/heavy-bottomed bronze pan with 2 cups of milk and 1 cup of water over high heat. Bring to a boil, lower heat to medium and stir occasionally, till it is reduced to half the original quantity.
3. Add rice.
4. Add remaining 2 cups milk and 1 cup water. Simmer, stirring constantly, for about 40 minutes, till pāyasam thickens and has a pinkish colour.
5. Reduce heat, add sugar and stir well. Cook for 2–3 minutes more, stirring gently.
6. Remove from heat. Let the pāyasam settle and come together. It should have a gruel-like consistency.
7. Cool and serve.

EḶU KARI KUḶAMBU Seven-vegetable Kuḷambu

Makes: 10–12 servings
Serving size: 125 gms
Calories per serving: 127

INGREDIENTS

French beans 50 gm
Tender dolichos beans 50 gm
Tender (yellow) pumpkin 100 gm
Plantain ½
Sweet potato 1 medium-sized
Colocasia 4
Tender dolichos seeds/Sem seeds ½ cup
Tamarind 50 gm
Water 5 cups
Turmeric powder ½ tsp
Asafoetida powder ¼ tsp
Salt 1½ tsp
Sesame seeds (white) 2 tsp, powdered

Spices for grinding
Oil 3 tsp
Asafoetida powder ¾ tsp
Bengal gram dal/chana dal ¼ cup
Dried red chillies 15
Coriander seeds ½ cup
Fenugreek seeds ½ tsp
Curry leaves 2 sprigs
Raw rice 1 tsp
Grated fresh coconut cup
Water 3 tbsp

Seasoning
Sesame oil 2 tsp
Fenugreek seeds ½ tsp
Dried red chillies ½ tsp
Asafoetida powder ¼ tsp
Curry leaves 1 sprig

METHOD

1. Trim all beans. Cut all French beans in half.
2. Cut dolichos beans in half if it is a big variety.
3. Peel pumpkin and cut into 1½-inch cubes.
4. Scrub sweet potato and plaintain and cut into ½-inch thick slices, with skin.
5. Scrub colocasia. In a pot, add enough water to cover and boil in their jackets. Once tender, set aside to cool. Peel and cut into quarters.
6. Extract tamarind juice, using 5 cups of water (see Pre-Cooking Processes).
7. Toast sesame seeds in a vānali over medium heat till aromatic. Remove and pound coarsely.
8. Heat 3 tsp of oil in wok. Fry all the ingredients for grinding over medium heat, stirring till the dal turns golden brown. Grind fried spice mix ingredients in a blender with 3 tbsp of water to a smooth paste. Set aside.
9. Heat 2 tsp of sesame oil in wok. Splutter fenugreek seeds, dried red chillies, asafoetida powder and curry leaves. Add all vegetables except boiled colocasia and sauté for 2 minutes to shrink vegetables a little.
10. Add tamarind water, turmeric powder, asafoetida powder and salt and boil, till the raw smell of tamarind disappears.
11. Check if vegetables are cooked. Add boiled colocasia, stir in the ground spice paste and bring to a boil. Remove from heat.
12. Add powdered white sesame.
13. If kuḷambu is too thick, add ¼ cup of boiling water and boil for a minute.

MENI TULĀ PĀYASAM Supreme Sweet Offering

Makes: 30 servings
Serving size: 100 gms
Calories per serving: 334

INGREDIENTS

Red rice 500 gm
Water 7½ cups + ½ cup
Grated jaggery 500 gm
Ghee 1¼ cups
Sugar 750 gm
Water 1½ litres

Garnish
Ghee 1 tbsp
Raisins 50 gm

(Recipe courtesy HH Sri Marthanda Varma, Pattom Palace, Thiruvananthapuram)

METHOD

1. Wash rice and soak in water for about 15 minutes. Drain and cook with 7½ cups of water till water is absorbed. The rice should not stick to the bottom of the vessel.
2. Boil ½ cup of water in a vessel, add grated jaggery. Stir continuously over medium heat till jaggery dissolves. Strain.
3. Mix strained jaggery with cooked rice in a heavy-bottomed vessel over medium heat. As it starts boiling, add ghee and sugar. Stir till sugar dissolves and is well-absorbed into the mixture. Remove from heat.
4. Heat 1 tbsp of ghee in a pan. Fry raisins over medium heat, till they puff up. Drain and garnish the pāyasam with the fried raisins.

AḶAGAR KOVIL DOSAI

Black Gram Dal and Rice Dosai

Makes: 12 servings
Serving size: 150 gms
Calories per serving: 421

INGREDIENTS

Raw samba rice 3 cups
Split black gram/Urad dal with skin 1¼ cup
Salt 3 tsp
Dried ginger 2-inch piece, coarsely pounded
Black pepper, broken very coarsely[1] 2 tsp
Whole black pepper 2 tsp
Jeera/cumin seeds 1 tbsp
Curry leaves 2–3 sprigs
Asafoetida powder 2 tsp

Mix ghee and oil
Ghee 1½ cups
Oil 1½ cups

Aḷagar Kovil is a Viṣṇu temple ten kilometres from Madurai where the dosai, crisp and golden, is very famous.

Many temple inscriptions detail the offerings made at the temples along with their ingredients and measurements. Some inscriptions, including one on the west wall of the prakaram of Tirupati temple, mention dosai as an offering.

METHOD

1. Wash rice and soak fully covered in water for 2 hours. Drain and pound finely.
2. Wash urad dal with skin and soak fully covered in water for about 4 hours.
3. Grind urad dal without water to make a smooth batter.
4. Add pounded rice to batter and beat well to a thick consistency. Batter should be very thick but not like a dough. If too thick, sprinkle 1 tbsp of water.
5. Add ginger, pepper, cumin seeds, curry leaves, asafoetida powder and salt to the batter. Stir once or twice. Keep aside for 2 hours for batter to get homogenized and settle down.
6. Put a heavy adai madaku (see Cooking Vessels) over medium heat. Pour 1-inch ghee-oil mixture on madaku. When the oil is hot, pour a cup of batter and spread to make an 8-inch round dosai. Pour 4 tbsp ghee-oil mixture on top.
7. Fry till the base is golden. Flip over and fry the other side.
8. Make remaining dosais in the same way.

[1] *Black pepper gently broken into two. If broken too much, the powder of the black skin will make the dosai look too dark and grey.*

JAGANNATHJI KA PEDA

Crisp Sugar-coated Biscuits

Makes: 20 servings
Serving size: 75 gms
Calories per serving: 565

INGREDIENTS

White flour/maida 500 gm
Ghee 3 tbsp + 3 tbsp + 2¼ cups
Fine rice powder 100 gm (see Pre-Cooking Processes)
Sugar 500 gm
Water ½ cup

This is one of many offerings in Jagannathji temple, the famous twelfth-century CE temple in Puri, Odisha. This is a popular prasādam offered to Sri Krishna in many homes, too.

METHOD

1. Mix maida and 3 tbsp of ghee in a bowl. Gradually add a little water at a time to make a smooth, tight dough. Knead well.
2. Mix rice powder with 3 tbsp of ghee to form a paste.
3. Take half the dough and roll it into a 12–14 inch disc.
4. Smear half the rice powder paste evenly over disc.
5. Roll disc tightly to form a cylinder. Cut cylinder into 1-inch thick pieces. Take each piece; seal 2 open ends by pinching gently with hands. Press very gently with a rolling pin to elongate it to 2–3 inches—this is the peda.
6. Make more pedas in the same way with the remaining dough and rice paste.
7. Mix sugar in 2 tsp of water over high heat and boil till it reaches one-thread consistency (see Pre-Cooking Processes). Remove from heat.
8. Place a vānali/wok over low heat. Add 2¼ cups of ghee. When it is frying hot, fry pedas in batches till crisp and light golden.
9. Remove fried pedas with a slotted spoon to drain oil and add to the warm sugar syrup. Immerse them fully in syrup and transfer to a serving dish. Once cool, they appear to be dusted with icing sugar powder.

KĀNCHIPURAM IDLI

Rice and Black Gram Dal Cakes Steamed in a Bamboo Basket

Makes: 24 servings
Serving size: 150 gms
Calories per serving: 272

INGREDIENTS

Rice 1 cup
Black gram dal/Urad dal 1 cup
Water 1½ cups
Thick curd ½ cup, whisked smooth
Black pepper, 1 tbsp, coarsely broken
Dried ginger 1-inch piece, crushed
Sesame oil ¼ cup
Ghee 4 tbsp
Jeera/cumin seeds 1 tsp
Asafoetida powder ¼ tsp
Curry leaves 2–3 sprigs
Salt 2–3 tsp

A fermented food offering is never made in the temple for reasons of ritual purity. Idli in its secular role is now fermented. Kānchipuram idli is the prasādam at Sri Varadaraja Perumal temple at Kānchipuram, Tamil Nadu. This 'idli' is not fermented.

METHOD

1. Wash rice and urad dal and soak them together in water for about 4 hours. Drain and grind with 1½ cups of water to make a thick, slightly grainy batter. Set aside for about 2 hours.
2. Add curd to the batter, mix well. Add remaining ingredients.
3. Keep the steamer ready with boiling water.
4. Steam for 40 minutes in a cylindrical bamboo basket or any basket lined with dried leaves or a flat-bottomed plate with 1½-inch rim or a 1½-inch deep perforated flat plate.
5. Once firm and cooked through, remove from steamer. Cut into cubes or slices and serve.

Note: Nowadays, when these idlis are made at home, an equal quantity of parboiled and raw rice is used. The batter is fermented overnight with salt. The other ingredients are added just before cooking. Just a tbsp of curd is added.

TERALIAPPAM

Cinnamon-flavoured Rice Appam

Makes: 12 servings
Serving size: 125 gms
Calories per serving: 270

INGREDIENTS

Rice 1 cup
Ripe bananas 5 (preferably the pūvan variety)
Grated jaggery 1 cup
Cardamom 4, powdered
Fresh terali/Cinnamon leaves 12

Teraliappam is made on Tuesdays in the month of Sravana to offer as prasādam to Devi, the goddesses Lakshmi and Bhagavati.

METHOD

1. Wash rice and soak in water for about 30 minutes. Drain rice through a bamboo basket. Pound to a fine semolina/ravā consistency.
2. Lightly roast the pounded rice in a vānali/wok over low heat, tossing all the while. Cool.
3. Mix the roasted rice flour, banana, jaggery, and powdered cardamoms, mash well by hand. The dough should be quite thick.
4. Wash cinnamon leaves and pat dry.
5. Place 1 tbsp of dough at the stem end of a leaf and roll into a cylinder. Insert stem into side of leaf. Repeat with remaining batter and leaves.
6. Steam appams for 15 minutes. Remove from steamer and cool.
7. Serve the whole leaf roll.

Note: Use leaves of Cinnamon zylanicum or Cinnamon malabaricum.

UNNI APPAM

Tiny Banana Appam

Makes: 36 servings
Serving size: 125 gms
Calories per serving: 419

Appam, indigenous to south India, is the earliest food offering known here and is mentioned in ancient epigraphs. The epigraph of 948–949 CE found on the slab near the Srirangam temple museum records that Brahmādhirajan, alias Achchiyan-Bhattan, gifted two pieces of land in Sāsanamangalam for sweet cake offerings (appam) to the deity on Ekadasi day during the Panguni festival. Literary references place the āppam much earlier than this inscription.

INGREDIENTS

Rice 1 cup
Water ½ cup
Grated jaggery 1 cup
Ripe bananas 2 (preferably pūvan variety)
Ghee ½ cup
Oil ½ cup

METHOD

1. Wash rice and soak in water for about 2 hours. Drain and grind to a fine paste with ½ cup of water.
2. Add jaggery and bananas. Grind and mix well.
3. Place an appam mould[1] over medium heat.
4. Mix ghee and oil together. Fill a quarter of each depression in the mould with the mixture.
5. When hot, pour a spoonful of batter into each depression. When the appams rise, flip over to fry the other side. Remove when golden brown.
6. Make the remaining āppams in the same way.

[1] *The appam griddle is called an appakarai (maker of appam). It is an iron griddle with circular depressions ¾-inch deep.*

KSHEERANNAM Rice with Sugar Candy

Makes: 4 servings
Serving size: 125 gms
Calories per serving: 329

INGREDIENTS

Milk 3 cups
Nutmeg powder 1 pinch
Mace powder 1 pinch
Rice ¾ cup
Powdered sugar candy ¾ cup
Saffron 2–3 pinches + 20 strands
Ghee ¼ cup

METHOD

1. Boil 3 cups of milk in an uruli/heavy-bottomed bronze vessel. When it foams up, stir well. Remove 1 cup of milk and keep aside.
2. Add nutmeg powder and mace powder to the 2 cups of hot milk in the vessel and bring to boil again.
3. Add washed rice. Simmer over medium heat. Stir often, till the rice is half cooked.
4. Now add the 1 cup of milk that was set aside earlier.
5. Stir to prevent the rice from sticking to bottom of the uruli.
6. When the rice is well cooked, add powdered sugar candy.
7. The sugar candy will start to melt. Cook till mixture is well blended. Stir.
8. Soak 2–3 pinches of saffron in 1 tbsp of water and make a paste with a pestle and mortar.
9. Add the ground saffron paste to the sweetened rice and mix well. Remove from heat.
10. Stir in saffron strands and ghee.
11. Serve hot.

TIRUVALLIKENI PULIYŌDARAI Tiruvallikeni Tamarind Rice

Makes: 10 servings
Serving size: 150 gms
Calories per serving: 275

INGREDIENTS

Spice Powder
Fenugreek seeds ½ tsp
Oil 1 tsp
Dried red chillies 3

Pulikachal: Tamarind paste
Tamarind 250 gm
Water 3½ cups
Sesame oil ½ cup
Mustard seeds 1 tbsp
Black gram dal/Urad dal 1 tbsp
Bengal gram dal/Chana dal 1 tbsp
Dried red chillies 15–18 (short, fat variety)
Asafoetida powder 2 tsp
Turmeric powder 1 tsp
Salt 2 tbsp

Rice
Rice 1 kg (long grain variety)
Water 2½ cups
Ghee 2 tsp

Seasoning
Sesame oil 1 cup
Cashewnuts 12, broken
Roasted peanuts 2 tbsp
Curry leaves 2 sprigs
Turmeric powder ¼ tsp

METHOD

Spice powder
1. Place a vānali/wok over low heat. Roast fenugreek seeds till they are aromatic. Remove.
2. Add 1 tsp of oil to vānali/wok and fry red chillies till they turn black. Drain excess oil and set aside to cool.
3. Grind the fried red chillies with the roasted fenugreek seeds to a fine powder.

Pulikachal
1. Extract tamarind water, using 3½ cups of water (see Pre-Cooking Processes).
2. Take a little oil in a heavy-bottomed vessel. Splutter mustard seeds over medium heat. Add red chillies, fry to a dark red colour. Add both dals, fry till golden. Remove from heat. Add asafoetida at once.
3. In the same heavy-bottomed vessel, add tamarind extract with turmeric powder and salt, put back on the stove and bring to a boil.
4. Add half the ground spice powder. Mix well.
5. Boil over medium heat for 20–30 minutes, till gravy reduces to a sauce-like consistency. This jelly-like tamarind mixture is pulikachal.

Rice
1. Wash rice and cook in 2½ cups of water in a steamer. Spread rice on a large platter and cool.
2. Fry cashewnuts in a little ghee over medium heat. Remove.
3. Add turmeric powder, oil, fried cashewnuts, peanuts, curry leaves and remaining ground spice powder to rice.
4. Add the tamarind jelly by spoonfuls and mix gently with rice. Use what is required and refrigerate the remaining jelly.

Note: Use 3 tsp freshly ground black pepper instead of red chillies to make the spice powder. In this case, roast the pepper, grind and mix.

MELKOTE PULIYŌDARAI Spicy Tamarind Rice

Makes: 25 servings
Serving size: 150 gms
Calories per serving: 438

INGREDIENTS

Oil 2 tbsp

Spices for powdering
Dhania/coriander seeds 10 tbsp
Cumin seeds 5 tsp. Dried red chillies 30
Bengal gram dal/Chana dal 5 tsp
Black gram dal/Urad dal 5 tsp
Sesame seeds 2½ tsp. Fenugreek seeds 2½ tsp
Whole black pepper 2½ tsp
Cinnamon 5-inch stick
Asafoetida 3-inch piece

Pulikachal
Tamarind 300 gm. Water 2½ cups
Turmeric powder 5 tsp
Salt 2½ tsp. Grated jaggery 3 tsp

Rice
Rice 1½ kg. Water 3½ litres
Turmeric powder 1 tsp. Oil 1 tsp

Seasoning
Oil 5 cups. Mustard seeds 10 tsp
Bengal gram dal/Chana dal 10 tsp
Black gram dal/Urad dal 10 tsp
Dried red chillies 30
Asafoetida powder 2 tsp
Curry leaves 6–10 sprigs

Garnish
Oil 5 tbsp. Peanuts 100 gm
Copra, 150 gm, diced fine
Curry leaves 2 sprigs

METHOD

1. Place oil in a vānali/wok over medium heat. When hot, add all spices for powdering and roast, till aromatic. Spices should not be over-fried. Remove from heat and cool. Grind to make a fine powder.

Pulikachal

1. Extract tamarind juice using 2½ cups of water (see Pre-Cooking Processes).
2. Take tamarind juice in a vessel with turmeric powder and salt. Boil over medium heat, till gravy reduces to a sauce-like consistency.
3. Add jaggery and cook for a few minutes longer. It should have a jelly-like consistency.

Rice

1. Wash rice and cook in 3½ litres of water. Grains should be fluffy and not stick together. Cool and separate with a fork.
2. Spread cooked rice on a large platter. Mix in turmeric powder and oil.
3. Heat oil in wok. Add seasoning ingredients except asafoetida powder, splutter over medium heat. Stir in asafoetida powder.
4. Pour seasoning over cooled rice. Add ground spice powder and pulikachal. Mix well. Taste and add salt, if required.
5. Heat oil in a wok over medium heat, fry groundnuts and copra, till light brown, stir in curry leaves.
6. Pour over rice. Mix well.

Note: The spice powder and pulikachal should not be mixed into the rice while it is hot. This puliyōdarai tastes better the next day as it has more time to absorb the flavours of the powder and tamarind sauce.

(Recipe courtesy Tiru Nārayana Temple, Melkote, Karnataka)

MILAGU VADAI Pepper Vadai

Makes: 80 servings
Serving size: 50 gms
Calories per serving: 312

INGREDIENTS

Black gram dal/Urad dal 7½ cups
Coarsely ground black pepper ¼ cup
Salt to taste
Oil for deep-frying 5¼ cups

METHOD

1. Wash urad dal and soak in water for 5–7 minutes. Drain completely. Set aside for about 20 minutes.
2. Grind dal to make a thick batter. Sprinkle in 1–2 tsp of water, as required. Add pepper and salt and mix well.
3. Take a small lime-sized ball of batter and flatten it into a 3-inch disc on a cotton cloth. Make a hole in the centre. Repeat with remaining batter.
4. Heat oil in a vānali/wok. When hot, gently drop vadai into hot oil and fry, in batches, till crisp. Drain.

ŚELVARAPPAM Crisp Fried Patties

Makes: 40 servings
Serving size: 75 gms
Calories per serving: 708

INGREDIENTS

Rice 2 cups
Salt ½ tsp
Ghee 2 cups

METHOD

1. Wash rice and soak in water for about an hour. Drain and spread on a cloth to dry. Grind to make a fine powder.
2. Sift fine rice flour into a bowl. Reserve coarse flour in sieve.
3. Measure the coarse flour. Take water in the ratio of 1 part rice flour to 3 parts water. Mix water and flour without lumps.
4. Take this mixture in a vessel and cook to make a thick porridge. Remove from heat.
5. Add the fine rice flour (prepared earlier) and salt into the prepared porridge, and mix well. The consistency should be that of a dough. Set aside overnight or for about 8 hours.
6. The next day, pinch off gooseberry-sized balls of dough. Pat each ball into a disc like a thick puri on a muslin cloth.
7. Take ghee in a vānali/wok over medium heat. Gently drop the appam into hot ghee and deep-fry in batches till crisp. Drain.

SUJI APPAM Semolina and Jaggery Puris

Makes: 25 servings
Serving size: 100 gms
Calories per serving: 1061

INGREDIENTS

Cover for filling
White flour/Maida 2 cups
Semolina/Ravā 1 tsp
Salt 1 pinch
Oil 2 tbsp

Filling
Ghee ½ cup + 1 tsp
Cashewnuts 10–15, broken
Semolina/Ravā 1 cup
Water 1 cup
Grated jaggery/Sugar 1½ cups
Cardamom 2–3, powdered
Oil for deep frying 2–3 cups

METHOD

Cover for filling

1. Mix maida, semolina and salt. Add oil and mix well till absorbed. Add a little water at a time and knead to make a soft, firm dough.
2. Set aside for about 2 hours.

Filling

1. Heat 2 tsp of ghee in a vānali. Fry cashewnuts over medium heat till golden. Slot out.
2. Add rest of ghee to wok, and roast semolina for 4 minutes without browning.
3. Add 1 cup of water and cook semolina over low heat, stirring continuously, till half cooked.
4. Add jaggery or sugar and stir till it thickens. Add 1 tsp of ghee and stir.
5. Mix in powdered cardamoms and remove from heat. Cool.

Appam

1. Divide dough and filling into 25 portions.
2. Smear a little oil on a banana leaf.
3. Roll a portion of dough into a ball and flatten into a small disc of 2-inch diameter. Place one portion of filling in the centre. Pull up edges and cover.
4. Place, sealed side down, on the banana leaf and press to make a 4-inch disc.
5. Make 2–3 appams at a time.
6. Place 1½-inch of oil in a wok over medium heat. Drop āppams into hot oil and fry till both sides are a light golden colour. Drain.
7. Make remaining appams in the same way. Cool and serve.

KONDAKADALAI SUNDĀL

Whole Bengal Gram Dal Sundāl

Makes: 12–15 servings
Serving size: 100 gms
Calories per serving: 318

Distribution of prasādam in the temple is an intrinsic part of the Srivaiṣnava tradition. We usually find throngs of children in the temple during the morning and evening distributions. Many amusing tales are told in this connection. A young lad, wanting double the prasādam and thinking himself to be clever, hides behind a pillar and stretches both his palms out to seem like two hands. The priest, knowing the nature of boys, brings both palms together and fills them up with sundāl, the prasādam for the day. You can understand the plight of this poor 'clever' boy! Like the greedy monkey in the story that has his hand stuck in the narrow-necked jar, this boy is caught in his own clever trap!

INGREDIENTS

Chickpeas (whole Bengal gram dal) 500 gm
Water 7 cups
Salt 1 tbsp
Lime juice 1 tbsp

Seasoning
Oil 1 tbsp
Mustard seeds ½ tsp
Black gram dal/Urad dal ½ tsp
Dried red chillies 4
Asafoetida powder 1 pinch
Curry leaves 1 sprig
Finely chopped ginger 1 tbsp
Finely chopped green chillies ½ tbsp
Grated fresh coconut 2 tbsp
Finely chopped unripe mango 1 tbsp (optional)

METHOD

1. Soak chickpeas in water overnight. Drain. Pressure-cook chickpeas with salt and 7 cups of water for 20 minutes after cooker reaches full pressure. Drain and cool.
2. Heat oil in a vānali/wok. Splutter mustard seeds. Add remaining seasoning ingredients and sauté for 1–2 minutes.
3. Add cooked chickpeas and stir a few times. Remove.
4. Stir in lime juice. Mix well and serve.

Note: Use the same method to prepare black-eyed beans, mochai/dolichos seeds and peanuts. A different sundāl, using a variety of beans, is prepared every day during Navaratri.

TIRUVALLIKENI TÉNKUḶAL

Temple Ténkuḷal

Makes: 51 servings
Serving size: 100 gms
Calories per serving: 1545

The crisp, savoury snack ténkuḷal appears to be a misnomer as it bears within it the sobriquet 'tén' or 'honey'. Initially, ténkuḷal referred to sweet fried flour tubes rolled in jaggery syrup; hence the name. Later it became the salt snack we know today. Interestingly, the original sweet survives as manoharam, the very same jaggery tubes rolled into a ball.

INGREDIENTS

Rice 8 kg
Black gram dal/Urad dal 7.5 kg
Pepper ¼ cup
Jeera/Cumin seeds 1 tbsp
Asafoetida 1 tsp. Salt ⅓ cup
Ghee for frying 5.6 kg
Canvas icing cone 1

METHOD

1. Wash rice and urad dal and soak in water for 2 hours.
2. Drain rice and dal and grind to a fine batter. Batter must be soft enough to pass through a canvas icing cone.
3. Add salt to dough before frying each ténkuḷal .
4. Heat 1½-inch deep ghee in a 12-inch wide vānali/wok over medium heat. Press a ténkuḷal in concentric circles through canvas cone into ghee to fill the wok, fry till both sides are golden brown. Drain and place in a colander.
5. Make remaining dough into tenkuḷals in the same way.

SUKHIYAN Sweet Balls with Coconut and Jaggery Filling

Makes: 18 servings
Serving size: 150 gms
Calories per serving: 1135

INGREDIENTS

Grated fresh coconut 1 cup
Grated jaggery ½ cup
Green cardamom powder ½ tsp
White flour/Maida ½ cup
Salt ¼ tsp
Refined oil 2 cups

METHOD

1. Place coconut and jaggery in a vānali/wok over medium heat. Mix well and stir continuously to prevent mixture from burning. Cook till mixture thickens and binds well. Mix in cardamom powder.
2. Remove from heat and cool on a platter.
3. Roll into marble-sized balls and set aside.
4. Add salt to maida and make a thick dipping batter with enough water.
5. Heat 1½-inch oil-ghee in a vānali over medium heat. Dip a ball of filling in the batter and drop into hot oil. Fry 4–5 sukhiyans at a time. Fry till crisp and golden brown. Remove from pan and drain.
6. Make remaining sukhiyans in the same way.

Note: Instead of a coconut and jaggery filling, green gram dal/Bengal gram dal and jaggery filling can be used, as for poḷi.

ATIRASAM Rice and Jaggery Vadai

Makes: 25–30 servings
Serving size: 100 gms
Calories per serving: 826

INGREDIENTS

Rice 2 cups
Grated jaggery 2 cups
Ghee 1 cup
Oil 1 cup
Banana leaf or polythene sheet

METHOD

1. Wash rice and drain. Spread on a clean cloth and dry in shade for about 2 hours. Do not let it dry completely. Grind to a fine powder. Sift the flour and set aside.
2. Dissolve jaggery in water and strain.
3. Boil strained jaggery over medium heat till it has a foamy consistency. Test syrup by pouring a teaspoon into a cup of water. The syrup should settle to the bottom, but not form a ball. (The consistency of syrup is very important to make perfect atirasam.)
4. Add rice flour gradually, continuously stirring, till all the flour is absorbed. It will form a soft dough. Let it cool.
5. Cover and keep for 2–3 days in a cool place.
6. Combine ghee and oil together.
7. Roll a lime-sized portion of dough into a ball. Place ball on a polythene sheet or banana leaf smeared lightly with oil and flatten it into a disc, about ⅛-inch thick, 3-inch diameter discs.
8. Heat 1½-inch oil-ghee mixture in a flat wok, slide 3–4 atirasam discs at a time, splash hot oil over it from the sides. When the underside is light brown, turn over and fry the other side, till it is a rich chestnut brown.
9. Remove with a slotted spoon and press out excess oil. A good atirasam has a crisp look.
10. Make the remaining atirasams in the same way, adding more ghee and oil as required.

DADHIYŌDANAM Curd Rice

Makes: 4 servings
Serving size: 150 gms
Calories per serving: 151

INGREDIENTS

Long-grained rice 1 cup
Water 3 cups
White butter 1 tbsp
Milk 2 cups
Thick fresh curd 1 cup, whisked smooth
Salt ½ tsp
Asafoetida powder 2 pinches dissolved in 2 tsp of water

Seasoning
Sesame oil 1 tbsp
Mustard seeds ½ tsp
Dried red chillies 2
Green chillies 2, cut into thirds
Ginger ½-inch piece, julienned
Asafoetida powder ¼ tsp
Curry leaves 1 sprig

METHOD

1. Wash rice, drain and cook in 3 cups of water in a steamer for 20 minutes.
2. Mash rice coarsely. Add salt and butter, mix. Then add milk, curd and asafoetida dissolved in 2 tsp of water.
3. Place oil in a vānali/wok over medium heat. Splutter mustard seeds. Add remaining seasoning ingredients and sauté for a few seconds. Add to rice, mix well and serve.

All temples have strict rules and regulations about the daily offerings made to the deity within. The great temples of India have an elaborate timetable for the nivedyams (offerings) made to the lord every day.

DAILY OFFERINGS TO THE DEITY AT SRIRANGAM TEMPLE, TAMIL NADU

7.00 A.M.

- Roti with jaggery and ghee
- Cooked whole green gram
- Vennai—butter
- Fresh cow's milk (not boiled)

10.00 A.M.

- Venpongal
- Dosai with dry ginger, pepper, long pepper, ghee and jaggery
- Kariamudu—vegetable
- Urukāi—pickle

1.00 P.M.

- Śuddhannam—cooked white rice
- Cooked whole green gram dal
- Uppuchāru—rasam
- Kūtu—vegetable with pepper, tamarind
- Atirasam
- Tirukannalamudu—green gram and jaggery pāyasam

For the goddess

- Mashed greens
- Uppuchāru—rasam seasoned with fenugreek, pepper
- Cooked white rice

6.15–6.45 P.M.

- Ksheerannam—sweet milk rice
- Ténkuḷal—crisp rice pretzels
- Appam
- Tirumāl vadai
- Kariamudu—vegetable

For the goddess

- Sweet puttu

8.00–8.30 P.M.

- Aravanai cooked in terracotta pots
- Cooked white rice
- Cooked green gram dal
- Condensed milk with saffron, cardamom and jaggery

DAILY OFFERINGS TO THE DEITY AT TIRUMALA TEMPLE, ANDHRA PRADESH

TIRUPATI NAIVEDYAM

Time	Sevas	Naivedyam
3.30 a.m.	Suprabhatha Seva Awakening of Lord	
3.30–4.30 a.m.	After Suprabhatha Seva	Navaneetam—freshly churned butter with a little sugar
4.30 a.m.	Dharbar/Kolu Seva	Sesame powder with jaggery
5.30 a.m.	First bell	Mathirai—mixture of butter, ginger and hot cooked rice (inside the Kulasekara threshold), Venpongal, Śarkarai Pongal, Kadambam, Puliyōdarai, Dadhiyōdanam
7.30–11.30 a.m.	Second bell at 7.30 a.m.	Ravā Kesari, Venpongal, Śarkarai Pongal, Kadambam, Betel leaves folded with rose petals, arecanut in silver kinnam
11.30 a.m.	Kalyana Utsavam	Daily appam for Kalyana Utsavam, Chinna Dosai
7.30 p.m.	Night bell	Milōgarai, Tomalai Dosai, Kadambam, Vakuladevi Ammavaru Pāyasam (Akkāra Adisil)
1.30 a.m.	Ekanta Seva	Milk and mixed fruits
7.30 a.m.	On Mondays Second bell	Big Laddu, Vadai, and Homa Sesa Appam. Out of 51 appams, 6 are for the homam and the remaining 45 appams are distributed
	Every Ekadasi	Dosai/a special rice nomattarici and kadambamn
7.30 p.m.	On Punarvasu Nakshatram day	Nei dosai/Punarvasu Dosai
7.30 p.m.	On Sravana Nakshatram day	Nei Dosai
7.30 p.m.	On Arudhra Nakshatram day	Puliyōdarai—special offering by the Maharaja of Mysore
7.30 p.m.	On Rohini Nakshatram day	Nei Dosai for small Krishna
7.30 a.m.	On Wednesdays after the second bell	Vadai Paruppu, Panagam, and Pālpāyasam
7.30 a.m.	On Thursdays	Jangiri, Thenkulal, Pāyasam, Puliyōdarai, Thiruppavadai Dosai
7.30 p.m.		Vadaiparuppu, pānakam—within Kulasekara Padi
3.30 a.m.	On Fridays First bell	Pongal, Śarkarai Pongal and Mathirai
7.30 a.m.	Second bell	Routine Prasādam and poḷi
	During Dhanur masam	Vella Dosai and Sundāl every day
7.30 p.m.	Adhyāyana Utsavam	Bagalabath
Every day at 7.30 p.m.	Sahasra Deepalankara Sevai	Ravā Kesari

Note: Earlier the prasādam was distributed in big pot sherds

OFFERINGS AT SRI PADMANABHA SWAMY TEMPLE–THIRUVANANTHAPURAM, KERALA

SRI PADMANABHA SWAMY SHRINE

- Pongal—twice a year Ratna Pāyasam is offered
- Śarkarai Pongal/ Śarkarai Pāyasam Ottavadai
- Appam
- Meni Tulā Pāyasam
- Pāl Pāyasam
- Kilikinnam—served in a round gold tray: rice, pulisseri, erusseri and śarkarai pongal, slightly liquid in consistency
- Mānga Pāl—twice a year

SRI NARASIMHA SWAMY SHRINE

- Pānakam
- Pāl Pāyasam
- Meni Pāyasam
- Aval

SRI KRISHNA SWAMY SHRINE

- Aval (puffed rice) with sugar/jaggery
- Appam
- Vennai (butter)
- Kadāli (bananas)

FOURTEEN POOJAS FOR SRI KRISHNA AT UDUPI

Pooja Name	Naivedhya Offering
Nirmālya Visherjana Pooja	Beaten rice, curd, groundnut, ginger, jaggery, coconut, tāmboolam
Ushas Kala Pooja	Cooked rice (naivedhya), milk, curd, tender coconut, coconut, banana, tāmboolam
Akshaya Pātra Pooja—Go Pooja	Haralu (nelpori), jaggery, banana
Panchamirtha Abhisheka Pooja	Cooked rice (naivedhya), coconut, banana, tāmboolam
Udvarthana Pooja	Cooked rice (naivedhya), milk, butter, tender coconut
Kalasa Pooja	Cooked rice (naivedhya)
Thirtha Pooja	Cooked rice, dosa, butter, jaggery pāyasam, coconut, banana, tāmboolam
Alankāra Pooja	Cooked rice, pāyasam, haralu ladu
Avasara Sanakadi Pooja	Cooked rice
Maha Pooja	Cooked rice, pāyasam, huggi (pongal), appa, vadai, chakkuli, undluga (seer), holige, athirasa, sweet unde (kadalaparuppu, coconut, sugar, ghee, cardamom), milk, curd, hanna kai, fruits, coconuts, tāmboolam, ukku theli, akki roti
Chāmara Seva Pooja	Haralu (nelpori), jaggery, haralu ladu, milk, fruits, coconuts, tāmboolam
Rathiri Pooja	Cooked rice, puliyōdarai, pancha kajjaya, dosai, milk, tender coconut, coconut, fruits, tāmboolam
Mantapa Pooja—Astāvadana Pooja	Haralu, jaggery

Note: Ukku Theli—the light first kanji (gruel) of rice, seasoned with green chillies, ginger, coriander leaves and shredded mango, a dish eaten by the poor, is also one of the offerings to Sri Krishna at Udupi. This was the offering made by the poet–devotee Sri Kanakadasa and is continued to this day in his honour.

OFFERINGS AT SHRI JAGANNATHJI TEMPLE, PURI

The 56 items (Chappan Bhog) of Mahaprasada are offered to Lord Jagannathji daily. The items offered are as follows:

Rice preparations

1. Sadha Anna—simple rice
2. Ghee Anna—rice mixed with ghee
3. Kanika—rice, ghee and sugar
4. Khecedi—rice mixed with lentils
5. Dahi pakhala—curd, rice and water

6. Mitha Pakhala—rice, sugar and water
7. Ada Pakhala—rice, ginger and water
8. Oria Pakhala—rice, ghee, lemon, and salt
9. Thali Khecedi—lentils, rice with sugar and ghee

Sweets

(Usually shaped in small balls and deep-fried)

10. Khaja—made of wheat
11. Gaja—made of wheat, sugar
12. Laddu—made of wheat, sugar and ghee
13. Magaja Laddu
14. Jira Laddu
15. Jagannatha Ballava—made of wheat, sugar and ghee
16. Khuruma—made of wheat, ghee and salt
17. Mathapuli—made of ghee, ginger and a kind of beans ground into a thick paste
18. Kakara—made of ghee, wheat and molasses
19. Marici Laddu—made of wheat, sugar
20. Luni Khurama—made of wheat, ghee and salt

Burfies

21. Suara Pitha—made of wheat and ghee
22. Cadei Ladda—made of wheat, ghee and sugar
23. Jhilli—rice flour, ghee and sugar
24. Kanti—rice flour and ghee
25. Amalu—made of wheat, ghee and sugar
26. Puri—made of wheat and ghee and deep fried, like a small thin pancake
27. Luci Puri—rice, flour and ghee
28. Bara—made of ghee and a kind of beans (gram)
29. Dahi Bara—gram, ghee and curd
30. Arisa—a flat cake made of rice, flour and ghee
31. Tripuri—another flat cake made of rice, flour and ghee
32. Rosapaik—cake made of wheat and ghee

Milk preparations

33. Khiri—rice, milk and sugar
34. Papudi—prepared only from the cream of milk
35. Khua—prepared out of pure milk slowly boiled over many hours to a soft custard
36. Rasabali—made of milk, sugar and flour
37. Tadia—made of cheese, sugar, ghee
38. Chena khai—made of fresh cheese, milk and sugar
39. Papudi kahaja—cream of milk, sugar and ghee
40. Khua manda—made of milk, wheat and ghee
41. Sarapuli—pure milk, boiled slowly for hours and spread into a large pizza-shaped pan in thin sheets

Curry with vegetables

42. Dali
43. Bindali
44. Urid dal
45. Muga dal
46. Dalama dal, vegetables, coconut, etc.
47. Mahura
48. Besara
49. Saga
50. Potala rasa
51. Goti baigana
52. Khata
53. Raita
54. Pita
55. Baigini
56. Bhaja—fried vegetable

ANNAM

ANNAM

Annam is from the root word 'ad' in Sanskrit, which means to eat, the noun form being annam. Annam in Vedic sources refers to that which is eaten, consumed; that which is, in fact, eaten by all— devas (the gods), men, animals, all beings.

Ancient Indian thought characterized Brahman the undifferentiated cause as annam (food): 'From space, wind; from wind, fire; from fire, water; from water, earth; from earth, plant-life. Plant-life is nourishment; from this, man. Indeed, man is the essence of food. The essence of everything is Brahman.'—*Taittiriya Brahmanandavalli I*

Brahman and annam are interchangeable: 'I am that annam for the Brahman to enjoy and be experienced by him, and that Brahman is my experience so he is annam.'—*Taitreya Upanishad, Anandavalli lines 3–6*

The Chandogya Upanishad also reiterates the same idea.

Annam nourishes the body and the intelligence, so it is the duty of everyone to grow more food so that all may attain this nourishment. Annam bahu kurvita: let food proliferate! Only such an excess of grain can help us carry out annadānam, the gift of food and water which is still considered the highest of gifts. This bestowal is not necessarily only to the poor or needy. It encompasses all of humanity which might be hungry at any given moment, including the wealthy.

This great belief in annadānam continues to the present day in the Indian emphasis on hospitality.

Indian Hospitality

The rigours of hospitality have existed in India for more than 3,500 years. Tiruvalluvar, in his moral treatise Tirukkural, extols the man who receives a continuous line of guests with an open heart and an open hand:

> *Śelvirundu Ōmbi varuvirundu pārtiruppān*
> *Nalvirundu vānat tavarku*
> Who hosts the passing guests and waits
> for more
> Will be the honoured guest of the gods

The hospitality followed by the householder in this couplet proceeds from the ancient Vedic injunction.

> न कञ्चन वसतौ प्रत्याचक्षीत। तद्व्रतम्।
> One should not turn away anybody who approaches (one's) door. That is the vow.

Every day the householder is expected to come out of his house and look for anyone who is unfed, whichever community he might belong to. He must bring him in and feed him. We see this practice among many orthodox Hindus even today, certainly in many ashrams, to wait for an atithi (a guest), before partaking of the morning meal. Till the atithi has eaten (an atithi could be a stranger, a wayfarer, not necessarily a known visitor), the householder and his family will not eat.

The householder is encouraged to extend this kind of hospitality to as many people as possible. This encompasses the samāradhana, which is public feeding. It is also called tadiyāradhana, arising from Tad (Brahman) and iya (those who belong) meaning people who are sātvik. When such good people are fed, one accumulates merit.

Besides the householder whose discipline is to offer food, there are ootupirais (food halls), chatrams (shelters), matams (places of religious order) and ashrams which give refuge and food to the public.

The temples in India have always specialized in feeding pilgrims and the general populace at temple festivals. When food is distributed to the poor during festivals or other important ritual occasions, it is referred to as Sri Nārayana Seva. On ritual occasions like Dwadasi samāradhana, on the acharyas' birth-star days, on completion of the reading of the epics, the Ramayana or Srimad Bhagavatam, or after the recital of Vedic scriptures, food is distributed on a mass scale.

The early epigraphs of the Tirumalā temple speak of endowments to the temple with the specific purpose of feeding pilgrims. A little later, free feeding halls for Śrivaiṣṇava pilgrims called Rāmanuja-kūtams were set up by Saluva Narasimhadeva Maharāya. These had an organization of their own separate from that of the temple.

The same tradition continues today in several maths and ashrams like the Sringeri math under Sringeri Śankaracharya, Sri Raghavendra math in Mantralayam and in Dharmasthala where thousands are fed every day. Annadānam is an important practice at the Jagannath and Ananta Vasudeva temples in Puri. Jain temples and ashrams continue to feed numerous pilgrims daily. All these religious centres perform this compassionate duty throughout the year. Food served for annadānam is always vegetarian.

The most extensive and elaborate public feeding programme, however, is the samāradhana at the temple in Udupi. It is also an occasion for wealthy patrons to distribute new clothes and other necessities. The importance given to this noble practice might have had its origins in the age-old custom when the whole village was fed on festive days or ceremonial occasions. It was a common practice to lay four full plantain leaves for one person and fill them with delicious and sumptuous food.

Tanneer pandals (water canopies) where water is distributed to pilgrims have been in existence for more than 1,000 years. The practice continues to this day when individuals and charitable organizations set up such stations on public roads during the summer and during major temple festivals where anybody can stop and have cool water, buttermilk or pānakam (a drink with jaggery, dried ginger and lime that is cooling to the system). Cucumber and bananas are also distributed sometimes.

I had a touching experience when I was welcomed as a guest in an ashram. Some years ago, while travelling back from Badrinath, tired and hungry, I reached Rishikesh. Passing by a building that looked like a place of rest, I entered. Immediately, I was welcomed and given a room and a bathroom with running hot water to refresh myself. Then, I was met with a big plate with six or seven small bowls all filled with a variety of vegetables and other food. This spontaneous hospitality has remained in my memory since then as a truly Indian spiritual tradition of welcoming the guest. Everyone was treated as an honoured guest without regard to their status or background. When I wanted to make a donation to the ashram, it was turned down gently but firmly since accepting it would be at odds with the philosophy of 'atithi devo bhava' (consider the guest as God).

This incident reminded me of the Indian belief that the name of the person who is ordained to eat it is inscribed on every grain of food in this world, *dāne dāne par khānewāla kā nām likhā hai.*

Āhāraśuddhi: Purity of food

The seeker of truth or one whose goal is self-realization should take great care to consume only the purest of foods. Pure food here means sātvik food. The Chandogya Upanishad points out the reason why man should be particular about the food that he consumes. As 'food is man', pure food clears his intelligence and leads to his final liberation. Brahmanāndi, a great seer, prescribes āhāraśuddhi for one who wishes to pursue emancipation of the self. To do this, he has to eat proper food, which fulfils the following three conditions:

1. Avoid that which is non-sātvik
2. The ambience of eating should be peaceful and happy
3. The one who cooks and serves the food should possess a sātvik quality

In addition to this, the hygiene of the food and its preparation should be of paramount importance.

Akshayapātram—the inexhaustible vessel of food

Though ancient Indian direction laid emphasis on the supreme responsibility of the householder to provide food for all his dependents and to carry out daily feeding of all other created beings like animals and birds, kings were also expected to bear the responsibility of feeding their subjects.

Banished to the forest after an ill-fated gambling game, King Yudhisthira in the Mahabharata is torn by the anxiety of failing in this duty. Finally he is advised to pray to the sun who is the provider of all sustenance on earth who, pleased by his devotion, gives him the akshayapātram, which then helps him look after the family during their time of exile.

The oldest of Indian beliefs was that no one in this world should starve. An early Buddhist tale of Āputran emphasizes this belief in graphic terms. The story describes the tragedy that befell Āputran, who was proud that he possessed the akshayapātram, which helped him feed anyone he met and satisfy their hunger. Finally he was stranded on an uninhabited island and had no one to feed. The discipline of sharing before eating had become so ingrained in his character that Āputran dropped the bowl in the sacred waters of the river and fasted unto death. This could also be read as a cautionary tale about the destructiveness of pride, especially in the matter of feeding others.

This overwhelming importance given to food, its proliferation and its distribution in India is seen in the following injunction:

> *Annam na nindyāt.tadvratam. prāno vā annam.*
> Do not scorn annam the food. It is life itself! This is the inviolable discipline for the one who knows.

MORE ABOUT RICE

The Odisha region has been a supreme rice grower from ancient times. Even today it is famous for many fine varieties of rice. Indigenous communities of the province continue to cultivate many kinds of rice and are the guardians of the wild rice available in the region. We believe there are more than sixty varieties of wild rice available there.

As the giver of sustenance, and hence of life itself, rice has come to hold a sacred place in the Indian consciousness.

The poet Tiruvalluvar remembers the lifelong service that his beloved wife Vasuki rendered to him, and mourns her death with adisirkiniyalai anbudayālai—'she who was as sweet to me as rice and [who] served [it] with love is not any more here…'

Rice smeared with turmeric called akshatā (uninjured) is the one outstanding symbol of sacredness and blessing in Indian tradition. It is part of all auspicious functions and much sought after from acharyas (gurus) and elders. Akshata completes the verbal blessing for longevity, wholesomeness, health and wealth.

With so much emotional and cultural connectedness with rice, it is not surprising to note that India during the Vedic period had as many as four lakh varieties of rice. Rice experts say that even today there are at least two lakh kinds of paddy (whole grain) growing across the country, assimilating the special characteristics of each region's locale and climate. The very names of these varieties of rice sound rich and fragrant.

Thus we have, in Tamil Nadu, jeeraga cambā (redolent of cumin), sirumani (tiny jewels), vayalkondan (that which fills the fields), kichidi camba, toppi camba (that which curls up like a hat when boiled!) and yānaikomban (curved like an elephant tusk). In Mysore, we find varieties like rājabhogam, chandrabhogam, indrabhogam, names that remind us of luxury and opulence. The names of Andhra Pradesh rice varieties sound artistic and musical, as in chitimuthayulu or kakirekhulu.

In the states of Bihar, Odisha and West Bengal, extensive rice-growing and rice-consuming regions, we find many more special varieties and lovely names like badal pughi (a drop of cloud), kala jeera (with the fragrance of black cumin), kala namak (aroma of black salt), and sona chur (gold dust). In UP a popular variety is ādamchini (Adam's sugar)!

Bāsumati, the rice that stands for fragrance most completely, more than any other rice, has become the king of rice internationally. We can trace the origin of the name to vasu or the richness of the earth, hence vasumati, carrying the rich fragrance of the earth, and then to basumati, the name that the whole world applauds now.

In contrast to these traditional names that trip off our tongues sweetly, we now have hybrids that are unfortunately known by numbers, IR8, IR52 and the stupefying number IR1116 and so on. These new varieties of rice are not as fragrant or tasty as the older varieties.

The guna pātham section of the Materia Medica, a therapeutic compendium of therapeutic plants and cereals found in India and published in the tenth century CE lists twenty-two different types of rice and their different properties. Their varied effects for health or otherwise for consumption are also categorized. One does not know if all these varieties are still extant in the country.

According to the compendium, rice comes under the grouping of 'sweet'. Its taste is sweet and its effect is cooling on the system. It is a nutrient. The gruel made from rice is a demulcent (soothing) and a refrigerant (cooling). Kanji, rice gruel, is a light nutritious food especially for those who are ill. The gruel can be mixed in milk, buttermilk, curds. It can be.

Many-splendoured Rice

The Materia Medica refers to the following varities of paddy grown in India:

- Kārarisi
- Karunkuravai
- Eerkucamba
- Pulugucamba
- Koraicamba
- Kuruncamba
- Milagucamba
- Jeeragacamba
- Kālancamba
- Maicamba
- Malligaicamba
- Kadaicamba
- Iluppaipoocamba
- Manicamba
- Valaithadicamba
- Kaivaraicamba
- Chencamba
- Kallundaicamba
- Gunducamba
- Kundrimanicamba
- Annamālagi

Some coarse varieties of rice, such as phisini and pichikar, were also known to have been cultivated.

FOOD SERVING ORDER

The rules of Ayurveda, once familiar to all but now known only to those who are inclined to disciplined eating habits, nevertheless seem to have been assimilated into the consciousness of many Indians, especially vegetarians.

Ayurveda sees food and spices as medicinal substances and good digestion as one of the main factors for good health. In Ayurveda, taste (rasā) is all important. The six rasās are madhura (sweet), amla (sour), lāvana (salty), katu (pungent), tikta (bitter) and kasayā (astringent).

The six rasās are made up of permutations and combinations of the five bhutās, the five elements—water, wind, light, earth and space. A correct balancing of these six rasās is considered essential for good health. In other words, a healthy diet must contain a combination of all six tastes. Thus, even a simple everyday meal will be planned to include lentils, a tamarind preparation, a green vegetable, a root vegetable, something sour, and something bitter.

The normal everyday meal pattern is heightened or amplified for ceremonial occasions. A characteristic plotting of such a pattern would be as follows:

The dining room is washed and a kolam or rice flour design for each guest is drawn on the floor. A wooden plank is placed for each guest with enough space on either side. A banana leaf (easily disposable after the meal) with its tapering edge to the left of each diner is placed before the guest. The water tumbler is to his left (he eats with his freshly washed right hand).

First bananas, jackfruit, or mango with honey and sugar according to the season is laid on the diner's leaf to the extreme left, with pāyasam at the centre. Until recently the rice would be served first, having been purified by ghee (clarified butter)—called annasuddhi, literally, the purifier of food. Then the person who eats, takes around the leaf a spoonful of water in the palm of his hands and says, 'Water (amirtham) be the basic layer.' The ritual of annasuddhi brings calmness to one's entire system, enabling one to start eating in peace. Then he eats his meal, at the end of which he again takes a little water and says, 'you are the cover.' ('amrtopastaranamasi ... amrtapidhanamasi').

Cooked dal is served before the vegetables as it is considered auspicious. This is followed by freshly cut vegetables (kosumalli seasoned with soaked mung dal) and pacchadis (fresh vegetables seasoned in a curd sauce). Then two or three different vegetables, mostly steamed and then sautéed with mustard and urad dal, are served. Some are dry, some fried, some soft, some crisp while others are differently spiced. A vegetable and dal preparation (negil kariamudu) is next. This is a savoury gravy to be mixed with rice.

Rice is served three times: the first course is with kuḷambu (which is a thick sauce.) The second course is with sātramudhu, a thin soup delicately spiced (the gourmet capabilities of the cook are gauged with this dish). This is accompanied by the appalam. Sweet preparations and mixed rice (chitrannam) follow. Rice with curd brings the meal to its conclusion. A variety of pickles and savoury condiments may bring the total number of dishes up to fifty-six. An aromatic betel leaf enclosing sweet spices may follow the meal as a digestive.

A menu that is quite common is given below:

1. Fruits with honey or sugar
2. Fresh vegetables finely cut and seasoned, two varieties
3. Fresh vegetables in curds, two varieties
4. Pulippu kūtu (gourd-like vegetables cooked with tamarind, dal, red chillies)
5. Poritta kūtu (dal, coconut, green legumes or gourds)
6. Puli kariamudu (okra/raw banana/brinjal)
7. Plain kariamudu (steamed vegetables with fresh coconut and seasoning)
8. Paruppusili (vegetables cooked with ground dal and seasoned)
9. Vadakkal (sautéed in oil gently)
10. Varuval/chips (made of raw banana/yams/jackfruit)
11. Appalam (fried dal wafers)
12. Vadām and vatral (dried wafers of rice, fried)
13. Vadai (ground urad-dal batter fried [like a doughnut] plain or with vegetables)
14. Tayir vadai (same as above in curd)
15. Plain rice with ghee
16. One or two mixed rices (spiced and seasoned in different ways)
17. Kuḷambu (a thick sauce with dal)
18. Sātramudhu (rasam—a delicate and thin liquid made with red gram dal and spices)
19. Tirukannamudu (milk cooked with rice and sugarcane juice)
20. Laddu, barfi (sweet balls and fudges)
21. Tirattipāl (a concentrated milk sweet)
22. Dadhiyōdanam (rice and curds, seasoned)
23. Pickles (both preserved and freshly cut ginger, mango, a slice of lime and so on)
24. Tāmbulam (areca nut, betel leaves and spices)

The śadrasās or 'six essences of palatal distinction' that constitute the aesthetics of the gastronomic experience are hereby accounted for; not only by the vegetables themselves, but also by the different spices; ginger, mint, green coriander, asafoetida, pepper and lemon, for instance. The six tastes are: sweet, sour, salt, bitter, hot (spicy) and astringent.

ETYMOLOGY

Though the origin of the word 'annam' may mean anything that is consumed over time, annam has come to mean 'cooked rice' in popular usage. Annam or cooked rice, being at the heart of nourishment, as being pure and sacred, is always served first with a bit of ghee, which is the purifier. The reason is that one can make an offering of annam to the household deity even if one cannot offer up the entire menu of the day. This becomes prasādam, blessed by the lord. Hence cooked rice came to be referred to as prasādam and later shortened to sādam. All rice preparations are called sādam, reinforcing the importance of 'blessed'.

The term for spiced cooked rice arises from the manipravalam (Tamil–Sanskrit) word 'odanam', which becomes 'odaram', then 'odarai' changing to 'ohorai' in some regions.The Dravidic adisil becomes arisil. Thus we have akkāravadisil (an ancient sweet preparation which is like the śarkarai pongal of today), puliyōdarai (tamarind rice), ellōdarai (sesame rice), dadhiyōdanam (curd rice), and ukkōrai (a rice and jaggery preparation).

KADAMBA SĀDAM

Mixed Vegetable Rice

Makes: 4 servings
Serving size: 100 gms
Calories per serving: 83

INGREDIENTS

Vegetables 2 cups
Long-grained raw rice 1 cup
Water 3 cups
Tamarind 15 gm
Water 3 cups
Green gram or tuvar dal 2 tbsp
Water ½ cup
Salt 1 tsp
Grated jaggery 1 tsp
Green chillies 2
Pepper corns 3–4
Sesame oil 1 tbsp

For vadai
Turmeric Powder
Urad dal ½ cup, soaked and ground
Oil for frying ½ cup

Spices for powdering
Sesame oil 1 tbsp
Dried red chillies ¾
Coriander seeds 2 tbsp
Asafoetida 5 gm

Seasoning
Sesame oil 1 tbsp
Mustard seeds ½ tsp
Curry leaves 1 sprig

Use a mix of the following vegetables: tender (yellow) pumpkin, plantain, colocasia, yam, tender amaranth stems and cluster beans.

METHOD

1. Extract tamarind juice with 2 cups of water (see Pre-Cooking Processes).
2. Boil colocasia in their jackets. Peel and slice into ½-inch pieces.
3. Peel yam, cut into cubes and boil in 1 tbsp of tamarind juice.
4. Peel and cube pumpkin and plantain. Cut greens into 1-inch pieces.
5. Wash rice and cook with 3 cups of water in a steamer.
6. Cook green gram dal or tuvar dal in ½ cup of water in steamer.
7. Heat ½ cup oil in a vānali. Make berry-sized pakodas from ground urad dal and fry. Keep aside.
8. Heat oil in a vānali. Add spices for powdering and sauté till aroma rises.
9. Take tamarind juice in a deep vessel, add salt, turmeric powder and jaggery. Add pumpkin, plantain and greens. Boil till vegetables are three-quarters done. Add colocasia and yam, boil for a minute or two.
10. Add the cooked tuvar dal, green chillies and pepper.
11. Add the vadais to the kuḷambu.
12. Add the ground spice powder. Boil till kuḷambu thickens.
13. Heat oil in a wok. Splutter mustard seeds. Add curry leaves and pour over kuḷambu.
14. Add 1 tbsp sesame oil to the rice, add the required kuḷambu to the rice, mix well and serve. Reserve some kuḷambu.

Note: Remove some of the cooked vegetables and add on top of rice before serving. Vegetables should not become mushy. Kabuli chana/chickpeas can be soaked overnight, cooked and added to kuḷambu.

BISI-BĒḶE BHĀTH Spicy Red Gram Dal Tamarind Rice

Makes: 4 servings
Serving size: 100 gms
Calories per serving: 142

INGREDIENTS

Raw rice ½ cup
Red gram dal/tuvar dal ½ cup
Water 3 cups
Turmeric powder 1 tsp
Tamarind 1 packed tsp
Water 1 ½ cups. Salt 1 tsp
Grated jaggery ½ tsp
Ghee 1–2 tbsp

Spices I
Sesame oil 1 tbsp. Dried red chillies 5
Fenugreek seeds ¼ tsp
Dhania/Coriander seeds ½ tbsp
Whole black pepper ¼ tsp
Jeera/Cumin seeds ¼ tsp
Asafoetida powder ½ tsp
Bengal gram dal/Chana dal ½ tbsp
Black gram dal/Urad dal ¾ tbsp
Water to grind ¼ cup

Spices II
Ghee 2 tsp. Cloves 5
Cardamoms 3
Marathi moggu (kapok buds) 1
Cinnamon ½-inch stick
Cashewnuts 8
Grated copra 1½ tbsp
Khus khus/Poppy seeds 1 tsp

Seasoning
Ghee ½ tbsp
Mustard seeds ¾ tsp
Curry leaves 1 sprig

METHOD

1. Wash rice and tuvar dal. Cook with turmeric powder and 3 cups of water in a rice steamer. Transfer to another vessel and set aside.
2. Extract tamarind juice using 1½ cups of water (see Pre-Cooking Processes) and boil till raw aroma disappears. Remove from heat.
3. Heat oil in a vānali/wok on medium heat. Add ingredients under Spices I, each separately in the given order, till dals turn golden. Grind with a little water to a fine consistency.
4. Heat ghee in wok. Add Spices II and fry in the order given for a minute. Grind to a fine powder.
5. Add boiled tamarind juice and salt to cooked rice and cook for a few minutes. Add jaggery.
6. Add ground Spices I and simmer for about 3 minutes, stirring a bit.
7. Add Spices II powder and mix well.
8. Heat ghee in a wok. Splutter mustard seeds, add curry leaves and sauté. Pour over rice and mix.
9. If the bisi-bele is too thick, add some hot water. The consistency of bisi-bele is like that of oats porridge.
10. Before serving, add a few spoons of ghee and mix.

TAKKĀLI SĀDAM Tomato Rice

Makes: 4 servings
Serving size: 100 gms
Calories per serving: 252

INGREDIENTS

Long-grained rice 1 cup
Water 2 ½ cups
Tomatoes 400 gm
Turmeric powder ½ tsp
Salt 1 tsp

Spices for grinding
Oil 1 tbsp
Dried red chillies 5
Dhania/Coriander seeds 1½ tbsp
Jeera/Cumin seeds 1½ tsp
Poppy seeds 2 tsp
Cashewnuts 10
Toasted Bengal gram dal/Pottu Kadālai 1¼ tbsp
Water 2 tbsp

Seasoning
Ghee 3 tbsp
Mustard seeds 1 tsp
Asafoetida powder ¼ tsp
Curry leaves 1 sprig

METHOD

1. Wash rice and cook in 2½ cups of water in a steamer. Set aside.
2. Blanch tomatoes (see Pre-Cooking Processes). Chop fine.
3. Heat ghee in a vānali/wok. Add cashewnuts, fry to a light brown and remove. In the same wok, add spices, sauté over medium heat for a minute. Grind spices finely along with cashewnuts with about 2 tbsp of water.
4. In a heavy bottom vessel heat oil, splutter mustard seeds. Lower heat, add asafoetida and curry leaves and sauté for a second.
5. Add tomatoes, turmeric powder, and salt. Sauté over medium heat, till ghee/oil separates.
6. Add ground spices and stir for about 3 minutes.
7. Add rice and mix well. If mixed rice is too dry, add very little hot water to moisten it.

MENTHIYA KEERAI SĀDAM Fenugreek Greens Rice

Makes: 4 servings
Serving size: 100 gms
Calories per serving: 256

INGREDIENTS

Long-grained rice 1 cup
Water 2½ cups
Tamarind 1 packed tsp
Water 1 cup
Turmeric powder ¼ tsp
Ghee 2 tsp
Cashewnuts 6, broken
Salt 1 tsp
Grated jaggery ¼ tsp
Chopped fenugreek leaves 2 cups
Tomatoes (medium) 3, deseeded and chopped fine

Spices I
Oil 2 tsp
Dried red chillies 4
Dhania/Coriander seeds 1 tbsp
Bengal gram dal/Chana dal 1 tsp
Black gram dal/Urad dal ½ tsp

Spices II
Cardamom 1
Cloves 2
Grated copra 1 tbsp

Seasoning
Sesame oil 1 tbsp
Mustard seeds 1 tsp
Curry leaves 1 sprig
Asafoetida powder ½ tsp

METHOD

1. Wash rice and cook in 2½ cups of water in a steamer. Set aside.
2. Extract tamarind juice using 1 cup of water (See Pre-Cooking Processes). Stir in turmeric powder.
3. Heat ghee in a vānali/wok on medium heat and fry Spices II till light brown. Remove and grind to a fine powder.
4. Add ghee and fry cashewnuts till golden and remove.
5. Heat oil in wok, add Spices I, fry till golden. Grind to a fine powder.
6. Heat oil in a vessel. Splutter mustard seeds, add asafoetida powder and curry leaves and sauté for a few seconds.
7. Add fenugreek leaves and sauté till well cooked.
8. Mix in tomatoes and sauté till oil separates.
9. Add tamarind juice, jaggery, Spices I powder and boil to a thick sauce.
10. Add cooked rice and salt and mix gently with a fork.
11. Stir in Spices II powder and fried cashewnuts and mix well.

MOCHAIKĀI MENTHIYA KEERAI PULAO

Fenugreek Leaves and Dolichos Beans Rice

Makes: 4 servings

Serving size: 100 gms

Calories per serving: 242

INGREDIENTS

Basumati rice/long-grained rice 1 cup
Curd, whisked smooth 1 tsp
Water (boiling) ¾ cup
Ghee 2 tbsp + 1 tbsp
Tomatoes (medium) 2, chopped
Jeera/Cumin seeds ½ tsp
Cardamom 2
Cloves 4
Bay leaf 1, halved
Asafoetida powder tsp
Whole green chillies slit at the tip 2
Ginger ½-inch piece, cut in fine juliennes
Chopped fenugreek leaves ½ cup
Chopped coriander leaves ¼ cup
Dolichos lablab beans (peeled) ½ cup
Turmeric powder ¼ tsp
Red chilli powder ½ tsp
Salt 1 tsp

METHOD

1. Soak rice for half an hour.
2. Heat 2 tbsp of ghee in a vānali/wok. Sauté tomatoes over medium heat till ghee separates. Set aside.
3. Heat 1 tbsp ghee in a vessel, add cumin seeds, cardamom, cloves, bay leaf and asafoetida powder and sauté over medium heat for a few seconds.
4. Add green chillies, ginger, fenugreek leaves and coriander leaves and sauté, till raw smell of greens disappear.
5. Stir in dolichos beans, turmeric powder and chilli powder and sauté for about a minute.
6. Mix in cooked tomatoes, add drained rice, salt, and curd.
7. Transfer to a vessel (which fits into a steamer) and steam for 15–20 minutes.

SĀDAM TURNS TO BHĀTH!

With north Indian influences entering south Indian cuisine, the everyday Tamil word 'sādam' came to be replaced with the Hindi word 'bhāth' lending it an exotic feel, first in the hotelier's perception, then in that of the general populace.

Telugu practices and etymology were part of Tamil culture during the days of the composite Madras Presidency. So, many terms and titles for food and recipes were Telugu and used as such. So, we have venkaya (kattrikai) sādam becoming vāngi bhāth.

Every language came under this diktat. The Sanskrit dadhiyōdanam became bagalābhāth, the Kannada bisi-bēḷe bhāth became bisi-bēḷe bhāth and the lowly uppuma acquired the striking title kharabhāth!

VĀNGI BHĀTH Brinjal Rice

Makes: 4 servings
Serving size: 100 gms
Calories per serving: 281

INGREDIENTS

Tender brinjals 250 gm
Long-grained rice 1 cup
Water 2 ½ cups +1 cup
Tamarind 1 tbsp
Ghee 1 tbsp
Cashewnuts 8, broken
Turmeric powder ½ tsp
Salt 1 tsp
Grated jaggery 1 tsp
Oil ½ tbsp
Tomatoes 3, chopped fine

Spices I
Oil 2 tsp
Dried red chillies 4
Dhania/Coriander seeds 1 tbsp
Bengal gram dal/Chana dal 1 tsp

Spices II
Cardamom 2
Cloves 2
Grated copra 1 tbsp

Seasoning
Oil 2 tsp
Mustard seeds 1 tsp
Curry leaves 1 sprig
Asafoetida powder ¼ tsp

METHOD

1. Cut brinjals into ¼-inch julienne strips and immerse in water.
2. Wash rice and cook it in 2½ cups of water in a steamer. Keep aside.
3. Extract tamarind juice using 1 cup of water (See Pre-Cooking Processes).
4. Heat oil in a vānali/wok. Add Spices I and sauté for a minute. Grind to a fine powder.
5. Heat ghee and sauté cashewnuts till golden brown. Remove.
6. Fry Spices II in oil till aromatic. Grind to a fine powder.
7. Heat oil again, splutter mustard seeds over medium heat. Stir in curry leaves and asafoetida and sauté for a few seconds, add drained brinjals, salt, jaggery and sauté till cooked. Remove.
8. Heat ½ tbsp of oil. Sauté tomatoes over medium heat, till oil separates. Add brinjals and mix well.
9. Spread cooked rice on a platter.
10. Mix in Spices I.
11. Pour brinjal tomato mix over rice along with Spice Powder II and cashewnuts. Mix well with a fork and transfer to a serving bowl.

ELUMICHAIPAḶA SĀDAM Lime Rice

Makes: 2–3 servings
Serving size: 100 gms
Calories per serving: 171

INGREDIENTS

Long-grained raw rice ½ cup
Water 1½ cups
Oil 2 tbsp
Cashewnuts 5, broken
Lime 1½
Turmeric powder ¼ tsp
Salt 1 tsp

Seasoning
Mustard seeds ½ tsp
Black gram dal/Urad dal 1 tbsp
Bengal gram dal/Chana dal ½ tbsp
Whole dried red chillies 2
Asafoetida powder ¼ tsp
Green chillies 2, slit
Curry leaves 2 sprigs

METHOD

1. Wash rice and cook in 1½ cups of water in a steamer. Remove, spread rice on a platter.
2. Heat oil in a vānali/wok. Fry cashewnuts over medium heat, till golden brown. Slot out.
3. Splutter mustard seeds in the same wok. Add remaining seasoning and fry till the dals turn golden.
4. Turn off heat, extract lime juice and add to wok with turmeric powder and salt.
5. Pour contents of wok over rice. Mix well.
6. Garnish with fried cashewnuts.

ELLORAI Sesame Rice

Makes: 4 servings
Serving size: 100 gms
Calories per serving: 241

INGREDIENTS

Long-grained raw rice 1 cup
Water 2 ½ cups
Oil 1 tsp
Cashewnuts 10, broken
Grated fresh coconut 3 tbsp (optional)
Salt ½ tsp

Spices for grinding
Dried red chillies 2
Black gram dal/Urad dal 1 tsp
Black sesame seeds 2 tbsp
Asafoetida powder 1 pinch

Seasoning
Sesame oil 1 tbsp
Mustard seeds ½ tsp
Dried red chillies 2
Bengal gram dal/Chana dal ¼ tsp
Black gram dal/Urad dal ¼ tsp
Asafoetida powder 1 pinch
Curry leaves 1 sprig
Copra 1 tsp (optional)

METHOD

1. Wash rice and cook in 2½ cups of water in a steamer.
2. Heat oil in a vānali/wok. Fry cashewnuts over medium heat, till golden brown. Slot out.
3. Add red chillies to wok and fry for a few seconds. Add remaining spices to be ground and sauté till light brown. Remove and grind to make a coarse powder.
4. Spread rice on a platter.
5. Heat oil in wok. Splutter mustard seeds over medium heat. Add remaining seasoning and fry till dals turn golden.
6. Pour seasoning over rice. Add spice powder, grated copra (optional) and salt. Mix gently with a fork. Garnish with cashewnuts.

Milagorai (Pepper Rice): For milagorai use powdered whole black pepper instead of black sesame seeds. Grind with dried red chillies, black gram dal/urad dal, Bengal gram dal/chana dal, and coriander seeds. Preparation is the same.

PACHAI MILAGĀI-TAYIR SĀDAM

Green Curd Rice

Makes: 4 servings
Serving size: 100 gms
Calories per serving: 351

INGREDIENTS

Green chillies 8–10
Green capsicum ¼
Salt ½ tsp
Ghee 1 tsp
Curd 2 tbsp, whisked smooth
Cooked rice 2 cups

Nandita was vivacious and full of life. She opened out her heart to everything and everybody. A green chilli here, some pepper there and presto! There was a lip-smacking dish! Her innovations seemed to spill out of her joyous character. Her 'green rice recipe' is one such.

METHOD

1. Grind green chillies, capsicum and salt together coarsely.
2. Place a pan over low heat and add ghee. When it is hot, add ground paste.
3. Immediately add curd, followed by cooked rice. Remove from heat.
4. Mix well and serve immediately. The rice should be bright green, not changed to a dull gray.

GUNA PĀTAM

An indigenous pharmacopeia called Guna Pātam (maybe 1500 CE) not only talks about the properties of various herbs for medicinal use but also talks of many prepared foods which are known by the same name even today.

The properties of many common food preparations like dosai, sambar dosai, puttu, modakam, ténkuḷal , atirasam, murukku, pāl annam (pāyasam), nei annam (ghee rice), pongal, rice kept in water overnight, buttermilk rice, blackgram rice, puliyōdarai, ellōdarai, tayir annam, mulaikeerai (greens), pulippu keerai, siru keerai and many other keerais, different kinds of rice—raw rice, parboiled rice, old rice and kanji are given in this. A few exmples:

Ghee rice—Improves digestion, reduces anger, and is suitable for special diets and elderly.

Curd rice—Removes the discomforts caused by bile, improves the digestive system and strengthens the immune system.

Green Gram dal pongal—Gives energy, reduces anger, and produces wind.

Śarkarai pongal—Reduces bile and controls vomiting.

Puliyōdarai—Reduces nausea, tastelessness, and biliousness.

Ellōdarai—Reduces arthritis and diseases due to excessive phlegm.

Cooked rice kept overnight in water—Is not good for young children and older persons.

A WORD ABOUT 'COOKING'

The difference in perception between north India and south India about what constitutes 'sacred' food and is therefore suitable as an offering in temples and to the deity at home, throws some light on the way that different societies mediate nature from culture.

In his book, *The Raw and the Cooked* and his article, 'The Culinary Triangle', anthropologist Claude Lévi-Strauss explains how culinary habits are expressions of social conventions and communicate symbolic value. There are three categories that designate foods consumed by humans—the raw, the cooked and the rotten. While much organic matter is biologically edible, every society designates only certain foods as culturally edible. The decomposition of food also subjects it to a natural process that could render it edible, as, for instance, cheese or in the Indian context, fermented foods like dough for idli, dosai, āppam. Similarly, boiling or steaming alters food with water and frying changes its structure with hot oil. Lévi-Strauss speculates that in Western societies the roasting of meat was considered patrician, whereas boiling gave the same food a plebeian status.

Applying some of these ideas to Indian cuisine, we can see that the Sanskrit term from the root 'pach' meaning 'to cook', hence 'pak' for 'cooking', has been applied differently in multiple regions. In north Indian cooking, pakā khānā designates fried food as 'cooked', whereas steamed food is (surprisingly to south Indians) designated as kacchā khānā (raw). In Tamil, taligai, cooked food, is generally that which is boiled or steamed.

From Odisha downwards to all over south India, steamed food is considered suitable for sacred offerings and for festivals. In north India, however, only talava, meaning fried foods, is offered in temples or to the deity at home or on festival days like Deepāvali.

The word talikai (cooking) is from the Sanskrit word talita meaning 'fried'. This is one more onomatopoeic word as it denotes the dancing of the food in the oil—tala tala. In the south of India, in temple madaipallis (kitchens) sacred offerings are called talikai vidudal, to mean an offering by devotees. The word talikai is still in vogue in some communities but samaiyal is more commonly used.

TĀLITTAL/TĀLIPPU: SEASONING

For many centuries right up to the present day, seasoning (tālippu) of food is called tirumanapārrudal by some groups of people. This word literally means the act of inducing good fragrance. In Indian cuisine, the seasoning is that which enhances the taste and look of the dish. A Sangam poem also describes how the sweet smoke of the seasoning, kuipugai (kuing, the onomatoepic sound of the mustard spluttering) gets into the maiden's eyes, and this pleases the lover.

A folk poem from Uttaranchal gives us another charming reference to the importance of seasoning. A poem of Giridha explains how even in the poorest hovel, the heart rises in joy, savouring the spices of the seasoning:

The evening's dark
With open skies
O little darling!
From the cowdunged hut
Smoke slowly rises,
O little darling!
The wet fire sputters.
Gran's wood is damp,
And the smoke is too.
Her spices splutter,
And the fragrance wafts.
What fresh savour!
...My heart is caught,
O little darling!

SEASONING AND GHEE

The use of good ghee is essential for the perfect seasoning. What is 'good' ghee? Butter should be clarified every few days so that it is always fresh. A good ghee will flow like silk and is golden in colour. When it settles, the sediment is like fine sand. Commercial sweet sellers usually melt the butter partially as they use the same ghee several times. This solidifies the ghee, like margarine. This has no flavour nor is it good for health. An Ayurvedic precept for good health is easily remembered in a saying in Tamil, '*Neyyai urukki, neerai churukki, morai perukki*', meaning 'melt the ghee, reduce (intake of) water and dilute buttermilk (for good health)'. This dictum is to be followed while eating.

Ghee for seasoning has to be melted with precision. It should not be overheated as the high temperature burns the ghee and changes the flavour. For seasoning vegetables and rasam, ghee is used while sesame oil is preferred for kuḷambu. Coconut oil is the choice for certain vegetable dishes. Kasandu sādam is a favourite on days in which butter is clarified for ghee. Hot rice is added to the sediment that is left behind after ghee has been decanted. Lightly toasted urad dal and a few curry leaves are added to the rice.

Customarily, as soon as rice is served, ghee is spooned three times over it as ghee is known as annasuddhi, the purifier of food, in the Vedas.

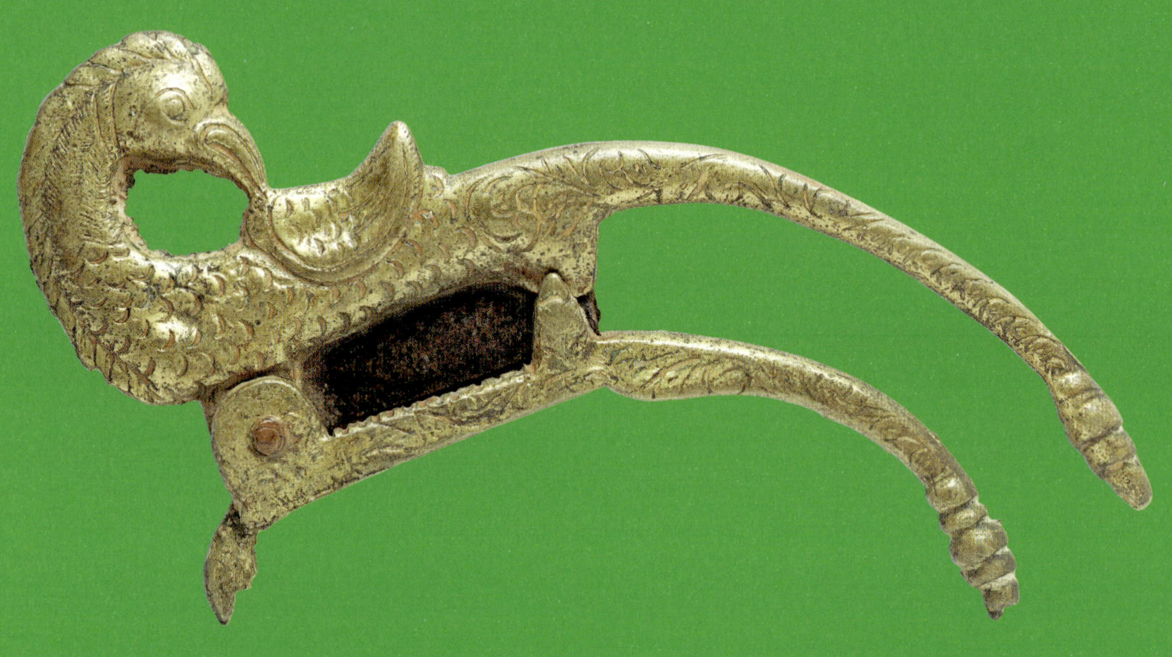

PACCHADIS/SALADS

In the food serving order, after fruit and honey, a pinch of salt in the corner of the leaf, and annam, pacchadi or kosumalli is served. Cooked dal is simultaneously served on the bottom half of the leaf.

VELLARIKĀI MILAGĀI KOSUMALLI

Cucumber Salad with Mung Dal

Makes: 4 servings
Serving size: 125 gms
Calories per serving: 361

INGREDIENTS

Green gram dal/Mung dal ¼ cup
Cucumber (medium) 1
Shredded ginger ½ tsp
Green chillies 1–2, seeded and slit
Coriander leaves 1 sprig, chopped
Grated fresh coconut 1 tbsp
Salt ½ tsp

Seasoning
Oil ½ tsp
Mustard seeds ½ tsp
Asafoetida powder 1 pinch
Curry leaves 1 sprig

METHOD

1. Wash mung dal and soak in water for about 30 minutes.
2. Wash cucumber and peel. Remove and discard seeds if they are mature. Grate cucumber.
3. Mix grated cucumber in a bowl with ginger and coriander leaves.
4. Heat oil in a vānali/wok. Splutter mustard seeds over medium heat. Add green chillies and stir.
5. Pour contents over cucumber.
6. Drain mung dal, rinse and add to bowl.
7. Add grated coconut and salt.
8. Mix well and serve.

Variation: Grated carrot can be used instead of cucumber and made in the same way.

அ. ச கோமு

VELLARIKĀI PACCHADI Cucumber in Curd

Makes: 4 servings
Serving size: 150 gms
Calories per serving: 83

INGREDIENTS

Cucumber (medium) 1
Fresh curd, whisked smooth ½ cup
Salt ½ tsp

Seasoning
Oil 1 tsp
Mustard seeds ½ tsp
Green chilli, slit 1
Curry leaves 1 sprig

METHOD

1. Peel cucumber. Remove and discard seeds, if mature. Dice cucumber finely.
2. Add curd and salt. Mix well.
3. Heat oil in a vānali/wok. Splutter mustard seeds over medium heat. Add green chilli and curry leaves.
4. Pour contents of pan over pacchadi.

Variations:

- *Grated coconut pacchadi: Grind 1 tbsp of grated coconut with a ½-inch piece of ginger and add to curd. Serve with or without adding cucumber.*
- *Capsicum and okra pacchadi: Use 4 tbsp of finely chopped capsicum and 8 finely chopped fried okra. Add to curd instead of cucumber.*
- *Ash gourd pacchadi: Boil 1 cup of chopped ash gourd in water and add to hung curd (see Pre-Cooking Processes) instead of cucumber.*

MAKKA CHOLA PACCHADI Corn in Curd

Makes: 4 servings
Serving size: 150 gms
Calories per serving: 202

INGREDIENTS

Tender fresh corn cobs 4
Curd, whisked smooth 2 cups
Red chilli powder ½ tsp
Dhania-jeera powder ¾ tsp
(see Podis/Readymade Powders)
Salt ¼ tsp

Seasoning
Oil 2 tsp
Mustard seeds ½ tsp
Green chillies 2, chopped fine

METHOD

1. Pressure cook corn kernels for 2 whistles (2 minutes) and drain water.
2. Beat curd in a bowl. Add chilli powder, dhania-jeera powder and salt.
3. Heat oil in a vānali/wok. Splutter mustard seeds over medium heat, stir in green chillies.
4. Add corn kernels and sauté for about a minute.
5. Pour contents of vānali/wok over spiced curd and mix well.

KOTTAMALLI PACCHADI Coriander Leaves in Curd

Makes: 4 servings
Serving size: 100 gms
Calories per serving: 63

INGREDIENTS

Curd, whisked smooth with ½ tbsp water
Coriander leaves 2 cups
Salt to taste
Asafoetida water ¼ tsp (see Pre-Cooking Processes)

Seasoning
Oil 1 tsp. Mustard seeds ½ tsp
Green chillies 2

METHOD

1. Whisk curd with ½ tbsp of water.
2. Grind coriander leaves with salt and asafoetida water. Add to curd and mix.
3. Heat oil in a vānali/wok. Splutter mustard seeds and green chillies and pour over pacchadi.

Variations:
Curry leaves (1 cup) or mint leaves (1 cup) can be used in the same way instead of coriander.

BEANS PACCHADI French Beans in Curd Sauce

Makes: 4 servings
Serving size: 125 gms
Calories per serving: 112

INGREDIENTS

French beans 250 gm
Salt ½ tsp + ½ tsp
Unsalted butter 1 tsp
Ginger ½-inch piece, crushed
Green chillies 1–2, sliced fine
Grated fresh coconut 2 tbsp
Coriander leaves 5–6 sprigs, chopped
Black pepper powder ¼ tsp
Hung curd, whisked smooth 1¾ cups (see Pre-Cooking Processes)
Almonds 3–5, chopped
Pistachios 2–5, chopped
Walnut 1, chopped. Raisins 5–8, chopped

METHOD

1. Trim beans and chop finely.
2. Boil beans with ½ tsp of salt and just enough water to cover, till tender.
3. Drain water and while beans are still hot, mix with butter, ginger, green chillies, grated coconut, coriander leaves and pepper.
4. Add beans and salt to curd.
5. Add nuts and raisins.
6. Transfer to a serving dish and refrigerate.

Note: This can be served without nuts and raisins.

DONGAR PACCHADI Black Gram Dal in Curd

Makes: 4 servings
Serving size: 75 gms
Calories per serving: 254

INGREDIENTS

Curd, whisked smooth ½ cup
Water ½ tbsp
Black gram dal/Urad dal 2 tsp, lightly toasted and finely powdered
Salt to taste
Asafoetida water ¼ tsp
(see Pre-Cooking Processes)

Seasoning
Oil 1 tsp
Mustard seeds ½ tsp
Green chillies 2
Curry leaves 1 sprig

METHOD

1. Whisk curd with ½ tbsp of water.
2. Mix in powdered urad dal, salt and asafoetida water.
3. Heat oil in a vānali/wok. Splutter mustard seeds over medium heat. Add green chillies and curry leaves.
4. Pour contents of wok over pacchadi.

MĀNGĀI KOSUMALLI Raw Mango Salad

Makes: 4–6 servings
Serving size: 100 gms
Calories per serving: 231

INGREDIENTS

Whole green mango (medium) 1
Kāramani/very tender runner beans 3–4

Dressing
Dried red or fresh green chillies 2, chopped fine
Roasted peanuts 1 tbsp, coarsely pounded
Lime juice 2 tbsp
Light soy sauce 3 tbsp. Sugar 1 tsp
Whole cashewnuts (roasted) 2 tbsp
Salt ¼ tsp

METHOD

1. Peel and grate mango into long thin shreds and soak in cold water to remove resin of raw mango. Drain.
2. Trim beans and cut into 1-inch pieces.
3. Bruise beans in a mortar and mix with grated mango.
4. Add dressing ingredients.
5. Toss to blend, mix in roasted cashews and serve.

Note: If using red chillies, cut them crosswise into bits with scissors.

SINGHADA MILAGĀI SALAD

Indian Water Chestnut and Red Chilli Salad

Makes: 4 servings
Serving size: 150 gms
Calories per serving: 125

INGREDIENTS

Water chestnuts 500 gm
Sogri ⅓ cup
Dried red chillies 1–2
Salt ½ tsp
Charcoal 1 piece
Ghee 1 tsp

[1]Sogri is the tender fruit of white radish and is available only at the end of winter/early spring.

METHOD

1. Peel water chestnuts without breaking the nut inside. Remove thin membrane covering the nut.
2. Cut water chestnuts horizontally into half and soak in water.
3. Wash and clean sogri. Remove tip. Cut to same size as water chestnuts. Drain water chestnuts and add to sogri[1].
4. Pound red chillies into coarse flakes. Mix salt and add to water chestnuts and sogri.
5. Place a tiny bowl in the centre of a hot vessel. Arrange water chestnuts and sogri around the bowl. Place a red-hot charcoal piece in the bowl. Add a few drops of ghee on the charcoal and cover vessel immediately. Set aside for a few minutes.
6. Remove charcoal and transfer the salad to a serving bowl and serve.

CARROT MULLANGI KOSUMALLI

Carrot and Radish Salad

Makes: 4 servings
Serving size: 125 gms
Calories per serving: 106

INGREDIENTS

Sesame oil, toasted, ½ tsp
White radish 1 cup, finely shredded
Carrot ⅛ cup, finely shredded
Ginger 1 tsp, finely shredded
Green chilli 1, slit
Lime juice ¼ tsp
Salt ¼ tsp
Chopped coriander leaves 2 tsp
White sesame seeds 1½ tsp, fried
Coarsely powdered peanuts 1 tbsp
Soy sauce ½ tsp

METHOD

1. Mix radish, carrot, ginger and green chilli.
2. Add lime juice, salt and coriander leaves.
3. Just before serving, stir in sesame seeds, powdered peanuts, and soy sauce. Add toasted sesame oil. Mix well and serve.

Toasted sesame oil or fragrant sesame oil is available in stores under Chinese ingredients.

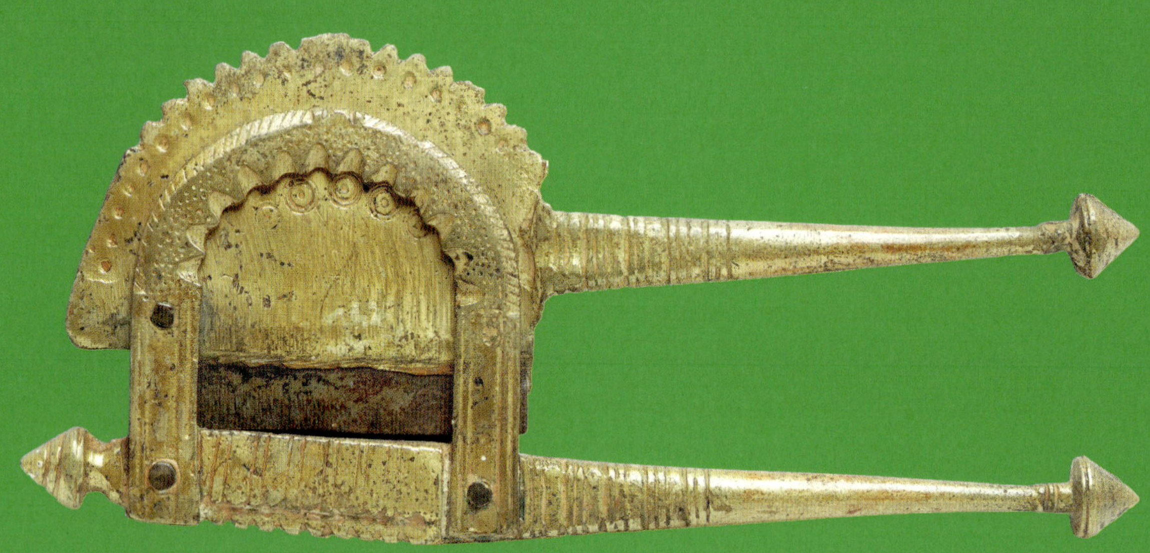

DALS AND GOJJUS

SĀDI DAL Basic Dal

Makes: 4 servings
Serving size: 150 gms
Calories per serving: 181

INGREDIENTS

Red gram dal/Tuvar dal or mung dal ½ cup
Water 2 cups
Turmeric powder ¼ tsp
Ghee or castor oil ¼ tsp
Tomato 1, chopped (optional)
Grated jaggery 1 tsp (optional)
Salt ½ tsp

Seasoning
Ghee or oil 1 tbsp
Mustard seeds ¼ tsp
Jeera/Cumin seeds ¼ tsp
Asafoetida powder ¼ tsp
Green chillies 2, slit
Curry leaves 1 sprig

Garnish
Coriander leaves 2–3 sprigs, chopped
Lime ½

METHOD

1. Wash dal and pressure-cook with turmeric powder, a drop of ghee or castor oil and 2 cups of water for 3 whistles (see Pre-Cooking Processes).
2. Remove dal and mash lightly.
3. Heat ghee or oil in a wok. Splutter mustard seeds, add cumin seeds and sauté. Add asafoetida powder and green chillies. Stir in curry leaves.
4. Add tomato (optional) and sauté for 1–2 minutes.
5. Mix in cooked dal, jaggery (optional) and salt.
6. Pour in some water if it is too thick and boil for about 2 minutes.
7. Before serving add a dash of lime juice.
8. Garnish with coriander leaves.

Variations:

- *Peel and cut 250 gm of tender ridge gourd. Cook in water to cover, till tender. Mix into cooked dal and add seasoning.*
- *Chop ½ cup of tender amaranth/paruppu keerai, fenugreek leaves or alfa-alfa leaves. Cook with dal in a pressure cooker for 3 whistles; when cooked, add seasoning.*
- *Chop 250 gm of tender green tomatoes and pan-fry lightly. Add them to dal and pressure-cook. Slice 50 gm of tender green chillies and pan-fry lightly. Mix into cooked dal and add seasoning.*
- *Peel and chop half a medium-sized green mango and add it to cooked dal. Boil till mango is tender. Omit tomatoes. Add seasoning.*

MĀMPAḶA DAL Ripe Mango Dal

Makes: 4 servings
Serving size: 150 gms
Calories per serving: 175

INGREDIENTS

Red gram dal/Tuvar dal ¾ cup
Water 4 cups + 2 cups
Turmeric powder ½ tsp
Ghee or castor oil ¼ tsp
Red chilli powder ½ tsp
Whole green chilli 1
Salt 1 tsp
Small, half-ripe, sour & sweet, flavourful mangoes 6

Seasoning
Ghee 1 tbsp
Mustard seeds ¼ tsp
Fenugreek seeds ¼ tsp
Asafoetida powder 1 pinch
Curry leaves 1 sprig

METHOD

1. Wash tuvar dal and pressure-cook with turmeric powder, ghee or castor oil and 4 cups of water for 3 whistles (see Pre-Cooking Processes).
2. Heat ghee in a vessel. Splutter mustard seeds over medium heat, add fenugreek seeds. When they turn brown, stir in asafoetida powder and curry leaves.
3. Add cooked dal and bring to a boil.
4. Mix in chilli powder, green chilli and salt.
5. Cut mangoes into 3 segments—two sides and kernel. Add to vessel and cook further.
6. Pour in 2 cups of boiling water and simmer till it thickens, and serve hot.

MULU ULUNDU DAL Whole Black Gram Dal

Makes: 4 servings
Serving size: 150 gms
Calories per serving: 244

INGREDIENTS

Whole black gram/Whole urad dal 1 cup
Water 3 cups
Turmeric powder ½ tsp
Cardamom 1
Clove 1
Ghee 1 tbsp
Salt ¾ tsp
Chopped tomatoes 1 cup
Red chilli powder 1 tsp
Roasted jeera/Cumin powder 1 tsp

Seasoning
Oil 1 tbsp
Cardamoms 2
Clove 1
Cinnamon 1-inch stick (optional)
Ginger 1-inch piece, chopped fine
Green chillies 1–2, chopped fine

Garnish
Coriander leaves 2 sprigs, chopped

METHOD

1. Wash whole urad dal and soak in water for about 2 hours.
2. Pressure-cook dal with turmeric powder, cardamom, clove, ghee, salt and 3 cups of water for 4 whistles (see Pre-Cooking Processes).
3. Heat oil in a vānali/wok. Add seasoning ingredients and sauté for about a minute.
4. Add tomatoes and sauté for 2–3 minutes.
5. Sprinkle in chilli powder and cumin powder.
6. Add cooked dal and simmer for 4–5 minutes.
7. Garnish with coriander leaves.

DINDIGUL GOJJU

Brinjal with Dal

Makes: 4 servings
Serving size: 150 gms
Calories per serving: 121

INGREDIENTS

Red gram dal/Tuvar dal 1 cup
Turmeric powder ½ tsp + ¼ tsp
Ghee or castor oil ¼ tsp
Water 3 cups
Tamarind 5 gm
Water 2 cups
Small onions 100 gm (optional)
Brinjal 1

Seasoning
Ghee 2 tbsp
Mustard seeds 1 tsp
Fenugreek seeds ½ tsp
Red chillies 6
Green chillies 8
Curry leaves 2 sprigs
Salt 1 tsp

Garnish
Coriander leaves 2–3 stems
Cashewnuts 6, broken

Gojju is a sauce-like dish, which is mushy and liquid and is made as an accompaniment to pongal, vadai, dosai, etc. This is another onomatopoeic word in Tamil culinary vocabulary. It is descriptive of the squishy nature of this vegetable preparation, somewhat like cooked sago.

The most mouthwatering gojju was made by a well-known hotelier from Dindigul who used to wait for us at the station with this delectable unforgettable dish, along with his signature dosais, idlis and pongal.

METHOD

1. If using onions, peel and cut each into two. Cut brinjal into fine pieces, immerse in water.
2. Extract tamarind juice (see Pre-Cooking Processes).
3. Pressure-cook red gram dal with turmeric powder and castor oil or ghee for 3 whistles (see Pre-Cooking Processes).
4. Heat ghee in a vānali. Fry cashewnuts over medium heat till golden brown and slot out. Splutter mustard seeds. Add fenugreek seeds and fry till golden brown. Add red and green chillies and curry leaves.
5. Add onions and sauté till onions are cooked and appear transparent.
6. Add brinjal pieces, sauté till done.
7. Add tamarind juice, turmeric powder and salt and boil for 5–6 minutes.
8. Add dal. If the consistency is thick, add a little boiling water.
9. Garnish with fried cashewnuts and coriander leaves.
10. If gojju is not spicy enough, add 1 tsp red chilli powder in hot oil and pour over gojju.
11. Serve with pongal, ravā dosai and any other dosais/idlis.

KATRIKKĀI RASAVĀNGI Brinjal Rasavāngi

Makes: 3 servings
Serving size: 150 gms
Calories per serving: 132

INGREDIENTS

Gothsu powder
Cooking oil 2½ tsp
Mung dal 2 tsp
Urad dal 1¼ tsp
Salem round dry red chilli 8
Fenugreek seeds ¼ tsp
Dhania/Coriander seeds 2 tsp
Asafoetida ½ tsp

Gothsu
Gingelly oil 2 tbsp
Mustard seeds 1 tsp
Curry leaves 1 sprig
Brinjal 2, cubed
Tomato 1, chopped
Turmeric powder ½ tsp
Boiled mung dal 100 gm
Tamarind pulp 25 ml
Jaggery, crushed 1 tsp
Salt 1 tsp
Coriander Leaves 2-3 stems
Water 2 cups

METHOD

Gothsu powder

1. Heat 1 tsp cooking oil in a pan.
2. Add 2½ tsp moong dal in low flame.
3. When it turns golden in colour, add 1¼ tsp urad dal, 2 tsp dhaniya seeds, 8 round red chillies, ¼ tsp fenugreek seeds and fry them till they turn light brown.
4. When it is roasted well, turn off the gas and add ½ tsp asafoetida.
5. Mix well and cool the ingredients. Then grind into a fine powder.

Gothsu

1. In a vānali, take 2 tbsp gingelly oil, splutter 1 tsp mustard seeds and 1 sprig curry leaves.
2. Add chopped tomato and ½ tsp turmeric powder. Cook the tomato for a couple of minutes.
3. Once it is cooked, add brinjals. The flame can be slightly increased now.
4. Pour some water for the ingredients to cook well.
5. Once the tomato and brinjal come to a boil, add the turmeric powder and 1¼ ladle of thick tamarind water. (Soak 50 g tamarind in hot water and squeeze. Use half of it). Add salt and jaggery.
6. Once all the ingredients have cooked well, add 2 tsp of the Gothsu powder. (The dal will thicken the Gothsu). Add 100 gm boiled moong dal and 1 tumbler water.
7. Gothsu for pongal shouldn't be very thick. Thicker than sambar but not as thick as kurma.
8. Bring it to a slight boil and add a lavish sprinkle of coriander leaves. Don't let it boil for too long. Gothsu is ready.

KOIYYAPAḶA GOJJU Guava Gojju

Makes: 3 servings
Serving size: 150 gms
Calories per serving: 58

INGREDIENTS

Guavas (large, firm, ripe) 2
Salt ½ tsp
Sugar 2 tsp
Water ½ cup

Spices
Ghee 1 tbsp
Mustard seeds ½ tsp
Jeera/Cumin seeds ¼ tsp
Cloves 2. Cardamom 1
Dried pomegranate seeds 1 tsp (optional)

Spice powders
Dhania/Coriander powder ¾ tsp
Red chilli powder ¾ tsp
Turmeric powder ½ tsp
Asafoetida powder ¼ tsp

METHOD

1. Cut guavas into large chunks.
2. Heat ghee in a vānali/wok. Splutter mustard seeds, then add the rest of the spices and sauté for a few seconds. Moisten spice powders with a drop of water and mix. Add to wok.
3. Add guavas. Add salt and ½ cup of water. Bring to a boil. Remove.
4. Serve hot with roti.

PACHAI MANITAKKALI GOJJU

Raw Solanum Nigrum Berries Gojju

Makes: 4 servings
Serving size: 150 gms
Calories per serving: 89

INGREDIENTS

Unripe Manitakkali[1] 1 cup

Seasoning
Sesame oil 2 tbsp

METHOD

1. Extract tamarind juice using 1 cup of water (see Pre-Cooking Processes).
2. Heat oil in a vānali/wok. Splutter mustard seeds over medium heat. Add remaining seasoning and sauté, till dal turns golden.
3. Add manitakkali and sauté till tender.

Mustard seeds ½ tsp
Black gram dal/Urad dal 1 tsp
Fenugreek seeds ¼ tsp
Asafoetida powder 1 tsp
Green chillies 4, slit
Curry leaves 1 sprig

Gojju
Tamarind ¾ tbsp
Water 1 cup
Turmeric powder ¼ tsp
Sambar powder[2] 2 tsp
Salt ½ tsp
Grated jaggery 1 tsp

4. Crush manitakkali slightly in wok with a potato masher.
5. Add tamarind juice, turmeric powder, sambar powder, salt and jaggery.
6. Boil till mixture thickens. Remove from heat.

Variations: Plantain flower and yam can be made in the same way.

[1]*The Hindi name for manitakkali is makoi, while its botanical name is* solanum nigrum. *This belongs to the same botanical family as chilli, tomato or brinjal.*
[2]*To make sambar powder, (see Podis/Readymade Powders). Also available in the market.*

TAKKĀLI GOJJU Tomato Gojju

Makes: 4 servings
Serving size: 150 gms
Calories per serving: 101

INGREDIENTS

Tomatoes 250 gm
Salt ½ tsp
Grated jaggery 1 tsp (optional)

For grinding
Mustard seeds ¼ tsp
Green chillies 2
Grated coconut 2 tbsp

Seasoning
Oil 1 tbsp
Mustard seeds ½ tsp
Dried red chillies 2
Asafoetida powder ¼ tsp
Curry leaves 1 sprig

METHOD

1. Finely chop tomatoes.
2. Grind mustard seeds, green chillies and grated coconut to a smooth consistency.
3. Heat oil in a vānali/wok. Splutter mustard seeds over medium heat. Add remaining seasoning and fry for a second or two.
4. Add tomatoes and sauté.
5. When tomatoes are slightly cooked, add salt, jaggery (optional) and ground spices. Simmer over low heat, till oil separates.
6. Remove from heat.

Variation: Pachai Takkāli Gojju (Unripe Tomato Sauce): Use 250 gm of unripe tomatoes instead of ripe ones and proceed as given.

VEGETABLES

VEGETABLES

The place of vegetables in Indian vegetarian cuisine is unique. The astonishing variety of vegetables available in India, the incredible diversity of recipes from the various regions, the almost continuous use of many of these vegetables for more than 2,000 years and the effortless adaptation of many new vegetables from other parts of the world, gives Indian cuisine a distinction that cannot easily be won by any other country in the world.

But what did ancient India have by way of vegetables? Greens were in plenty as testified by many literary sources, tender leaves of many wild plants and trees were used and berries were an important part of the menu. Both greens and berries were recommended by Ayurveda as health-giving. The berries were not only eaten raw and cooked in tamarind stews, but were also dried and preserved.

Sesame and eggplant, as well as different kinds of yams and melons were known to have existed during the early Vedic period. Several varieties of gourds were known, so were beans. Tender cluster beans, runner beans and dolichos seeds were considered delicacies and were eaten lightly flavoured with spices. Turmeric, ginger and many varities of rhizome and cardamom have been part of the Indian menu since at least 3000 BCE. A 2 CE poem from the Sangam Age details the kind of menu that was followed in a Brahmin household of the time. A troubadour advises a traveller to avail the kind hospitality of one such household:

> *Manaiyurai koliyodi jñamali tunnādu*
> *Valaivai r Killaiyodi maraivili payatru*
> *Maraikappal ...*
> *Cudarkadaip paravaip peyarpadu vattanj*
> *Cedā marumōr vaivennaiyin matuali t*
> *Turuppuru paśungaip polodu karikalandu*
> *Kanjaga narumuriyalai ip paindunar*
> *Nedumara kokka naruvadi vidirtta*
> *Tagaimān kadiyin vagaippadap peruguvir.*

> Where you see houses that have neither hen nor dog, where the parrot with the curved beak is taught the sounds of the Vedas by Brahmins who reside there, in such places, you will find women … with pleasant mien, wearing bangles on their arms (who) will feed you with the best rice and lentils. Further, they will give you tender pomegranate fried in butter, made from cow's milk curds, mixed with pepper and garnished with curry leaves. They will offer you the abundant tender mangoes and various other pickles from large pots.
>
> —Perumpānātrupadai, Verses 299–310

The poem marks the simplicity of the food consumed then. It also shows us how some of those food combinations, like curds and rice with tender mango pickles, are still a fundamental part of the south Indian menu today.

Differences in micro-climates in peninsular

India have contributed to a vast array of vegetables and spices. The semi-arid Deccan plateau, the fertile river basins of the Andhra region and the lush tropical vegetation of the Western Ghats yield us diverse crops, vegetables and spices which have helped to make south Indian vegetarian cuisine unique. For the vegetarian who revels in the abundance of vegetables, the interest lies in the way the accent falls on the vegetables that are special to a region, the emphasis laid on one spice more than the other. The entire grammar of food in a particular region depends a great deal on the climate and the tastes that have developed over centuries.

There are no taboos at the Indian table where vegetables are concerned. The only guidelines in choosing vegetables and the proper time for their consumption are those that are found in ancient Ayurvedic texts and in other texts like the fourteenth century *Āhara Niyamam*, a manual on right eating.

Vegetables like carrot, cabbage, capsicum, peas, radish, etc., popularly known as 'English' vegetables, have now become a part of the Indian kitchen and are made in the same way as Indian vegetables. It is interesting to note that 'English' vegetables are never part of the menu for religious occasions. This includes the multi-faceted potato too! Though it is not accepted for rituals, this late import from South America brought into India by the Portuguese is now the indisputable king of vegetables. Its versatility is unassailable, lending itself for use in all forms and in every preparation. It is the cook's friend as it can be made very quickly and no one has been known to turn down a potato dish!

Of Garlic, Onion and Spices

India can boast of a variety of vegetables and the vegetarian cuisine of south India reflects the imagination and skill of cooks in hundred years past who have invented and innovated numerous ways of cooking these vegetables—in salads, in yoghurt sauces, freshly and simply sautéed, pan-fried or deep-fried.

The recipes in this book do not use either onion or garlic. First, the cuisine of the traditional groups of south Indian vegetarians was extremely simple with a sparing use of spices and condiments as many were either unknown or unavailable. Earlier generations depended to a great extent on the natural taste and flavour of the vegetables that were available at the time.

Ayurveda divided all foods into three kinds based on the effects they had on the constitution, outlook and behavior of those who ate them. Ayurveda advocates sātvik (pure) food for a healthy life. Orthodox groups adopted these ideas and believed that only sātvik foods can promote pure thought that would help them in the contemplative life which was their goal. This belief was intensified with the spread of Jainism in south India.

Ayurveda characterized rajasic foods as those promoting anger and aggression leading to hyperactivity, in turn leading to sleeplessness while tamasic foods were those that induced lethargy and produced flatulence. Garlic was not totally taboo as it was allowed for medicinal purposes. It is a popular natural medicine for lactating mothers and is routinely used to offset any infection like a cold that babies might suffer from. It is an antiseptic, an antidote for congestion of the lungs.

This practice of not using garlic is not uniquely Indian. Princess Gabriella of Liechtenstein often spoke about how European royalty did not use garlic and used onions very sparingly. This was because, she said, they could afford exotic spices like cardamom, cloves and saffron to flavour their food while the commoners had to be content with garlic or onion to add zest in theirs!

Royalty and spices seem to have gone together since ancient times. More than Indian silk and ivory, it was pepper that captured the imagination of aristocracy from Greece and Rome and later, that of the Europeans of the Middle Ages. Spices like pepper, cinnamon, cardamom, ginger and others, which were always sparingly used in India, led to a culinary extravaganza in these societies.

The 2 CE Roman cookbook by Apicius detailing 468 recipes uses pepper in 349 of them. The early fourteenth-century pantry of Jeanne, the widow of King Charles IV of France, continues this saga of spice. It was filled with 6 lbs of pepper, 13½ lbs of cinnamon, 5 lbs of grains of paradise, 3½ lbs of cloves, ¼ lb of saffron, ½ lb of long pepper, a small quantity of mace and 23½ lbs of ginger—a veritable spice market!

Pepper was used in conjunction with ginger, cumin, caraway, spikenard and other herbs, honey and dates to make sauces of various kinds to flavour a variety of meat dishes. The same interest in sauces continues in England, where, in the fifteenth century, the household of Humphrey Stafford, Duke of Buckingham, used 316 lbs of pepper and 194 lbs of ginger annually, apart from other spices like nutmeg and cloves. This works out to an average of 2 lbs of spices per day, a staggering figure. Spices were used not only in cooking but were also used to flavour dessert which were called 'dainties', a mixture of fruits, nuts and spices. (*Spice* by Jack Turner).

This excess, which is more like an addiction, is reflected in the present prevalence of onion and garlic in Indian cuisine today. Though some dishes may call for the presence of these bulbs to lend a distinct flavour, what is puzzling is the complete invasion of these vegetables into almost every part of our cuisine. This has led to market intervention in the form of readymade ginger-garlic paste available in packets of all sizes. Pressed for time to pound, powder and grind different combinations of spices, it is perhaps easy for the present generation of cooks to add a teaspoon or more of this paste to their vegetables and gravies hoping to infuse some flavour into them.

This overwhelming use of garlic and onion in present-day cooking might make us feel that we are back in Shakespearean days when one of Shakespeare's characters was forced to give this advice to his troupe:

> 'And most dear actors, eat no onions nor garlic, for we are to utter sweet breath'

This contrasts with Italian cuisine where the garlic is slotted out of the gravy or pasta as garlic there is used only as a catalyst to harmonize all the flavours of the dish.

Current medical opinion is in favour of eating a pod of garlic a day as a health measure as garlic has shown itself to be helpful in reducing the risk of some cancers and in preventing cardiovascular disease. It is not at all advisable for pregnant women or those who are to undergo surgery as it is a natural blood thinner.

In pure vegetarian cuisine, the cooking is so light and delicate, the vegetables fresh and the spices used minimal, that the use of garlic and onion overpowers the native taste of the vegetables and the spices.

Curry

British colonials have given the word 'curry'

a whole new connotation, differing from its original meaning of cooked vegetable or kari. 'Curry' for them came to mean a 'mess' of vegetables, meat and spices. Bright yellow turmeric was what they distinguished as representative of Indian spice which they referred to as Indian saffron. The variation in meaning may have been brought about by the cooks whom the British employed in India. Many Indians refused to work for the British in their kitchens as they were considered 'aliens'. The ones who did come forward to serve as cooks had no clear idea of cuisines. They would use all the spices in the spice box indiscriminately in a kuḷambu or in vegetable gravies, and the British came to understand that this was Indian 'curry'.

The best western definition of curry is to be found in that excellent cookery dictionary, *New Larousse Gastronomique*:

> [It is] 'a combination of spices, thoroughly dried, ground to a powder, and cooked slowly in clarified butter, vegetable oil or soured milk before adding the vegetables that are to be curried. The curry powders sold in grocery shops are usually a combination of fifteen or twenty herbs, seeds and spices. Those who really appreciate curry choose special combinations of spices to go with various dishes, some of which call for mild, subtle seasonings and others for hotter ones. The strength of a curry depends on how much chilli is used.

The principal ingredients of curry powder are allspice, anise, bay leaves, cinnamon, caraway, celery seed, cloves, coriander, cumin, curry leaves, dill, fennel, fenugreek (seeds and leaves), garlic, ginger, mace, mustard, nutmeg, pepper (white and black), paprika, poppy seeds, saffron, turmeric, mint, cubeb berries, sumach seeds, juniper berries, zedoary root, salt.

Almost 200 spices were powdered together to form the famous PV Chalam curry powder which was used at random for each and every Indian dish by the British or by those who cooked for them. To this day, in Britain the word 'curry' stands for a heavily spiced Indian gravy preparation with vegetables.

The famous PV Chalam curry powder popularly known as Madras Curry Powder has been exported since 1860 and still has a major presence overseas. PVS Vencata Subramanyam, grandson of the original P. Venkatachalam who started the business, says that though Madras Curry Powder is now known as Vencat Curry, it has lost none of its popularity in the export market.

Kari, Not Curry

Indians use the word 'curry', usually spelt 'kari' to mean a dry cooked vegetable, which is sautéed and seasoned. The origin of the word for the cooked dish is from the raw ingredient, karikāi, meaning uncooked vegetable in Tamil.

The word later came to be used for meat as well, which has made at least one squeamish pure vegetarian community in south India refer to cooked vegetables as kari-amudu (vegetable that is like nectar, 'amudu' being the Tamil word for the Sanskrit 'amritam'). The word 'kari-amudu' is of ancient usage. We find the word 'tiruvamudu' being used as early as the year 1013–1014 in an inscription by Rajaraja Chola I in the Sivayoganatha temple at Tiruvisanallur–Kumbakonam. The Airavatesvara temple, also at Kumbakonam (1215–1216), speaks of kariamudu.

CABBAGE AND PATTĀNI KARI Cabbage with Green Peas

Makes: 4 servings
Serving size: 100 gms
Calories per serving: 66

INGREDIENTS

Cabbage 200 gm
Green peas ⅓ cup
Salt ½ tsp + ½ tsp

Seasoning
Oil 1 tbsp
Mustard seeds ½ tsp
Dried red chilli 1
Black gram dal/Urad dal 1 tsp
Curry leaves 1 sprig
Grated fresh coconut 2½ tbsp

METHOD

1. Shred cabbage (2-inch in length).
2. Boil cabbage in just enough water to cover it, with ½ tsp of salt, till tender but crisp. Do not cover pan. Drain.
3. Boil peas in just enough water and mix with cabbage.
4. Heat oil in a vānali/wok. Splutter mustard seeds over medium heat. Add remaining seasoning and fry, till dal turns golden brown.
5. Add grated coconut and fry, till it releases its flavour.
6. Add vegetables and toss for a few minutes. Remove from heat.
7. Serve with rice and rasam/sambar.

Variations:

- *French beans, carrot, cauliflower, cluster beans, dolichos beans, plantain stem, runner beans and snake gourd can be made in the same way.*
- *Cabbage, beans, carrot, cauliflower of equal portion—all these can be mixed and made as one kari.*
- *Cut and boil drumsticks. Scrape out the pulp. Season the pulp in the same way.*
- *Cull stamens from plantain flower and immerse immediately in buttermilk to prevent oxidation, drain, chop finely and cook as above.*

KOTTHAVARANKĀI PARUPPUSILI

Cluster Beans with Ground Dal

Makes: 4 servings
Serving size: 100 gms
Calories per serving: 182

INGREDIENTS

Avarakai/Dolichos beans 200 gm
Red gram dal/Tuvar dal ½ cup
Dried red chillies 2–3
Turmeric powder ½ tsp
Salt ½ tsp

Seasoning
Oil 2 tbsp
Mustard seeds ½ tsp
Asafoetida powder ½ tsp
Curry leaves 1 sprig

This is a popular method of serving green vegetables, besides adding to the nutritional factor. Red gram dal/tuvar dal or green gram dal/mung dal, is ground with spices, steamed, crumbled and seasoned, hence the name usili (crumble).

METHOD

1. Wash tuvar dal and soak in water for about an hour. Drain and grind with red chillies and turmeric powder to make a coarse batter.
2. Place batter in a greased plate and steam for 10–15 minutes.
3. Cool, crumble and keep aside.
4. Trim cluster beans and cut into small pieces.
5. Boil cluster beans with salt and just enough water till tender but crisp. Do not cover pan.
6. Heat oil in a vānali/wok. Splutter mustard seeds, add asafoetida, stir in curry leaves and sauté.
7. Add crumbled dal and sauté for a few minutes.
8. Add beans, mix well, remove from heat and serve.

Variations: Use green gram dal/mung dal instead of red gram dal/tuvar dal. Cabbage, dolichos beans, lablab, fenugreek leaves, capsicum, snake gourd, and plantain flower (see Pre-Cooking Processes for its preparation) can be made in the same way.

VAḶAIKKAI TUVARAN Green Plantain Tuvaran

Makes: 4 servings
Serving size: 100 gms
Calories per serving: 313

INGREDIENTS

Green plantain (Vaḷaikkai) 4
Salt ½ tsp

Spices for grinding
Jeera/Cumin seeds 1 tsp
Dried red chillies 3–4
Grated fresh coconut 2 tbsp
Salt ½ tsp
Turmeric ¼ tsp
Water 2 tsp

Seasoning
Oil 4–5 tsp
Mustard seeds 1 tsp
Black gram dal/Urad dal ½ tsp
Curry leaves 1 sprig

METHOD

1. Peel and cut the plantains into small cubes.
2. Boil with salt and just enough water to cover, till tender.
3. Grind spices together with coconut and salt with 2 tsp of water.
4. Heat oil in a vānali/wok. Splutter mustard seeds; add urad dal and fry till golden in colour and add curry leaves.
5. Add ground spices turn over once or twice, add cooked plantain.

Variations:

- *Cabbage: Shred, boil till tender but crisp, drain and proceed as above.*
- *Runner beans and beans: Cut runner beans into 1-inch pieces and cut beans into ½-inch pieces and cook as above.*

VENDAKĀI VADHAKKAL Pan-fried Okra

Makes: 3–4 servings
Serving size: 100 gms
Calories per serving: 75

INGREDIENTS

Okra 400 gm
Salt ½ tsp

Spices to add
Black pepper 1 tsp, coarsely pounded
Jeera/Cumin seeds 1 tsp, coarsely pounded

Seasoning
Oil 1½ tbsp
Mustard seeds ½ tsp
Curry leaves 1 sprig

METHOD

1. Cut okras into ½-inch thick slanted pieces.
2. Heat oil in a vānali/wok. Splutter mustard seeds, stir in curry leaves.
3. Add okra and salt. Sauté, turning a few times till slightly cooked. It should not change colour.
4. Add spice powders and turn over the vegetables.
5. Remove from heat and serve.

Variations:
Kovakāi (Coccinia grandis), snake gourd and brinjal can be made in the same way. For colocasia, plantain, potato and yam, boil till tender, remove skin and slice or cubes.

Optional: Use red chilli powder, dhania-jeera powder.

BRINJAL

The etymology of the words for kattrikāi (brinjal) in Indian languages is from bandagi (Sanskrit) and its various mutated forms—vandaki, venkayulu, baingan, etc.

In India, the Spanish 'brinjal' is commonly used, though 'eggplant' and the French sophisticate 'aubergine' occur occasionally in cookbooks.

LAVANGA KATRIKĀI Brinjal with Cloves

Makes: 4 servings
Serving size: 100 gms
Calories per serving: 169

INGREDIENTS

Long, thin brinjals 500 gm
Salt ½ tsp
Gram flour/Besan 1 tbsp
Ghee for frying 2½ tbsp

Spices for powdering
Ginger 1½-inch piece, chopped
Cloves 1-inch stick, powdered
Big black cardamom 1, powdered
Whole black pepper powder from 15 corns
Red chilli powder 1 tsp
Salt ½ tsp

Divide the above powder into 2 portions

Seasoning
Cloves 4
Salt ¼ tsp
Sugar 2 tbsp
Lime juice 2 tbsp

METHOD

1. Slit the brinjals into quarters, halfway through—rub salt and keep for half an hour.
2. Chop the ginger finely.
3. Mix the powder of cloves, black cardamom, black pepper and red chilli powder and divide into 2 portions.
4. Toast the besan.
5. Heat ½ tbsp of ghee in a wok in low–medium flame, add ginger, and salt and besan and mix well.
7. Stuff the brinjals with half the spice mix. Close well.
8. Heat 1½ tbsp ghee and season with 3 cloves to dark brown. Add brinjals and salt and place them evenly on wok, cook on low fire.
9. When cooked, mix sugar and lime juice, cover and cook on low heat, till juice dries up.
10. Open the lid, add remaining half of spice powder and stir gently. Remove.

MASALA KATRIKKĀI VADHAKKAL

Spicy Pan-fried Brinjal Slices

Makes: 4 servings
Serving size: 100 gms
Calories per serving: 129

INGREDIENTS

Brinjal (large variety) 1, roughly 350 gm
Oil 1 tsp + ¼ cup

Spice powder
Gram flour/Besan 1 tbsp
Dried mango powder 1 tsp
Red chilli powder 1 tsp
Asafoetida powder ½ tsp
Dhania/Coriander powder 1 tsp
Turmeric powder ¼ tsp
Ajwain ¼ tsp
Salt ½ tsp

METHOD

1. Cut brinjal into ½-inch thick slices.
2. Mark slices deeply with a knife to form a diamond pattern on one side.
3. Combine all spice powders in a bowl. Add 1 tsp of oil and mix well.
4. Coat spice powder into brinjal slices on both sides.
5. Put ¼ cup of oil in a frying pan over medium heat. When oil is hot, place brinjal slices in pan. Fry till well cooked. Turn over and fry the other side.
6. Remove, drain on kitchen paper and serve.

TINDA TAYIR KARI Indian Round Gourd with Curd

Makes: 4–5 servings
Serving size: 100 gms
Calories per serving: 83

INGREDIENTS

Tinda/Indian round gourd 500 gm
Cornflour 1 tsp
Sour curd ¾ cup, whisked smooth
Water 1 cup

Seasoning
Oil 2 tbsp
Ginger 1½-inch piece, crushed well
Whole green chillies 4, slit at tip
Curry leaves 1 sprig
Asafoetida powder 1 pinch
Salt 1 tsp
Finely chopped coriander leaves 1 cup

Garnish
Toasted jeera/Cumin powder ½ tsp
Turmeric powder ½ pinch

METHOD

1. Whisk cornflour with curd and 1 cup of water thoroughly and set aside.
2. Cut tinda cap, peel and cut into quarters and steam for 8 minutes.
3. Heat oil in a vānali/wok on low heat. Add seasoning and sauté for 1–2 minutes.
4. Add coriander leaves and salt and sauté over medium heat for 1 minute.
5. Add steamed tinda and cook over low to medium heat.
6. Add turmeric powder and toasted cumin powder and mix well.
7. Add curd with cornflour, cook further till most of the liquid is absorbed (some gravy should remain).

PUDALANGĀI PIDITAN Snake Gourd Fistfuls

Makes: 4 servings
Serving size: 100 gms
Calories per serving: 222

INGREDIENTS

Pudalankāi/Snake gourd 180 gm
Besan/Bengal gram flour 2 tbsp
Rice flour 2 tbsp
Grated coconut 1½ tbsp
Dried red chilli 1, deseeded and coarsely powdered
Green chilli 1, cut fine
Turmeric powder 1 tsp
Asafoetida 1 tsp
Salt ½ tsp
Curry leaves 1 sprig

Seasoning
Oil 1 tbsp
Mustard seeds 1 tsp
Curry leaves 2 sprigs

METHOD

1. Cut snake gourd into 2 halves along the length. Cut these into thin crescents.
2. Mix besan flour, rice flour, green chilli, red chilli, turmeric, asafoetida, salt and curry leaves.
3. Add snake gourd to mixture and lightly knead with hand without using water.
4. Take a dessert spoon of the vegetable mixture and shape into an oblong roll.
5. Shape remaining mixture into oblongs/fistfuls (piditan).
6. Arrange them on a plate and steam for 5 minutes.
7. Remove steamed piditans.
8. Heat oil in a vānali/wok. Splutter mustard seeds and curry leaves. Add piditans and turn once or twice gently till all of them are coated evenly with oil.

VAḶAIPŪ KADUGU ARAITHA KARI

Plantain Flower with Ground Mustard

Makes: 4 servings
Serving size: 100 gms
Calories per serving: 103

INGREDIENTS

Banana flower 1
Curd 1 tsp
Water 2 cups
Turmeric powder 1 pinch
Salt ½ tsp

For grinding
Mustard seeds 2 tsp
Grated jaggery 1 pinch
Green chilli 1, chopped
Grated fresh coconut 3 tbsp

Seasoning
Oil 1½ tbsp
Mustard seeds ½ tsp
Curry leaves 1 sprig

METHOD

1. Prepare banana flowers (see Pre-Cooking Processes). Chop fine and immerse in 2 cups of water mixed with curd in a vessel.
2. Add turmeric powder and salt. Boil banana flowers till tender. Drain and set aside.
3. Grind mustard seeds, jaggery, green chilli and grated coconut.
4. Heat oil in a vānali/wok. Splutter mustard seeds, stir in curry leaves.
5. Add ground mix and sauté for about a minute.
6. Add cooked banana flowers. Sauté for a few minutes for flavours to blend.
7. Remove from heat and serve.

CAULIFLOWER KARI Cauliflower Sauté

Makes: 6 servings
Serving size: 100 gms
Calories per serving: 149

INGREDIENTS

Cauliflower (medium) 500 gm
Salt 1 tsp + 1½ tsp + ¾ tsp
Boiling water 1 cup
Coriander leaves ½ cup
Green chillies 2

Seasoning
Oil 4 tbsp
Jeera/Cumin seeds ½ tsp
Ginger 1-inch piece
Curd ⅓ cup

METHOD

1. Remove stem of cauliflower, cut into small florets and wash in water with salt and drain.
2. Cut ginger into julienne pieces.
3. Grind coriander leaves and green chillies with a little salt to a paste.
4. Heat 2 tbsp oil in a vānali/wok over low heat and sauté cauliflower till golden spots are formed on all sides.
5. Add boiling water and cook till tender. Drain and keep aside.
6. Heat oil in wok over medium heat and splutter cumin seeds, add ginger and sauté for a minute.
7. Add ground paste, sauté for a minute or two.
8. Lower heat, add curd and cook, stirring continuously till oil separates.
9. Add cooked cauliflower to the green masala and cook till slightly moist.
10. Remove and serve hot with rotis and rice.

BROCCOLI ELLU KARI Broccoli with Sesame Seeds

Makes: 4 servings
Serving size: 100 gms
Calories per serving: 71

INGREDIENTS

Broccoli florets 250 gm
Salt ½ tsp

Seasoning
Oil 2 tsp
Dried red chillies 2
White sesame seeds 1 tsp

METHOD

1. Boil broccoli with salt and just enough water to cover, till tender but crisp.
2. Heat oil in a vānali/wok. Fry red chillies.
3. Add sesame seeds and sauté for a few seconds.
4. Add cooked broccoli florets.
5. Sauté over medium heat for about 2 minutes.
6. Remove from heat and serve.

KOS MUTTIA Cabbage Muttia

Makes: 4 servings
Serving size: 100 gms
Calories per serving: 87

INGREDIENTS

Cabbage 400 gm
Oil 1 tbsp
Suji/Semolina 100 gm
Besan/Bengal gram flour 1 tbsp
Turmeric ¼ tsp
Asafoetida 2 pinches
Chopped coriander 1 tbsp
Salt 1 tsp
Hung curd 2 tsp

Spices for grinding
Inji/Ginger 1-inch piece
Green chillies (medium) 3

Seasoning
Oil 2 tsp
Mustard ⅓ tsp
Jeera/Cumin seeds 1 tsp
Curry leaves 1 sprig
Green chillies 2, deseeded and slit

Garnish
Chopped coriander ½ tbsp

METHOD

1. Clean and shred cabbage.
2. Grind spices to a paste. In a separate bowl place semolina, besan, turmeric, asafoetida, chopped coriander, salt and oil. Add the ground paste. Mix well.
3. To the above mixture, add shredded cabbage and hung curd and knead to a soft mixture. Form fist sized rolls even in size.
4. Steam the rolls for 30 minutes.
5. Remove and cool.
6. Heat oil in a vānali/wok. Splutter seasoning and pour over muttias.
7. Garnish with chopped coriander and serve.

DUM PARWAL Slow-cooked Pointed Gourd

Makes: 4 servings
Serving size: 100 gms
Calories per serving: 248

INGREDIENTS

Parwal 12
Ghee and oil mix ½ cup
Water 1 cup

Seasoning
Ghee and oil mix 2 tsp
Jeera/Cumin seeds ½ tsp
Cloves 4
Asafoetida powder ¼ tsp

Spices
Dried ginger powder 1 tsp
Ginger 1-inch piece, crushed
Garam masala 1 tsp
Sukhi badi[1] ½ tsp
Green chillies 2, chopped fine
Red chilli powder 1 tsp
Dhania/Coriander powder 1 tsp
Salt ¾ tsp
Ghee1 tsp

Garnish
Coriander leaves 2–3 sprigs, chopped

METHOD

1. Wash and scrape parwal. Make a slit along one side without separating segments. Discard seeds.
2. Heat ½ cup ghee and oil mix in a vānali/wok. Fry the gourd over medium heat, till light brown. Drain and remove from wok.
3. Add more ghee and oil in vessel. Add seasoning and fry over medium heat for about a second.
4. Add fried gourds, spices, salt and 1 cup of water.
5. Pour a tsp of ghee over the vegetable.
6. Cover vessel with a lid. Lower heat and place a red-hot charcoal piece on the lid.
7. When gourds are tender, after about 5 minutes, sprinkle with coriander leaves.
8. Remove from heat and serve.

Variations: Bitter gourd, bottle gourd, lotus stem, okra, tinda can be made in the same way.

[1]*Sukhi badi is also known as Kashmiri badi. It is a small, dried disc, 2–3 inches round, ½-inch thick, made up of different spices.*

URULAI MADRAS KĀRAKARI Spicy Potatoes

Makes: 4 servings
Serving size: 100 gms
Calories per serving: 140

INGREDIENTS

Baby potatoes 400 gm

Spices for grinding
Dhania/Coriander seeds 2 tsp
Dried red chillies 5
Turmeric powder ½ tsp
Salt 1½ tsp
Asafoetida powder ¼ tsp
Water 2 tbsp

Seasoning
Oil 4 tbsp
Mustard seeds 1 tsp
Black gram dal/Urad dal 1 tsp
Curry leaves 2 sprigs

METHOD

1. Scrub potatoes and boil them in their jackets, till tender. Peel and set aside.
2. Grind spices with about 2 tbsp of water to a fine consistency.
3. Coat potatoes with ground spices and set aside for 30 minutes.
4. Heat oil in a vānali/wok. Splutter mustard seeds, add urad dal and fry, till it turns golden brown. Stir in curry leaves.
5. Add spiced potatoes.
6. Reduce heat, spread potatoes evenly all over vānali/wok.
7. After 2 minutes turn potatoes over and again spread all over till all edges are sligthly roasted.
8. Remove from heat and serve.

CHUTNEY URULAI KIḶANGU KARI Chutney Potatoes

Makes: 4 servings
Serving size: 100 gms
Calories per serving: 248

INGREDIENTS

Baby potatoes 600 gm
Oil for deep-frying 1½ cups
Salt ½ tsp
Chopped coriander leaves 2 cups
Mint leaves ¾ cup
Cashewnuts 20
Curd 1½ cups, whisked smooth

METHOD

1. Scrub potatoes and boil in their jackets for about 25 minutes, till tender but firm. Peel potatoes and prick all over with a fork.
2. Heat oil in a vānali/wok and deep fry potatoes, till glossy and pale yellow. Sprinkle in some salted water while frying. Drain and set aside.
3. Grind coriander leaves and mint leaves a little coarsely.
4. Grind cashewnuts finely with a little water and mix with curd.
5. Heat oil in wok. Sauté cumin seeds, ginger paste and red chilli powder mixed with 1 tsp of water for about a minute.

Finely shredded green mango (not too sour)[1] 1 tbsp
Tomato purée[2] ¾ cup

Seasoning
Oil 1 tbsp
Jeera/Cumin seeds 1 tsp
Ginger paste 1 tbsp
Red chilli powder 1 tsp
Water 1 tsp

6. Add tomato purée, sauté till raw smell disappears, then add shredded mango and then coriander mint chutney; cook together for about 3 minutes.
7. Reduce heat, add curd cashewnut mixture and cook for about a minute.
8. Add fried potatoes. If it is too dry, add ¼ cup of boiling water and mix well.
9. Taste and add more salt, if required.
10. Serve with rice or roti.

[1]*Instead of green mango add 1 tsp of lime juice just before serving.*

[2]*Instead of readymade tomato puree, fresh tomatoes can be pulped and used.*

CABBAGE WITH TAKKĀLI AND OMAM KARI

Cabbage with Tomato and Carom Seeds

Makes: 4 servings
Serving size: 100 gms
Calories per serving: 39

INGREDIENTS

Cabbage 500 gm
Tomato 1, medium
Oil 2–3 tsp
Omam/Ajwain/Carom seeds 2 tsp
Salt ⅛ tsp/2 pinches
Sugar 1 pinch (optional)
Water 2 tbsp (from blanching)

METHOD

1. Remove cabbage leaves one by one and wash.
2. Cut leaves in 1½-inch square pieces.
3. Cut tomato, remove seeds and chop finely.
4. Blanch cabbage leaves in boiling water 1 minute and drain. Keep aside.
5. Pour oil in a vānali/wok and heat to (medium). Splutter omam/ajwain seed without burning.
6. Add tomato pieces, add salt and sugar, sauté for 2–3 minutes, till oil separates.
7. Add cabbage, mix well and reduce heat.
8. Add 2 tbsp of blanched water and cover and cook for 2–3 minutes.
9. Open once or twice and sauté and serve.

APPALAM KARI Papad Kari

Makes: 3–4 servings
Serving size: 100 gms
Calories per serving: 131

INGREDIENTS

Medium-sized papads 4, cut into 1-inch squares
Green chilli 1, deseeded and chopped
Mustard seeds 1 tsp
Cumin seeds 1 tsp
Asafoetida ½ tsp
Turmeric powder ½ tsp
Red chilli powder 1 tsp
Curd 2 tbsp
Besan/Bengal gram flour 1 tsp
Water 2 cups
Ghee 2 tbsp
Chopped coriander 2 tbsp
Salt ½ tsp

METHOD

1. Heat the ghee in a heavy-bottomed pan on medium heat and crackle the mustard and cumin seeds.
2. Drop in the asafoetida and green chilli and fry lighty.
3. Add the red chilli powder and curd. Mix well and stir fry on medium heat for about a minute or two.
4. Mix in the turmeric powder, besan, water and salt.
5. Bring to a boil. Add the papads and coriander leaves. Cook on low heat for about 3 minutes or till the papads are nicely cooked.

SEPPANKIḶANGU KĀRA KARI Spicy Colocasia

Makes: 4 servings
Serving size: 75 gms
Calories per serving: 158

INGREDIENTS

Seppankiḷangu/Colocasia 16, 2½-inches long
Mustard oil to deep-fry 22 ml
Mustard seeds 2.5 gm
Curry leaves 8
Ginger 17.5 gm, cut finely, like thread
Turmeric powder 2 gm
Red chilli powder 1.5 gm
Curds cheese[1] 125 gm, whisked in a bowl
Lemon juice 30 ml

METHOD

1. Wash, scrape the colacasias and put in a pan full of boiling water and blanch for 10 minutes. Drain and keep aside.
2. Heat the vānali/wok, add all the spices and seeds, except asafoetida, one at a time and broil over low heat until each spice emits its unique aroma and the seeds begin to crackle. Cool and put all the spices and seeds in a mortar, add asafoetida, pound with a pestle into a fine powder, add salt and mix well. Sieve and keep aside.
3. Heat mustard oil to a smoking point in a wok. Reduce to low heat. Add the blanched colocasias and deep fry until light brown. Remove and keep aside. Strain the oil and reserve 45 ml for the gravy.

Garnish

Mint leaves 8

For pickle masala

Big green cardamoms 2

Cloves 3

Black cardamoms 2

Bay leaf 1

Coriander seeds 3.7 gm

Fennel seeds 2.5 gm

Cumin seeds 1.5 gm

Kalonji 1.5 gm

Asafoetida 1 gm

Mustard seeds 2.5 gm

Fenugreek seeds 1.5 gm

Salt 1 tsp

4. Heat the reserved mustard oil (45 ml) in a kadāi, add mustard seeds, curry leaves and stir for 10 seconds. Then add the ginger, stir for 15 seconds, add turmeric, red chilies and salt, stir for another 15 seconds. Remove kadāi from heat, stir in curds, and return the kadāi to heat. Stir fry until the fat leaves the sides. (Approx. 7–8 minutes)
5. Now add the pickle masala. Add water (approx. 240 ml) and cook, stirring occasionally for 2 minutes or until gravy is of sauce consistency. Remove and adjust the seasoning.
6. Arrange 8 colacasias on each of 4 individual plates, garnish with mint leaves and serve with strained rice or phulka.

[1]*In a muslin cloth pour the curds—gather the sides of the cloth and hang for ½ hour to drain the water and use the cheese.*

KNOLKOHL-PĀLAK KARI Knolkohl and Pālak

Makes: 4 servings

Serving size: 100 gms

Calories per serving: 153

INGREDIENTS

Tender knolkohl with leaves 4–5

Pālak 2 cups, whole leaves

Milk ¼ cup

Salt ½ tsp

Seasoning

Mustard oil 2 tbsp (see Pre-Cooking Processes)

Fenugreek seeds ½ tsp

Mustard seeds ½ tsp

Jeera/Cumin seeds ½ tsp

Whole dhania/Coriander seeds ¾ tsp

Green chillies 2

Dried red chilli 1

METHOD

1. Remove knolkohl stalks. Wash knolkohl, remove leaves and reserve. Cut knolkohl into quarters and then into thin slices.
2. Wash pālak leaves thoroughly.
3. Pressure-cook knolkohl slices and leaves, and pālak with milk for 2 whistles.
4. Heat mustard oil in a vānali/wok. Splutter mustard seeds over medium heat, add fenugreek seeds. When they start to turn dark brown, lower heat, add remaining seasoning and fry for about 2 seconds.
5. Add cooked vegetables, salt and mix well.
6. Remove from heat and serve.

URULAI KOLKATA KARI Potatoes Kolkata Style

Makes: 4 servings
Serving size: 100 gms
Calories per serving: 174

INGREDIENTS

Baby potatoes 500 gm
Oil 1½ cups
Tamarind ½ tsp
Water ½ cup
Salt ½ tsp
Grated jaggery ¼ tsp

Spices for powdering
Cloves 3
Tej patta/Cinnamon leaf 1
Cinnamon ½-inch stick
Dhania/Coriander seeds 1 tbsp
Cardamoms 2
Turmeric powder ¼ tsp
Red chilli powder 1 tsp
Garam masala ¼ tsp
Water 1 tsp

Seasoning
Oil 2 tsp
Jeera/Cumin seeds ½ tsp
Asafoetida powder ¼ tsp

Garnish
Toasted jeera/Cumin powder 1½ tsp
Finely chopped coriander leaves 1 tbsp

METHOD

1. Scrub potatoes and boil in their jackets, till tender but firm. Peel potatoes.
2. Extract tamarind juice using ½ cup of water (see Pre-Cooking Processes).
3. Grind spices to make a coarse powder.
4. Heat 1½ cups of oil in a vānali/wok. Deep-fry potatoes till glossy and pale yellow. Drain and set aside.
5. Heat oil in wok. Sauté seasoning for 2–3 seconds.
6. Mix 1 tsp of water to ground spices, add to vānali/wok and sauté for about 2 minutes.
7. Add fried potatoes and toss, till well-coated with spices.
8. Stir in tamarind juice and jaggery. Cook over low heat, till liquid is absorbed.
9. Sprinkle toasted cumin powder and garnish with coriander leaves.

MULAKEERAI AND MIXED VEGETABLE KARI

Amaranth, Black-eyed Bean, Cauliflower and Carrot Kari

Makes: 4 servings
Serving size: 100 gms
Calories per serving: 51

INGREDIENTS

Amaranth 150 gm
Cauliflower 75 gm
Carrot 75 gm
Black-eyed bean or white kabuli chana 50 gm
Sugar 1 pinch
Water 1–2 tbsp

Spices
Cloves 2
Jeera/Cumin seeds ¼ tsp
Asafoetida powder 1 pinch

For grinding
Green chilli 1 long
Ginger ½-inch piece
Salt ½ tsp

METHOD

Step I

1. Cut roots of amaranth and remove. Wash all stems with leaves thoroughly and drain. Chop stems and leaves finely.
2. Cut cauliflower into 1½-inch florets.
3. Peel carrots and cut into ¾ inch cubes.
4. Soak black-eyed beans for 20 minutes in water and cook. If using kabuli chana, soak overnight and cook.
5. Steam carrots and cauliflower, remove when ¾ cooked.
6. Boil amaranth with 1 tbsp of water, salt and sugar. Cook well, add a pinch of asafoetida and remove.

Step II

1. Grind finely the amaranth with ginger and chilli into a fine paste.
2. Heat oil in a vānali/wok, toast cloves and jeera and powder them coarsely.
3. Place a vessel on heat, add ground amaranth and steamed vegetables and black-eyed beans/kabuli chana. Simmer for 2 minutes.
4. Add toasted jeera and clove powder on top. Mix well and serve.

Variations: Green peas and kabuli chana can be added instead of black-eyed beans.

PARANGIKAI PĀLAK KARI

Black Pālak and Tender Pumpkin

Makes: 4 servings
Serving size: 100 gms
Calories per serving: 69

INGREDIENTS

Tender (yellow) pumpkin 400 gm
Pālak 200 gm
Small walnut with shell 1
Mustard oil 2 tsp

Seasoning
Mustard oil 1½ tbsp
Methi seeds/Fenugreek seeds ⅓ tsp
Cloves 3
Asafoetida powder ½ tsp
Saunf/Fennel ½ tsp
Jeera/Cumin seeds ⅓ tsp
Dhania/Coriander powder ⅔ tsp
Red chilli powder ½ tsp
Turmeric powder ¼ tsp
Water 1 tsp
Asafoetida powder ⅛ tsp or 2 pinches
Ginger 1-inch piece, grated
Salt ½ tsp
Jaggery ⅛ tsp

Garnish
Coriander 1–2 tsp, chopped

METHOD

1. Wash pumpkin and make 1½-inch cubes with peel.
2. Clean, wash pālak, chop finely and grind to a fine paste.
3. Mix spice powders (dhania, red chilli and turmeric) with a tsp of water.
4. Burn the whole walnut on red-hot charcoal/gas evenly by rotating the walnut till it glows red.
5. Remove and place in a small plate and drizzle 2 tsp of mustard oil. Cool and grind the burnt walnut to a fine paste.
6. In a vānali/wok, pour mustard oil (see Pre-Cooking Processes) and when ready, splutter methi seeds/fenugreek seeds, cloves, saunf and cumin. Lower heat, add asafoetida and ginger.
7. Add spice powder paste (dhania, red chilli and turmeric).
8. Add salt and pumpkin pieces and sauté for a minute. Sprinkle a little water, cover and cook on low heat. Open and turn a few times.
9. When half-done, add ground pālak and the ground walnut paste and cook further. Remove when still moist. If too dry, add 1 tbsp of hot water.
10. Garnish and serve.

The present term kūtu refers to vegetables cooked with spices and dals in a thick liquid base. It was originally called negil kariamudu, meaning vegetables in thick liquid.

The Kannada word sagu, now currently used for vegetables, is popular and easily understood in south India. A funny story goes with the word:

At a temple feast, an attendant carrying a twin-cup serving vessel asked a guest, who did not speak Kannada, '*Sagu bega*?' to inquire if the guest wanted more sagu. The hungry guest, not wanting to forego any dish, thinking there were two different dishes, replied, 'Give me some sagu and some bega!' not realizing that bega means 'Do you want?'

Kūtu is like north Indian rasedar or dal. Kūtu is mixed with plain cooked rice and eaten quite often in lieu of sambar or rasam. It is an accompaniment to puri, paratha or roti.

CHOW-CHOW PATTĀNI KŪTU Chow-chow and Peas Kūtu

Makes: 4 servings

Serving size: 100 gms

Calories per serving: 159

INGREDIENTS

Chow-chow or custard gourd (medium) 1

Peas 100 gm

Water ½ cup

Spices for grinding

Oil 2 tsp

Black gram dal/Urad dal 2 tsp

Dried red chillies 4–5

Fenugreek seeds/Methi seeds ½ tsp

Sesame seeds ¾ tsp

Asafoetida powder ¼ tsp

Water 2–3 tsp

Copra (not to fry)

Seasoning

Cashewnuts 4, broken

Oil 1 tsp

Mustard seeds ½ tsp

Urad dal 1 tsp

Asafoetida powder ¼ tsp

Curry leaves 1 sprig

METHOD

1. Peel and cube chow-chow.
2. Shell the peas.
3. Heat oil in a vānali/wok over medium heat, add spices, and fry till golden, remove.
4. Grind spices with copra to a grainy consistency.
5. In a pan bring ½ cup of water to boil, add peas; when tender, keep aside.
6. In another pan, boil chow-chow, cook till tender, yet firm, add boiled peas with its water.
7. Add ground spices and stir well. Simmer for a minute. Remove from heat.
8. Heat oil in wok. Fry cashew to a light golden. Remove and keep aside. In the same oil splutter the other seasoning, pour over the kūtu.
9. Splutter mustard seeds with urad dal, asafoetida and curry leaves and pour into vegetables.

Variations: Cauliflower, carrot and peas can be made in the same way.

French beans and green peas can be made in the same way.

PULLIPPU KŪTU Mixed Vegetable Tangy Kūtu

Makes: 4 servings
Serving size: 100 gms
Calories per serving: 70

INGREDIENTS

2 cups altogether
Carrots
Potatoes
French beans or avaraikkai
Chow-chow or custard gourd

Tamarind juice 2 tsp
Salt ½ tsp
Cooked mung dal 3 tsp

Spices for grinding
Oil 1 tbsp
Dhania/Coriander seeds 4 tsp
Dried red chillies 6
Bengal gram dal/Chana dal 2½ tsp
Black gram dal/Urad dal 1½ tsp
Cinnamon ⅛-inch stick
Asafoetida 2 pinches
Grated fresh coconut/Copra 3 tsp
Water to grind 1 tbsp

Seasoning
Oil 2 tsp
Dried red chillies 1–2
Mustard seeds ¾ tsp
Black gram dal/Urad dal ¾ tsp
Asafoetida 1 pinch
Curry leaves 1 sprig

METHOD

1. Cube carrots, potatoes, custard gourd. Cut French beans or avaraikkai into 1-inch pieces. All cut vegetables together should be 2 cups.
2. Heat oil in a vānali/wok and fry spices for grinding over medium heat, till aromatic. Remove.
3. Grind fried ingredients with fresh coconut to a grainy consistency.
4. Boil enough water to cook vegetables. First cook carrots and potatoes, when they are half cooked, add French beans/avaraikkai and cook for 1 or 2 minutes. Add gourd and cook till vegetables are tender but crisp. Ensure there is enough water in wok. Add more boiling water if required.
5. Add ground spices and mix.
6. Mix tamarind juice and salt and boil for 4 minutes.
7. Add cooked mung dal and boil for a minute or two.
8. Heat oil in wok. Splutter mustard seeds, add remaining seasoning and fry.
9. Pour contents of wok over kūtu.
10. Remove from heat and serve.

PĀVAKKAI MĀNGĀI KŪTU Bitter Gourd and Mango Kūtu

Makes: 4 servings
Serving size: 100 gms
Calories per serving: 229

INGREDIENTS

Bitter gourd 300 gm
Mangoes (not too sour) 150 gm
Oil 1½ tbsp
Ginger 1-inch piece, cut in fine juliennes
Green chillies 5, slit
Turmeric powder ½ tsp
Red chilli powder ½ tsp
Dhania/coriander powder ½ tsp
Fresh coconut 1, ground
Salt 1 tsp
Jaggery or sugar ½ tsp

Seasoning
Oil 1 tsp
Mustard seeds ½ tsp
Dried red chillies 2
Curry leaves 1 sprig

METHOD

1. Wash bitter gourd, scrape lightly. Discard seeds and cut lengthwise into quarters. Cut into ¾-inch pieces.
2. Bring water to boil over medium heat. Add bitter gourd and cook till soft.
3. Peel mangoes and cut into slices.
4. Heat oil in a vānali/wok. Add ginger and green chillies and sauté for about a minute.
   powder with 1 tsp of water. Lower heat and add to wok.
6. Add ground coconut and salt.
7. Mix in mango pieces and cook, till tender.
   coated.
9. Heat oil. Splutter mustard seeds, add red chillies, stir in curry leaves.
10. Pour seasoning over curry and serve.

Note: This dish goes well with rice, dosai, etc.

URULAIKIḶANGU PARANGIKAI RASEDAR

Potato Pumpkin Rasedar

Makes: 4 servings
Serving size: 100 gms
Calories per serving: 122

INGREDIENTS

Potatoes 500 gm
Pumpkin 300 gm
Tomatoes 250 gm
Tej patta 1
Asafoetida ½ tsp
Kasuri methi/Dried fenugreek leaves ½ tsp (optional)
Ginger cut into small pieces 1 tsp
Green chillies cut into small pieces 1 tsp
Coriander/Dhania powder 1 tbsp
Chilli powder 1 tbsp
Turmeric powder 1 tsp
Salt 1 tbsp
Cooking oil 2 tbsp

Garnish
Coriander leaves 1 tbsp

METHOD

1. Cut potatoes and pumpkin to the same size.
2. Heat oil in a vānali. Add tej patta, asafoetida, green chillies and ginger and sauté for a minute.
3. Add potatoes, cover the vānali with a lid and cook the potatoes in steam for a few minutes.
4. When half cooked, add the pumpkin pieces, salt, turmeric powder, coriander powder, chilli powder.
5. When the vegetables are almost cooked, add the tomato pieces.
6. Once cooked, add some hot water to form the gravy. Let it boil. Remove from fire.
7. Add coriander leaves as garnish.

PANCHMELA SĀG Mélange of Vegetables

Makes: 4 servings
Serving size: 100 gms
Calories per serving: 67

INGREDIENTS

Tender (yellow) pumpkin 75 gm
Dosaikāi 75 gm
Big cucumber (Malabar) 75 gm
Brinjal 50gm
Parwal/Pointed gourd 50 gm
Karamani/Runner beans 50 gm
Kothavarangai/Cluster beans 50 gm
Pālak leaves (whole) 75 gm
Tomato ¼ cup, juiced
Potato (medium) 1
Salt ¾ tsp
Water 1½ cups + 1 tsp
Red chilli powder 1 tsp
Dhania/Coriander powder 1 tsp
Turmeric powder ½ tsp
Green chillies 2, cut fine
Ginger 1-inch piece, cut fine
Garam masala ½ tsp
Ghee 1 tsp

Seasoning
Oil 2 tbsp
Methi seeds/Fenugreek seeds ¼ tsp
Mustard ¾ tsp
Tej patta/Cinnamon leaf ½ leaf
Lavang/Cloves 4
Kalonji/Nigella seeds ¼ tsp
Jeera/Cumin seeds ½ tsp
Sombu/Aniseed ¼ tsp
Omam/Ajwain 1 pinch
Asafoetida ¼ tsp

METHOD

Prepping the vegetables

1. Peel and dice cucumber, pumpkin and potato into 1½-inch cubes
2. Cut parwal and brinjal lengthwise into quarters.
3. Cut cluster and runner beans into 2-inch long pieces.
4. Discard pālak stems and cut the leaves in halves.
5. Mix water with chilli powder, turmeric powder and coriander powder. Stir and keep aside.

Cooking

1. Place oil in a vānali/wok, add methi seeds and when colour changes to light brown, add other seasoning ingredients one by one except ajwain and asafoetida. Remove from heat at once, add ajwain and asafoetida.
2. When oil is still hot, immediately add turmeric, dhania-chilli paste and cut chilli and ginger.
3. Now add vegetables that need the longest time to cook first like potatoes, cucumber, and sauté for a minute, stir and cover. Turn once or twice.
4. After a few minutes add brinjal and parwal, add 1½ cups of water and cover with a plate containing water.
5. After a few minutes, add yellow pumpkin, runner beans and cluster beans. If necessary add water from the plate.
6. When ready, add garam masala, ghee, stir well and serve.

Note: This is one of the most popular dishes of strict vegetarians. It varies a little from province to province. The origin is Marwar of Rajasthan.

KUḶAMBU/SAMBAR

KUḶAMBU/SAMBAR

Kuḷambu refers to a thick gravy with one or two vegetables to be mixed with rice as a main course of a south Indian meal. Sambar is a later, heavier version and the word refers to a dish loaded with spices. Originally from Sanskrit, the word 'sāmbharam' meant 'with heaviness'. In Gujarat a vegetable dish is called sāmbhariyā meaning 'that which is heavily laden with spices', for instance, baingan sāmbhariyā.

The Mahrattas who settled down in Thanjavur contributed to popularizing local dishes. An example would be the local araithu vitta kuḷambu (kuḷambu with ground spices) which they referred to as sambar to mean an intensity of spices, from 'sāmbhariya' (full of). The word and the kuḷambu have become so popular now that they have almost edged out the simple paruppu kuḷambu. A heavily spiced powder called sāmbhariyā is available now in Mumbai stores. Other imports from the Mahratta kitchen are the sweets jāngiri and bādushā.

Preparation of vegetables for kuḷambus:
Vegetables are cut in large pieces for use in kuḷambus. Most vegetables can be used for kuḷambus. A single vegetable or a combination of vegetables can also be used.

If using:

1) Red or white pumpkin: Peel and cut into 1-inch cubes. Cut drumstick into 2 pieces.
2) Brinjal: Remove stems and discard. Cut brinjal into quarters and long ones into halves.
3) Okra: Remove top and bottom ends of okra, and leave whole if small. Cut into half, if large.
4) Capsicum: Cut into 2-inch squares.
5) Chow-chow: Peel and cut into 2-inch-long pieces.
6) Lablab: Cluster beans or beans trim ends, remove fibre, cut into 2-inch-long pieces.
7) Amaranth leaves: Cut tender stems into 2-inch-long pieces.
8) Plantain: Peel and cut into 2-inch slices.
9) Colocasia or yam: Boil till tender. Peel and cut into 2-inch cubes.

All vegetables for kuḷambu should be sautéed with a teaspoon of oil in a vānali/wok over medium heat, then added to tamarind juice and cooked further.

PARUPPU KUḶAMBU

Red Gram Dal Kuḷambu

Makes: 4 servings
Serving size: 100 gms
Calories per serving: 119

INGREDIENTS

Red gram dal/Tuvar dal ½ cup
Water 1½ cups + 2 cups
Turmeric powder ¼ tsp
Ghee or castor oil ½ tsp
Tamarind 15 gm
Turmeric powder ¼ tsp
Vegetables of choice 150 gm
Oil 1 tsp (if required)
Kuḷambu/Sambar powder 3 tsp
Asafoetida powder ½ tsp
Salt 1 tsp
Rice flour ¼ tsp (if required)

Seasoning
Sesame oil 2 tsp
Dried red chilli 1
Fenugreek seeds 1 tsp
Mustard seeds ½ tsp
Whole green chillies 2
Curry leaves 1 sprig

Use any one of the following vegetables: tender (yellow) pumpkin, white pumpkin, brinjal, drumstick (2), okra, capsicum (2 medium-sized).

METHOD

Preparation of vegetables: See beginning of 'Kuḷambu' chapter.

1. Wash and pressure-cook tuvar dal with turmeric powder, ghee or castor oil and 1½ cups of water for 3 whistles (see Pre-Cooking Processes). Tuvar dal should be well-cooked but not mushy.
2. Extract tamarind juice using 2 cups of water (see Pre-Cooking Processes).
3. Heat oil in a heavy-bottomed vessel. Add seasoning and splutter over medium heat. Stir in curry leaves, add vegetable of choice, sauté for a minute. Add kuḷambu/sambar powder and immediately add tamarind juice, asafoetida powder and salt and boil for 15–20 minutes (till vegetables are cooked).
4. Add cooked dal and blend well. If kuḷambu is thick, add some water and bring to a boil once again.
5. Remove from heat and serve.

ARAITHUVITTA PARUPPU KUḶAMBU/ SAMBAR

Spicy Red Gram Dal Kuḷambu

Makes: 4 servings
Serving size: 100 gms
Calories per serving: 142

INGREDIENTS

Red gram dal/Tuvar dal ½ cup
Water 1½ cups + 2 cups
Turmeric powder ¼ tsp + ¼ tsp
Ghee or castor oil ½ tsp
Tamarind 12 gm
Vegetable of choice 100–150 gm
Oil 1 tsp (if required)
Asafoetida powder ½ tsp
Salt 1 tsp
Curry leaves 1 sprig
Rice flour ¼ tsp (if required)

Spices for grinding
Sesame oil 1 tbsp
Dried red chillies 2–3
Fenugreek seeds ½ tsp
Dhania/Coriander seeds 2 tsp
Whole black pepper ½ tsp
Bengal gram 1 tsp
Grated fresh coconut 3 tbsp
Water 2 tbsp

Seasoning
Sesame oil 2 tsp
Dried red chilli 1
Fenugreek seeds ¼ tsp
Mustard seeds ½ tsp
Green chillies 2, slit

Use any one of the following vegetables: tender (yellow) pumpkin, white pumpkin, brinjal, drumstick, okra, capsicum.

METHOD

Preparation of vegetables: See beginning of 'Kuḷambu' chapter.

1. Wash tuvar dal and pressure-cook with ¼ tsp of turmeric powder, ghee or castor oil and 1½ cups of water for 3 whistles.
2. Extract tamarind juice using 2 cups of water (see Pre-Cooking Processes).
3. Heat oil in a vānali/wok. Add spices for grinding except the grated coconut and fry till aromatic. Grind with grated coconut and 2 tbsp of water to a fine paste.
4. Heat oil in heavy-bottomed vessel. Add seasoning and splutter over medium heat. Stir in curry leaves, add vegetable of choice, sauté for a minute. Add tamarind juice, asafoetida powder and salt and boil for 15–20 minutes (till vegetables are cooked).
5. Add ground spices, cooked dal, and mix well.
6. Bring to boil and simmer for about 5 minutes.
7. If kuḷambu is too thick, add some boiling water and boil for a minute.
8. Remove from heat and serve.

PARUPPU URUNDAI KUḶAMBU

Red Gram Balls in Tamarind Kuḷambu

Makes: 4 servings
Serving size: 100 gms
Calories per serving: 151

INGREDIENTS

Red gram dal/Tuvar dal 1 cup
Dried red chillies 4
Water ¼ cup
Asafoetida powder ¼ tsp
Salt 1 tsp
Sesame oil 2 tsp
Mustard seeds 1 tsp
Curry leaves 1 sprig

Kuḷambu

Tamarind 15 gm
Water 5 cups
Sesame oil 2 tsp
Mustard seeds 1 tsp
Curry leaves 1 sprig
Fenugreek seeds ¼ tsp
Kuḷambu/Sambar powder 2 tsp (see Podis/Readymade Powders)
Asafoetida powder ½ tsp
Turmeric powder ¼ tsp
Salt 1 tsp

METHOD

Red Gram Balls

1. Soak tuvar dal and red chillies for about 30 minutes in ¼ cup to be in one line of water and grind coarsely to make a thick batter. Add asafoetida powder and salt and mix well.
2. Heat oil in a vānali/wok. Splutter mustard seeds over medium heat. Stir in curry leaves.
3. Add gram batter and stir, till well cooked.
4. Cool and shape into 18–20 small dumplings (urundai). Set aside.

Kuḷambu

1. Extract tamarind juice using 5 cups of water (see Pre-Cooking Processes).
2. Heat oil in heavy-bottomed pan. Splutter mustard seeds over medium heat. Stir in curry leaves.
3. Add fenugreek seeds, kuḷambu/sambar powder and asafoetida powder.
4. Add tamarind juice, turmeric powder and salt and simmer for 4–5 minutes, till raw smell of tamarind disappears.
5. Gently add dumplings, one at a time. Cook, till they rise to the surface. Lower temperature and simmer for 2 more minutes.
6. Remove from heat and serve.

MOR KUḶAMBU

Spicy Curd Kuḷambu

Makes: 6 servings
Serving size: 100 gms
Calories per serving: 106

INGREDIENTS

Vegetable of choice 250 gm
Oil 1 tsp
Thick curd 3 cups, whisked smooth
Water 4 cups
Turmeric powder ¼ tsp
Salt 1 tsp
Coriander leaves 2–3 sprigs, chopped (optional)

Spices for grinding
Red gram dal/Tuvar dal 1 tbsp
Sesame oil 1 tbsp
Fenugreek seeds ¾ tsp
Black gram dal/Urad dal 1 tbsp
Asafoetida powder ¼ tsp
Grated fresh coconut 3 tbsp
Jeera/cumin seeds 1 tsp
Green chillies 4–5
Water ¼ cup

Seasoning
Sesame oil 2 tsp
Dried red chilli 1
Fenugreek seeds ¼ tsp
Mustard seeds ½ tsp
Curry leaves 1 sprig

Use any one of the following vegetables or a mix: colocasia, potato, okra, white pumpkin, chow-chow, brinjal.

METHOD

Preparation of vegetables: See beginning of 'Kuḷambu' chapter.

1. Wash red gram dal and soak in water for half an hour.
2. Heat oil in a vānali/wok. Add fenugreek seeds, urad dal and asafoetida powder and fry over medium heat, till golden brown.
3. Drain tuvar dal and grind with fried spices, coconut, cumin seeds and green chillies in ¼ cup of water to a grainy mixture.
4. Blend curd with 4 cups of water, till smooth. Add ground spices and boil in a heavy-bottomed vessel over medium heat. Stir continuously to prevent lumps forming.
5. Add prepared vegetables. Simmer till a head of foam is formed. Remove from heat immediately.
6. Heat oil in a vānali/wok. Add seasoning ingredients, splutter over medium heat and pour over kuḷambu. Add coriander leaves.

Variations:

- *Māmpaḷa Mor Kuḷambu (for 6 servings): Wash 8 mangoes (preferably chandrakaran or any other small variety) and split them halfway through the stem and bottom. Cook them in water for about a minute and add to kuḷambu in place of the vegetables. Cook, till a head of foam is formed.*
- *Pondy Puliseri: A sour curd kuḷambu is made in a similar way. Use chana dal instead of tuvar dal for grinding.*

KURUNTHOKAI

Tamil Sangam literature, that which spans the years between the third century BCE and second century CE, is a treasure house of references to the food of the day. What is amazing is that many of those dishes have come down to us and are still as popular today as they were in that ancient time.

The Tamil poem 'Kurunthokai' by Kudalur Kilar gives us a poetic description of the making of Mor Kuḷambu, a thick spicy gravy with yoghurt:

Mulitayir piśainda kāndal melviral
Kaluvuru kalingam kalādu udiik
Kuvalaiyun kan kuyppugai kamala t
Tanrulandt tatta tīmpuli pāhar
Inidena Kanavan undalin
Nunnidin Mahilndan tonnudal mukame

With flower-like hands that mash the mature curds
With those hands, she wiped her apron
Eyes full of smoke from the seasoning of mustard
She came in haste as not to delay
in serving her husband
—'Kurunthokai' *167*, Kudalur Kilar
1–2 CE

PACHAI MOR KUḶAMBU Beaten Curd Kuḷambu

Makes: 4 servings
Serving size: 100 gms
Calories per serving: 59

INGREDIENTS

Curd 2 cups, whisked smooth
Water 4 cups
Salt 1 tsp

For grinding
Grated fresh coconut 3 tbsp
Green chillies 5–6, chopped
Rice ¼ tsp
Jeera/Cumin seeds ¼ tsp
Water ¼ cup

Seasoning
Sesame oil 1 tbsp
Mustard seeds ½ tsp
Fenugreek seeds ½ tsp
Curry leaves 1 sprig

METHOD

1. Mix curd with salt and blend with 4 cups of water, till smooth.
2. Grind grated coconut, green chillies, raw rice and cumin seeds with ¼ cup of water.
3. Add ground mixture to curd and mix well.
4. Heat oil in a vānali/wok. Splutter mustard seeds over medium heat, add fenugreek seeds. When they turn brown, stir in curry leaves. Pour contents of vānali/wok over kuḷambu.

Note: No vegetables are added in this mor kuḷambu.

PĀVAKKAI PITTLAI Bitter Gourd Kuḷambu

Makes: 4 servings
Serving size: 100 gms
Calories per serving: 93

INGREDIENTS

Bitter gourd 100 gm
Cooked red gram dal/Tuvar dal 1 cup
Cooked Bengal gram/Chana dal 1 tbsp
Grated jaggery 1 tsp
Curry leaves 1 sprig
Grated fresh coconut 1 tbsp
Tamarind ¾ tbsp
Water 3 cups
Turmeric powder ¼ tsp
Salt 1 tsp
Oil 2 tsp + 1½ tsp

Spices for grinding
Bengal gram dal/Chana dal 1 tsp
Black gram dal/Urad dal ¾ tsp
Dhania/Coriander seeds 2 tsp
Dried red chillies 4–5
Asafoetida powder ¼ tsp
Grated fresh coconut 1 tbsp
Water 2 tbsp

Seasoning
Oil 1 tsp
Mustard seeds ½ tsp
Dried red chillies 2
Black gram dal/Urad dal 1 tsp
Curry leaves 1 sprig

METHOD

1. Cut bitter gourd into ½-inch thick rounds or into ¼-inch quarters and wash.
2. Extract tamarind juice using 3 cups of water (see Pre-Cooking Processes). Mix in turmeric powder and salt.
3. Prepare cooked red gram dal/tuvar dal and Bengal gram/chana dal (see Paruppu Kuḷambu recipe).
4. Heat 2 tsp of oil in a vānali/wok and fry bitter gourd lightly over medium heat. Set aside.
5. Add spices for grinding, except grated coconut, to vānali/wok and fry over medium heat till golden brown. Remove.
6. Add coconut to vānali/wok and fry, till it just changes colour.
7. Grind fried spices and coconut to a fine paste with 2 tbsp of water.
8. Pour tamarind juice into a deep vessel and bring to a boil. Add gourd and simmer over medium heat, till tender.
9. Add cooked red gram dal and boil for about 5 minutes.
10. Stir in cooked chana dal, ground spice paste, jaggery and curry leaves and boil for 2 minutes. Remove from heat.
11. Heat oil in a vānali/wok. Splutter mustard seeds, add remaining seasoning and sauté till urad dal turns golden. Pour seasoning over pittlai.
12. Heat 1½ tsp of oil in a pan and fry grated coconut till golden brown. Add to pittlai and serve.

Note:

1. *Brinjal can be used instead of bitter gourd.*
2. *Pittlai can be served with rice like a sambar or kūtu.*
3. *Pittlai also makes a tasty accompaniment for idli, pongal, uppuma and dosai.*

PACCHAI CHUNDAIKĀI PORITHA KUḶAMBU

Green Solanum Torvum Kuḷambu

Makes: 4 servings

Serving size: 100 gms

Calories per serving: 58

INGREDIENTS

Pacchai Chundaikai

Green Solanum Torvum 2–3 tbsp

Tamarind 10 gm

Water 2 cups

Turmeric powder ¼ tsp

Salt 1 tsp

Grated jaggery 1 tsp

Oil 1½ tsp (optional)

Grated fresh coconut 1 tbsp (optional)

Spices for grinding

Dried red chillies 4

Black gram dal/Urad dal 1 tsp

Black pepper 1 tsp

Asafoetida powder 1 tsp

Grated fresh coconut 1 tbsp (optional)

Seasoning

Oil 1 tsp

Mustard seeds ½ tsp

Curry leaves 1 sprig

Use beans such as lablab beans (mochai), black-eyed beans (lobia/karamani), chickpeas (Kabuli chana/kondai kadalai) for this dish.

METHOD

1. Heat oil in a vānali/wok. Fry spices for grinding till aromatic. Grind with grated coconut to a fine paste.
2. Extract tamarind juice using 2 cups of water (see Pre-Cooking Processes). Mix in turmeric powder and salt.
3. Heat oil in vessel. Splutter mustard seeds. Stir in curry leaves. Add green chundaikai/solanum torvum.
4. Pour in tamarind juice and simmer for about 15 minutes.
5. Blend in ground spice paste and bring to a boil. Add ¼ cup water if consistency is too thick.
6. Stir in jaggery and mix well. Remove from heat.
7. To enhance flavour of kuḷambu, fry ½ tsp of grated fresh coconut lightly in ½ tsp of oil, till its aroma is released, add to vessel and serve.

Note: Instead of pacchai chundaikai, use bitter gourd, ridge gourd, brinjal, broad beans, amaranthus stems, and green plantain. Along with chundaikai, brinjal, snake gourd, bitter gourd and drumstick can be used in this kuḷambu. Instead of pacchai chundaikai, dried chundaikai can be used.

MĀMPAḶA KUḶAMBU Ripe Mango Kuḷambu

Makes: 4 servings
Serving size: 100 gms
Calories per serving: 88

INGREDIENTS

Mango juice (preferably from rasalu, alphonso, cherukurasa, peetar varieties) 2 cups
Curd 1 cup, whisked smooth
Water 1 cup
Salt ½ tsp
Sugar ½ tsp
Water 1 cup

Seasoning
Oil ½ tbsp
Mustard seeds ½ tsp
Fenugreek seeds ¼ tsp
Jeera/cumin seeds ¼ tsp
Dried red chilli 1
Green chillies, chopped 2–3

METHOD

1. Mix curd and mango juice, salt, sugar and 1 cup of water. Set aside.
2. Heat oil in a vānali/wok. Splutter mustard seeds over medium heat, add fenugreek seeds. When they start to turn brown, add cumin seeds. Add red and green chillies and sauté, turning once or twice.
3. Pour in curd-mango juice mix.
4. Simmer over medium heat for 3 minutes. When it starts to boil, remove from heat immediately.

MENTHIYA KUḶAMBU

Fenugreek Kuḷambu

Makes: 4 servings
Serving size: 100 gms
Calories per serving: 56

INGREDIENTS

Vegetable of choice 150 gm
Tamarind 15 gm
Water 5 cups
Dry papad 1, broken into pieces
Turmeric powder ½ tsp
Salt 1 tsp
Grated jaggery ½ tsp
Rice powder ¼ tsp (if required; see Pre-Cooking Processes)

Seasoning
Sesame oil 2 tbsp
Dried red chillies 5
Fenugreek seeds ½ tsp
Mustard seeds ½ tsp
Black gram dal/Urad dal 2 tsp
Bengal gram dal/Chana dal 2 tsp
Red gram dal/Tuvar dal 2 tsp
Asafoetida powder ½ tsp
Curry leaves 1 sprig

Use any one of the following vegetables: tender (yellow) pumpkin, white pumpkin, drumstick, colocasia, yam, cluster beans, French beans, brinjal, okra, capsicum, amaranth stem, green plantain.

METHOD

Preparation of vegetables: See beginning of 'Kuḷambu' chapter.

1. Extract tamarind juice using 5 cups of water (see Pre-Cooking Processes).
2. Heat oil in vessel. Add asafoetida powder, dried red chillies, rest of the seasoning and splutter over medium heat.
3. Add any uncooked vegetable and sauté for about 2 minutes.
4. Mix in tamarind juice, turmeric powder and salt. Bring to a boil and simmer for about 15 minutes.
5. If using a cooked vegetable, add it now.
6. Stir in jaggery. Simmer for about 2 minutes longer.
7. If kuḷambu is too thick, add some warm water and bring to a boil again.
8. If it is thin, add ½ tsp of rice flour mixed in 1 tbsp of water and boil, till thick.

Note: If using papad, break into pieces then add to vānali/wok and turn a few times.

KOMU, MY FRIEND

Komu was an expert in the Kallidaikurichi cuisine from the deep south of India that is even today famous for its atirasam, laddu, mysore pak, wheat halwa and murukku. Kallidaikurichi appalāms have yet to find their match.

Komu's affection was reflected in the immense variety and quantity of food that she would cook and keep ready for her guests. Once I, who was the lone guest on that trip, was greeted by her with a huge canister of sevai and what seemed like half a gallon of curds and rice! On another visit, my friends refused to continue with their itinerary as they said that after the impossible feast laid out by Komu, they had to sleep the afternoon off!

The Kallidaikurichi village had the noteworthy practice of creating a community kitchen made up of all the kitchens in the village for special occasions like weddings. As these houses were street houses, their backyards and kitchens were connected. This enabled them to have the use of four or five kitchens all of which had rows of old-fashioned stoves built of brick and mud which were specifically made for the use of wood as fuel, and on which the entire wedding feast was prepared.

On occasions like these, no fire would be lit in any individual kitchen as the whole village would be fed from the community kitchen. A special vessel known as the elu kuli in Tamil with seven different compartments was used to carry food to every household in the village along with a tooku (vessel with handle) of pāyasam and a bhogini (see Talking of Vessels) of cooked rice.

KATTRIKAI KĀRA KUḶAMBU Brinjal in Tamarind Kuḷambu

Makes: 4 servings
Serving size: 100 gms
Calories per serving: 45

INGREDIENTS

Tamarind 15 gm
Water 3 cups
White sesame seeds 1½ tsp
Small round brinjals 8
Tomatoes 3, chopped and mashed
Grated jaggery ½ tsp

Spice powders
Dhania/Coriander powder 3 tsp
Red chilli powder 2 tsp
Turmeric powder 1 tsp
Salt 1¼ tsp

Seasoning
Oil 3 tbsp
Fenugreek seeds ½ tsp
Mustard seeds ¼ tsp
Jeera/Cumin seeds ¼ tsp
Curry leaves 1 sprig

METHOD

1. Extract tamarind juice using 3 cups of water (see Pre-Cooking Processes).
2. Roast sesame seeds in a vānali/wok over low heat. Powder coarsely and set aside.
3. Wash brinjals and remove stalks, retaining calyx. Make 4 slits at base without cutting through. Do not separate segments.
4. Heat oil in a heavy bottomed vessel. Add seasoning and splutter over medium heat. Stir in curry leaves.
5. Add brinjals and toss a few times over medium heat for 2–3 minutes. Cover vessel and cook, till brinjals are almost tender.
6. Add tomatoes and sauté till oil separates.
7. Add spice powders and stir gently, till well blended. Add tamarind juice and salt and boil for a few minutes.
8. Mix in jaggery. Sprinkle sesame powder and mix well.

VATRAL KUḶAMBU Sun-dried Vegetable Kuḷambu

Makes: 6 servings
Serving size: 100 gms
Calories per serving: 82

INGREDIENTS

Tamarind 25 gm
Water 7 cups
Manitakkali vatral[1] 3 tbsp
Turmeric powder ½ tsp
Kuḷambu/Saṃbar powder 4 tbsp
Salt 1½ tsp

Initial seasoning
Sesame oil 4 tbsp
Fenugreek seeds 1 tsp
Mustard seeds 1 tsp
Asafoetida powder 1 tsp
Curry leaves 1 sprig

Final seasoning
Sesame oil 2 tbsp
Red chilli powder 1 tsp
Asafoetida powder ½ tsp
Curry leaves 1 sprig

METHOD

1. Extract tamarind juice using 7 cups of water (see Pre-Cooking Processes).
2. Heat oil in heavy-bottomed vessel. Add initial seasoning and splutter over medium heat.
3. Add vatral and sauté till light brown.
4. Mix turmeric powder, kuḷambu/sambar powder and salt into tamarind juice and pour into vessel. Bring to boil and continue to boil for about 2 minutes. Lower heat and simmer for about 45 minutes.
5. When kuḷambu thickens, remove from heat.
6. Heat oil in a vānali/wok. When hot, remove from heat, stir in curry leaves, add powders. Pour over kuḷambu and cover.

[1] *Vatral means sun-dried vegetables. Any of the following vatral may be used instead of manitakkali vatral: brinjal, sundaikkai, midukankai, bitter gourd, cluster bean and dolichos.*

MĀNKOTTAI VATRAL KUḶAMBU Sun-dried Mango Kuḷambu

Makes: 4 servings
Serving size: 100 gms
Calories per serving: 35

INGREDIENTS

Sun-dried mango stone (mānkottai) 1 kernel
Sun-dried mango pieces 4–5 pieces (30–35 gm)
Salt 1 tsp

METHOD

1. Break mango stone and take half the kernel.
2. Soak mango kernel and dried mango pieces in water for about an hour. Drain and set aside.
3. Heat oil in a vānali/wok. Add spices and fry over medium heat till aromatic. Grind fried spices with soaked and drained mango kernel and mango pieces to a fine consistency.

Spices
Oil 2 tsp
Dried red chillies 3
Whole black pepper ½ tsp
Black gram dal/Urad dal 1½ tsp
Asafoetida powder 1 pinch

Seasoning
Oil 2 tsp
Mustard seeds 1 tsp
Curry leaves 1 sprig

4. Place a heavy-bottomed vessel over medium heat. Add ground mango-spice mixture with 5 cups of water. Mix in salt. Bring to a boil, lower heat and simmer till kuḷambu thickens.
5. Heat oil in a vānali/wok. Splutter mustard seeds over medium heat. Stir in curry leaves. Pour seasoning over kuḷambu and cover.

Note: Green mangoes are cut, sliced and the sides separated and dried along with seed. This dried seed is cracked and the kernel is used with mango pieces. This kuḷambu can be prepared without the kernel also.

MILAGU KUḶAMBU Pepper Kuḷambu

Makes: 4 servings
Serving size: 100 gms
Calories per serving: 41

INGREDIENTS

Tamarind 25 gm
Water 4½ cups
Turmeric powder ¼ tsp
Salt 1 tsp

Spices
Sesame oil 1½ tbsp
Whole black pepper 1½ tsp
Dried red chillies 2
Asafoetida powder ½ tsp
Black gram dal/Urad dal 1 tsp
Red gram dal/Tuvar dal 1 tsp
Raw rice ¼ tsp
Water for grinding 2 tbsp

Seasoning
Sesame oil 1 tsp
Mustard seeds ½ tsp
Curry leaves 1 sprig

METHOD

1. Extract tamarind juice using 4½ cups of water (see Pre-Cooking Processes).
2. Heat oil in a vānali/wok. Add spices, fry over medium heat, till dals turn golden brown. Remove and grind with 2 tbsp of water to a fine consistency.
3. Heat oil in heavy-bottomed vessel. Splutter seasoning.
4. Mix turmeric powder and salt with tamarind juice and pour into vessel. Bring to a boil.
5. Add ground spices and simmer till kuḷambu thickens.

RASAM

RASAM

The second course in a south Indian meal, rasam has been called 'the elixir of life' by connoisseurs of flavour. It is called 'sāru' in both Karnataka and Andhra Pradesh and is also referred to as satramudu (from saramarta or essence of nectar). Satramudu is a term that is part of an esoteric vocabulary of a very small community in Tamil Nadu.

The order of serving rasam in the south Indian menu is exact and significant. Rasam is served after the heavily spiced kuḷambu and before the satiating sweet as it has an ameliorating effect on the palate and the digestive system.

The intrinsic quality of water (liquid) is in its flow. And it is this flow on the tongue that we taste with rasam, which is mostly water, but with a savour brought on by a delicate medley of spices.

In many ways, it is apt to compare rasam with south Indian classical music. south Indian classical music or Carnatic music has a strict grammar that forms the base, with exacting rules and ragas (tones). At the same time, the artist has every freedom to build upon this foundation with imagination and expertise to present a totally individual rendering.

Carnatic music is organized around precise combinations of tones each invoking a particular mood or emotion. These combinations called ragas are deep-rooted in the very philosophy of Indian cultural tradition and mythology. Every performance of Carnatic music requires the musician to explore ragas in-depth, examining the complex relationships of the notes with each other. This creative improvization is the hallmark of a Carnatic music performance.

If we bring this metaphor into the realm of cooking, we can say that while the vegetables and spices remain the same, the way an expert cook interprets and combines them brings out varied flavours from the same ingredients.

A cook's expertise is determined by the taste and quality of the rasam (s)he makes. From very simple ingredients, one should be able to provide the very acme of taste. This is really a tall order and many a great cook has lost his job for not being able to make a good rasam! A new applicant for the post of cook would always be asked to make rasam, and to toast an appalam. These are the benchmarks of culinary expertise where south Indian vegetarian cuisine is concerned.

A popular humorous folk story is often told around rasam. A young woman, a newly-wed, had been told to look after the guest well. So she plies him with rice and rasam continuously, thinking it impolite to stop till the guest is sated and says 'enough'. The guest too keeps on eating thinking it impolite to say 'enough', as reflecting on the quality of the rasam.

Trying her hand at conversation, the young woman asks the guest how many children his mother has. Filled to the brim, on the verge of collapse, the guest answers, 'If I'm still alive after drinking all this rasam, my mother will have eight children!'

The speciality of rasam is that even though it entices us with a variety of spices, seasonings, and souring agents, it also has an in-built restraint, mildness and lightness.

Rasam also has the meaning of satva, the true essence of things. Both rasam and sāram mean 'quintessence'.

Perunkāyam—Asafoetida

Asafoetida, perunkayam in Tamil, plays a stellar role in south Indian vegetarian cuisine. A resin from a shrub of the umbelliferae family in Afghanistan, mixed with gum arabic to tone down its intensity and make it more palatable, asafoetida is used very sparingly, only in pinches and drops. It is a digestive and is used with almost all kuḷambu, sambar and rasam (except jeeraka rasam), and in many mixed rice preparations. When asafoetida is forgotten, one misses the distinctive aroma and taste that it adds to the dish. At the same time, just a pinch or drop more can turn the dish 'poisonous'.

In the past, asafoetida was not available in grocery stores. It was hawked in the streets much like greens, vegetables, curd and buttermilk in those days. The hawker would trail the residential streets singing his high-pitched song describing the inimitable taste that perunkāyam brings to cooking:

Pāl perunkāyam pāl perunkāyam
Paruppu kuḷambukkum rasathukkum porutham
Poda maranditttal pusippadu varutham...

The pure milk sap of asafoetida
ideal it is for kuḷambu and rasam
indeed it's a sad state of affairs when forgotten!

How to serve rasam? Rasam is served on hot rice with ghee. It is also served alongside the main plate in small bowls.

PARUPPU RASAM

Dal Rasam

Makes: 4 servings
Serving size: 125 gms
Calories per serving: 73

INGREDIENTS

Red gram dal/Tuvar dal ½ cup
Water 1½ cups + 1½ cups
Turmeric powder ¼ tsp
Ghee or castor oil ½ tsp
Water to mix with cooked dal 2–2½ cups
Tamarind 8–10 gm
Tomatoes (small) 2, cut into pieces
Salt 1 tsp
Curry leaves 1 sprig
Rasam powder 2½ tsp (see Podis/Readymade Powders)
Asafoetida powder ¼ tsp

Garnish
Coriander leaves 2–3 sprigs, chopped

Seasoning
Ghee 1½ tsp
Dried red chilli 1 (optional)
Mustard seeds ½ tsp
Curry leaves 1 sprig

This paruppu rasam is the everyday rasam recipe. This rasam is made in many households daily and is considered indispensable after the kuḷambu, either to mix with hot rice and ghee or to drink from a bowl.

METHOD

1. Wash tuvar dal and pressure-cook with 1½ cups of water for 4 whistles. (See Pre-Cooking Processes)
2. Mash dal with a wooden mallet or a hand whisk with 2 to 2½ cups of water.
3. Separate the dal water and reserve the dal.
3. Extract tamarind juice using 1½ cups of water (see Pre-Cooking Processes).
4. In a heavy-bottomed vessel over medium heat, pour tamarind juice, add tomatoes, salt and curry leaves. Boil for about 8 minutes, till the raw smell of tamarind and tomatoes disappear.
5. Add rasam powder, turmeric powder and asafoetida powder. Simmer for 5 minutes.
6. Add cooked dal water and 1 heaped tbsp of the reserved dal. Mix well.
7. When foam rises to brim, remove from heat and add coriander leaves.
8. Heat ghee in a vānali/wok. Splutter seasoning, pour over rasam.
9. Serve hot.

RADHA PANIKKAR

A close friend, Radha Panikkar was yet another inspiration for me to learn new recipes. I learnt the famous kuḷal puttu of Kerala from Radha. The easy tomato rasam (without tamarind) of hers is still made in my kitchen, after well over thirty years.

Radha was an extremely organized person. This natural flair for organization was reflected in everything that she did. Once again, it was not only recipes that I learnt from her but the many intricacies of cooking. She knew shortcuts that saved time without compromising on the taste and quality of the food. In keeping with her direct and forthright character, Radha would insist on the exact way and length of the vegetables to be cut for avial. She held in contempt the slipshod way in which vegetables were cut in any size for this signature dish. She said that vegetables for avial should be neither longer nor thicker than a matchstick. No wonder that her dishes were such a feast for the eyes as well as the tongue.

EḶUMICHAI TAKKĀLI RASAM Rasam without Tamarind

Makes: 4 servings
Serving size: 125 gms
Calories per serving: 188

INGREDIENTS

Red gram dal/Tuvar dal ¼ cup
Water 1 cup
Turmeric powder ¼ tsp
Ghee or castor oil ½ tsp
Water to mix with cooked dal 4 cups
Black pepper 1 tsp, coarsely pounded
Jeera/Cumin seeds ½ tsp, coarsely pounded
Ghee 2 tsp
Ginger 1-inch piece, cut into fine juliennes
Green chillies 3, slit
Tomatoes 6–7, deseeded and chopped fine
Rasam powder 2 tsp (see Podis/Readymade Powders)
Asafoetida powder ¼ tsp
Salt to taste
Juice of lime/Lemon (squeezed from ½ lime or ¼ lemon)
Sugar ½ tsp

Seasoning
Ghee 1 tsp
Mustard seeds ½ tsp
Jeera/Cumin seeds ½ tsp
Curry leaves 2–3 sprigs

Garnish
Coriander leaves 2–3 sprigs, chopped
A thin slice of lime/lemon 1

METHOD

1. Wash tuvar dal and pressure-cook with turmeric powder, ghee or castor oil and 1 cup of water for 4 whistles.
2. Mash dal with a wooden mallet or a hand whisk with 4 cups of water. Reserve.
3. Place a heavy-bottomed deep vessel, over medium heat. Add 2 tsp of ghee. Add pounded pepper and cumin seeds, ginger and green chillies. Sauté for about a minute.
4. Add tomatoes and sauté for a few minutes, till well cooked.
5. Add cooked dal water, rasam powder, asafoetida powder and salt and simmer.
6. When foam rises to the brim, remove from heat and add coriander leaves.
7. Add a slice of lemon to rasam and toss out at once. Mix pinch of sugar to lime juice and pour over rasam.
8. Heat ghee in a vānali/wok. Splutter seasoning. Add to rasam and cover.

MYSORE RASAM

Makes: 4 servings
Serving size: 125 gms
Calories per serving: 53

INGREDIENTS

Green gram or red dal ¼ cup
Water 4 +1 cup
Tamarind 10 gm
Tomatoes (small) 2
Mysore rasam powder 1 tbsp (see Podis/Readymade Powders)
Asafoetida ½ tsp
Salt 1 tsp
Coriander leaves 2 sprigs, chopped
Grated jaggery 1 tsp

Seasoning
Ghee 1 tsp
Mustard seeds 1 tsp
Asafoetida ½ tsp
Curry leaves 2 sprigs

METHOD

1. Wash green gram dal or tuvar dal in 4 cups water and pressure-cook. Cook till the dal is soft.
2. Remove the dal water and reserve.
3. Extract 10 gm of tamarind juice in 1 cup of water (see Pre-Cooking Processes).
4. Remove the seeds of the tomatoes and cut into small pieces.
5. Place a heavy-bottomed vessel over medium heat. Add tamarind juice, cooked dal, salt and the tomatoes. Boil till the raw smell of tamarind disappears.
6. Add Mysore rasam powder and boil well.
7. Add the cooked dal water and simmer for some time.
8. Reduce the heat and add asafoetida.
9. When the rasam boils up, remove from heat.
10. Heat ghee in a vānali. Add seasoning and splutter over medium heat and pour over the rasam.
11. Add jaggery and coriander leaves.

Note: Dal has to be mashed well, water added, and dal water removed 2 or 3 times.

Variation: Mangalore rasam—Follow same method. Use Mangalore rasam powder (see Podis/Readymade Powders) instead of Mysore rasam powder.

UDUPI TOMATO RASAM

Makes: 4 servings
Serving size: 150 ml
Calories per serving: 67

INGREDIENTS

Tomatoes (medium) 2
Tamarind 25 gm
Water 100 ml + 1 cup + 3 cups
Red gram dal/Green gram dal ¼ cup
Jaggery 2 tsp
Turmeric ½ tsp
Coconut oil 3 tsp
Salt 1½ tsp
Udupi rasam powder 2½ tsp (see Podis/
Readymade Powders
Asafoetida)

Seasoning
Cooking oil 1 tbsp
Mustard seeds 1 tsp
Whole dry red chilli 1
Green chillies 2, slit lengthwise
Curry leaves 2 sprigs

Garnish
Coriander leaves, chopped

METHOD

1. Cut tomatoes into small pieces. Set aside.
2. Extract tamarind juice in 100 ml of water. (see Pre-Cooking Processes). Set aside.
3. Cook dal with 1 cup of water. Keep aside.
4. Take a vessel, add oil. Splutter mustard seeds, add green chillies and curry leaves.
5. Add tomatoes, turmeric powder and fry well for 3 minutes.
6. Add tamarind extract and cook till the raw smells of tomatoes and tamarind disappear.
7. Add jaggery. Boil for a minute.
8. Add cooked dal water, 3 cups of water and boil for 2 to 3 minutes.
9. Take 2½ tsp of Udupi rasam powder, mix with a little hot water, add to the rasam.
10. Add salt and 2 pinches of asafoetida.
11. Add the coriander leaves to the rasam. Remove from fire.

ELUMICHAMPAḶA RASAM Lime Rasam

Makes: 4 servings
Serving size: 125 gms
Calories per serving: 51

INGREDIENTS

Red gram dal/Tuvar dal ½ cup
Water 1½ cups
Turmeric powder ¼ tsp
Ghee or castor oil ½ tsp
Water to mix with cooked dal 4 cups
Asafoetida powder ¼ tsp
Green chillies 2 tsp, chopped fine
Ginger 1 tsp, chopped fine
Salt 1 tsp

Seasoning
Ghee 1 tsp
Mustard seeds ½ tsp
Jeera/Cumin seeds ½ tsp
Curry leaves 1 sprig

Garnish
Coriander leaves 2–3 sprigs, chopped
Lime 1

METHOD

1. Wash tuvar dal and pressure-cook with turmeric powder, ghee or castor oil and 1½ cups of water for 4 whistles (see Pre-Cooking Processes).
2. Mash dal with a wooden mallet or a hand whisk with 4 cups of water. Reserve.
3. Place a heavy-bottomed vessel over medium heat. Add cooked dal, asafoetida powder, green chillies, ginger and salt.
4. Bring to boil and simmer for about 5 minutes.
5. When foam rises to the brim, remove from heat.
6. Heat ghee in a vānali/wok. Splutter seasoning. Pour over rasam and cover.
7. Add coriander leaves and lime juice just before serving.

Note: Do not reheat rasam after adding lime juice. It will turn the rasam bitter.

ANNĀSIPAḶA RASAM Pineapple Rasam

Makes: 4 servings
Serving size: 125 gms
Calories per serving: 93

INGREDIENTS

Chopped pineapple 3 tbsp
Salt ¼ tsp +1 tsp
Sugar ¼ tsp
Red gram dal/Tuvar dal 1/3 cup
Water 1½ cups
Turmeric powder ¼ tsp
Ghee or castor oil ½ tsp
Water to mix with cooked dal 2½ cups
Black pepper 1 tsp, coarsely pounded
Jeera/Cumin seeds 1 tsp, coarsely pounded
Rasam powder 2 tsp (see Podis/Readymade Powders)
Salt 1 tsp
Green chillies 4–5, slit
Curry leaves 1 sprig
Grated jaggery ½ tsp
Pineapple juice ¼ cup
Lime juice from 1 lime

Seasoning
Ghee 1 tsp
Mustard seeds ½ tsp
Jeera/Cumin seeds 1 tsp

METHOD

1. Mix ¼ tsp of salt with sugar into chopped pineapple and set aside.
2. Wash tuvar dal and pressure-cook with turmeric powder, ghee or castor oil and 1½ cups of water for 4 whistles (see Pre-Cooking Processes).
3. Mash dal with a wooden mallet or a hand whisk with 2½ cups of water.
4. Place a heavy-bottomed vessel over medium heat. Add cooked dal and bring to a boil.
5. Add 1 tsp of salt, pounded pepper and cumin seeds, rasam powder, salt, green chillies and curry leaves. Bring to a boil and simmer for about 5 minutes.
6. When foam rises to the brim, add pineapple juice, lime juice and jaggery. Remove from heat. (After adding the juices do not reheat rasam.)
7. Heat ghee in a vānali/wok. Splutter seasoning over medium heat. Pour over rasam.
8. Add chopped pineapple.

Note: If using fresh pineapple, mix it with salt and sugar to taste and set aside. If using canned pineapple, drain syrup, wash pineapple and use. Sugar is not required when using canned pineapple.

JEERAGA RASAM Cumin Rasam

Makes: 4 servings
Serving size: 125 gms
Calories per serving: 36

INGREDIENTS

Tamarind 15 gm
Water 2 cups
Turmeric powder ¼ tsp
Salt 1 tsp
Curry leaves 1 sprig
Grated jaggery ½ tsp (optional)

Spices
Oil 2 tsp
Dried red chillies 3
Whole black pepper 1½ tsp
Jeera/Cumin seeds 1½ tsp
Red gram dal/Tuvar dal 1 tbsp
Water 3 cups

Seasoning
Ghee 2 tsp
Jeera/Cumin seeds ½ tsp

METHOD

1. Extract tamarind juice using 2 cups of water (see Pre-Cooking Procceses). Mix in turmeric powder.
2. Heat oil in a vānali/wok. Fry spices and dal over medium heat, for a minute. Grind and set aside.
3. Place a heavy-bottomed vessel over medium heat. Add tamarind juice, salt and curry leaves. Boil for about 5 minutes, till the raw smell of tamarind disappears.
4. Add ground spices. Add 3 cups of water. Boil till it foams up.
5. Add jaggery (optional).
6. When foam rises to the brim, remove from heat.
7. Heat ghee in a vānali/wok. Splutter cumin seeds over medium heat. Pour over rasam and cover.

INJI RASAM Ginger Rasam

Makes: 4 servings
Serving size: 125 gms
Calories per serving: 59

INGREDIENTS

Red gram dal/Tuvar dal ½ cup
Water 1½ cups
Turmeric powder ¼ tsp
Ghee or castor oil ½ tsp
Water to mix with cooked dal 2–2½ cups
Tamarind 12 gm
Water 2 cups
Salt 1 tsp
Curry leaves 1 sprig
Rasam powder 2 tsp (see Podis/Readymade Powders)
Asafoetida powder ¼ tsp
Ginger 1-inch piece, crushed

Seasoning
Ghee 1 tsp
Mustard seeds ¼ tsp
Jeera/Cumin seeds ¼ tsp

Garnish
Ginger ¼-inch piece, cut into fine juliennes (optional)
Coriander leaves 2–3 sprigs, chopped (optional)

METHOD

1. Wash tuvar dal and pressure-cook with turmeric powder, ghee or castor oil and 1½ cups of water for 4 whistles (see Pre-Cooking Processes).
2. Mash dal with a wooden mallet or a hand whisk with 2–2½ cups of water. Reserve.
3. Extract tamarind juice using 2 cups of water (see Pre-Cooking Processes).
4. Place a heavy-bottomed vessel over medium heat. Add tamarind juice, salt and curry leaves. Boil for a few minutes.
5. Add rasam powder and asafoetida powder. Boil till the raw smell of tamarind disappears.
6. Add reserved dal. Simmer till it foams up.
7. Add crushed ginger.
8. When foam rises to the brim, remove from heat.
9. Add ginger juliennes and coriander leaves (optional).
10. Heat ghee in a vānali/wok. Splutter seasoning. Pour over rasam and cover.

PORITTA RASAM Rasam with Lime and Fried Spices

Makes: 4 servings
Serving size: 125 gms
Calories per serving: 90

INGREDIENTS

Red gram dal/Tuvar dal ½ cup
Water 1½ cups
Turmeric powder ¼ tsp
Ghee or castor oil ½ tsp
Water to mix with cooked dal 2 cups
Asafoetida powder 1 pinch
Curry leaves 1 sprig
Salt 1 tsp
Lime 1

Spices
Oil 2 tsp
Dried red chillies 1–2
Dhania/Coriander seeds 2 tsp
Jeera/Cumin seeds ½ tsp
Whole black pepper ½ tsp
Red gram dal/Tuvar dal 1 tsp
Black gram dal/Urad dal 1 tsp
Grated fresh coconut 1 tbsp

Seasoning
Ghee 1 tsp
Mustard seeds ½ tsp
Dried red chillies 2

METHOD

1. Wash tuvar dal and pressure-cook with turmeric powder, ghee or castor oil and 1½ cups of water for 4 whistles.
2. Mash dal with a wooden mallet or a hand whisk with 2 cups of water. Reserve.
3. Heat oil in a vānali/wok. Add spices and dals and fry over medium heat, till dals turn golden brown. Grind with grated coconut.
4. Place a heavy-bottomed vessel over medium heat. Add cooked dal, ground spices, asafoetida powder, curry leaves and salt. Boil for a few minutes.
5. When foam rises to the brim, remove from heat.
6. Heat ghee in a vānali/wok. Splutter seasoning over medium heat. Pour over rasam and cover.
7. Serve with lime wedges on the side.

Note: Do not boil rasam after adding lime juice.

KHANDATIPPILI RASAM Long Pepper Rasam

Makes: 4 servings
Serving size: 125 gms
Calories per serving: 75

INGREDIENTS

Tamarind 15 gm
Water 2 cups
Salt 1½ tsp
Curry leaves 1 sprig

Spices
Ghee 2 tsp
Dried stems of long pepper 5
Long pepper seeds 5–6
Whole black pepper ¼ tsp
Red gram dal/Tuvar dal 1 tbsp
Jeera/Cumin seeds ¾ tsp
Water for grinding 2 tbsp
Water 3 cups

Seasoning
Ghee 2 tsp
Mustard seeds ½ tsp
Dried red chilli 1

METHOD

1. Extract tamarind juice using 2 cups of water (see Pre-Cooking Processes).
2. Heat ghee in a vānali/wok. Fry dried stems of long pepper and seeds separately over medium heat, till brown and aromatic. Set aside.
3. Add black pepper, dal and cumin seeds to vānali/wok and fry till aromatic.
4. Grind all fried spices together finely with water.
5. Place a heavy-bottomed vessel over medium heat. Add tamarind juice, salt and curry leaves. Boil for a few minutes till raw smell disappears.
6. Add ground spices. Add 3 cups of water.
7. Boil till foam rises to the brim and remove from heat.
8. Heat ghee in a vānali/wok. Splutter mustard seeds and red chilli over medium heat. Add to rasam and cover.

Note: The dried long pepper stems are called khandatippili in Tamil, and the seeds, arisi tippili. The botanical name is piper longinum.

VEPPAMBU RASAM Neem Flower Rasam

Makes: 4 servings
Serving size: 125 gms
Calories per serving: 82

INGREDIENTS

Tamarind 15 gm
Water 2 cups
Turmeric powder ¼ tsp
Salt 1 tsp
Curry leaves 1 sprig

Spices
Sesame oil 1 tsp
Dried red chillies 4–5
Red gram dal/Tuvar dal 1 tbsp
Asafoetida powder ¼ tsp
Water 2½ cups

Seasoning
Ghee 2 tsp
Jeera/Cumin seeds ½ tsp
Dried neem flowers 2 tbsp

METHOD

1. Extract tamarind juice using 2 cups of water (see Pre-Cooking Processes).
2. Heat oil in a vānali/wok. Fry red chillies and dal over medium heat, for 1 to 2 minutes. Grind to make a coarse powder.
3. Place a heavy-bottomed vessel over medium heat. Add tamarind juice, turmeric powder, salt and curry leaves. Boil till the raw smell of tamarind disappears.
4. Add ground spice powder. Add 2½ cups of water. Continue to boil.
5. When rasam foams to the brim, remove from heat.
6. Heat ghee in a vānali/wok. Splutter cumin. Add neem flowers and fry, till they turn golden brown.
7. Pour over rasam and cover.

MOR RASAM Buttermilk Rasam

Makes: 4 servings
Serving size: 125 gms
Calories per serving: 36

INGREDIENTS

Curd 1 cup
Water 4 cups
Salt ¾ tsp
Turmeric powder ¼ tsp
Fenugreek seeds ¼ tsp

Spices
Oil 1 tsp
Dried red chillies 4
Red gram dal/Tuvar dal 1 tbsp
Whole black pepper ½ tsp
Asafoetida powder 2 pinches

Seasoning
Oil 1 tsp
Mustard seeds 1 tsp
Curry leaves 1 sprig

METHOD

1. Mix curd with 4 cups of water to make buttermilk. Churn well and strain. Add salt and turmeric powder.
2. Place a vānali/wok over medium heat. When hot, roast fenugreek seeds, till golden brown. Grind to make a powder.
3. Add oil to vānali/wok. Add asafoetida, red chillies, dal and pepper and fry till aromatic. Grind to a powder. Mix in ground fenugreek seeds.
4. Mix ground spices with buttermilk in a heavy-bottomed vessel.
5. Place vessel over medium heat. Stir well for 2 or 3 minutes. When rasam foams, remove from heat.
6. Heat oil in a vānali/wok. Splutter mustard seeds over medium heat. Stir in curry leaves. Pour over rasam and cover.

KOLLU RASAM Horse Gram Rasam

Makes: 4 servings
Serving size: 125 gms
Calories per serving: 77

INGREDIENTS

Horse gram ½ cup
Water 1½ cups
Water to mix with cooked gram 2 cups
Tamarind 12 gm
Water 2 cups
Turmeric powder ¼ tsp
Salt 1 tsp
Curry leaves 1 sprig
Tomatoes 2, deseeded and chopped fine
Grated jaggery 1 tsp

Spices for grinding
Oil 2 tsp
Dried red chillies 5–6
Fenugreek seeds ½ tsp
Cinnamon ¼-inch stick
Dhania/Coriander seeds 1½ tsp
Jeera/Cumin seeds ½ tsp
Poppy seeds ½ tsp
Bengal gram dal/Chana dal 1 tsp
Black gram dal/Urad dal 1 tsp
Grated copra 2 tbsp

Seasoning
Oil 2 tsp
Mustard seeds ½ tsp
Dried red chillies 2
Asafoetida powder 1 pinch

METHOD

1. Wash horse gram and soak in water overnight. Rinse thoroughly and drain.
2. Pressure-cook horse gram with 1½ cups of water for 4–5 whistles (see Pre-Cooking Processes).
3. Cool and add 2 cups of water and blend well. Reserve.
4. Heat oil in a vānali/wok. Add spices and dals and fry over medium heat till dals turn golden brown. Grind coarsely with copra.
5. Extract tamarind juice using 2 cups of water (see Pre-Cooking Processes).
6. Place a heavy-bottomed vessel over medium heat. Add tamarind juice, turmeric powder, salt and curry leaves. Boil till the raw smell of tamarind disappears.
7. Add tomatoes and ground spices and boil further for 3 minutes.
8. Add reserved horse gram. Simmer till foam rises to the brim and remove from heat.
9. Heat ghee in a vānali/wok. Splutter mustard seeds over medium heat. Add red chillies and asafoetida powder. Pour over rasam and cover.

Note: Kollu Rasam is a good diuretic.

PANEER RASAM

Rose Petal Rasam

Makes: 4 servings
Serving size: 125 gms
Calories per serving: 32

INGREDIENTS

Red gram dal/Tuvar dal ¼ cup
Water ¾ cup + 2 cups
Turmeric powder ¼ tsp
Ghee or castor oil ½ tsp
Water to mix with cooked dal 2½ cups
Tamarind 10 gm
Salt ½ tsp
Curry leaves 1 sprig
Rasam powder 1 tsp (see Podis and Readymade Powders)
Asafoetida powder 1 pinch
Coriander leaves 1 sprig, chopped
Sugar ½ tsp
Rose water ¼ cup
Rose petals from 1 Edward rose (panneer rose)

Seasoning
Ghee 1 tsp
Mustard seeds ¼ tsp

This rasam is served separately (as a drink in cups) when the rasam and rice is served during weddings. It can be served as a welcome drink before a meal. Use the larger petals from an Edward rose (panneer rose); discard pollen and small petals.

METHOD

1. Wash tuvar dal and pressure-cook with turmeric powder, ghee or castor oil and ¾ cup of water for 4 whistles (see Pre-Cooking Processes).
2. Mash dal in a blender and mix with 2½ cups of water. Reserve.
3. Extract tamarind juice using 2 cups of water (see Pre-Cooking Processes).
4. Place a heavy-bottomed vessel over medium heat. Add tamarind juice, salt and curry leaves. Boil for a few minutes.
5. Add rasam powder and asafoetida powder. Boil till the raw smell of tamarind disappears.
6. Add reserved dal and simmer till it foams up.
7. When foam rises to the brim, remove from heat.
8. Heat ghee in a vānali/wok. Splutter mustard seeds and pour over rasam.
9. Add coriander leaves.
10. Add sugar and cover vessel.
11. Before serving, just warm the rasam (do not boil). Add rose water and the large rose petals.
12. Pour into kinnams/katoris (small bowls), garnish with a few rose petals and serve hot/serve with hot rice.

SWEETS

SWEETS

Sugarcane was widely used in ancient India. It is well known that sugarcane was also first refined into sugar in Bihar in 700 BCE. Persians of the sixth century CE refer to sugar as an 'Indian' luxury. Indian 'sugar' of the time was jaggery. Jaggery is still an important ingredient in numerous Indian sweets and is used in many dishes even today.

A sixteenth-century text, *Manasollasoa*, mentions many sweets which are made even today like polika, ladduka, payasa, bindu modaka, karanjika, purika, vataka and papara. Other sweets that the text refers to are phenika, kohari, bahrul, kasāra and jalebi, some of which seem to be of Turkish origin.

The variety of Indian sweets from the four southern regions is extensive, even though dessert is not an essential part of the everyday menu of the south Indian. Though some sweets are common to many regions, like the ravā kesari with its many variations, there are others that have been created or developed to suit the tastes of a particular area or ethnic group.

There are special sweets, those that are made for a particular festival, that have been adopted by regional communities beyond where they originated. Others are too complex or require extreme skill to make with any degree of professionalism. Into this latter category fall sweets like padar pheni (flaky pheni), semia pheni (vermicelli pheni), mandige (like flaky roti).

Mandige

Mandige is one of three light flaky pastry sweets that is served with saffron-almond milk. The other two are padar pheni (fine foam) and semia pheni (vermicelli foam). Made in a similar way, for semia pheni, the dough ball is dropped into hot ghee. It opens out into a fine-threaded pastry.

Ingredients

Whole wheat flour
Ravā (fine quality)
Sugar powder
Cardamom
Poppy seeds/Khus-khus
Ghee

Method

1. Make a roux (padar/pastry) of sugar powder and ghee.
2. Mix with wheat flour and fine ravā. Knead well and make a good dough.
3. Grind cardamom and khus-khus seeds to a thick paste, sprinkling a few drops of water.
4. Take an orange-sized ball of the wheat-ravā dough and roll into a big thin roti like a rumali roti.
5. Smear the cardamom–khus-khus paste all over the roti lightly.
6. Roll like a pencil. Twist it into a round. Flatten it.
7. Roll again into a large square.

8. Invert a newly made mud pot over a firewood stove.
9. Place the square roti over it.
10. When it fluffs up, turn over and cook for a minute.
11. Remove and serve with saffron milk.

North India has greater varieties of exotic sweets like halvas, son papri, burfi, jalebis, gulab jamun and others. Some of these originated in Turkey and Lebanon and can be found right across the Mediterranean even today.

The Bengalis are justly famous for their sweets, made mainly out of milk or chena (paneer). With no oil or ghee, using the freshest ingredients, Bengali sweets delight with their lightness and delicate flavours.

The famous sandesh grew out of the bride's desire to communicate with her husband in a large joint family. Perhaps back then the young bride would quietly curdle the milk, make sandesh out of the resultant chena and send it as a literal message of her love to her husband! The sandesh now takes several delicious forms with the addition of subtle flavourings like saffron, orange blossom, rose water, pandanus flower water, etc. Lately, it is stuffed with almonds and baked. Modern versions include savoury sandesh.

The iconic rasagulla was an invention of serendipity. It is said that K.C. Das, a chef from Kolkata, when faced with a large quantity of curdled milk, invented the dish and sent it as his signature preparation to the British durbar held in Delhi in 1911!

Sweets from all over India are now made professionally and are available in shops everywhere. Weddings now cater to this pan-Indian taste and celebrity weddings have been known to serve up to 108 sweets.

A Hierarchy of Nuts

There is a social hierarchy to the nuts used in Indian cooking.

A friend from a business community told me a long time ago about how, when the ladies of her community went on a picnic, there used to be sidelong glances to note whose preparations boasted of the maximum amount of almonds and saffron, both expensive ingredients from Kashmir. For some wealthy Indian women, almonds and saffron are as indispensable to their image as silks and diamonds.

In the Indian eye, the almond reigns supreme as the king of all nuts. Whether it is because of its exotic origins, its price or its taste, the almond, almond sweets and other almond-based preparations have attained a supreme status that remains unchallenged.

The superior almond is followed by its important but not as popular cousin, the pista. The pistachio, except when it is used to make halva or burfi, is used mostly for garnishing or to add colour to other sweets.

On the next tier is the cashewnut. Grown extensively in India and a common ingredient of Indian sweets and savoury dishes, its easy availability in spite of its heavy price has perhaps placed it lower than the almond and the pista.

Way down on the connossieur's list is the humble peanut and the sesame (technically a seed), both being a popular part of the poor man's diet, giving rise to a Tamil metaphor—'elaiketra ellurundai', or the sesame sweet that is fit for a poor person, as if to say 'cut your coat according to the cloth'!

Yet one more nut, the sāraiparuppu (*anacardium*), a cousin of the pista in the botanical sense, is used for garnishing when almonds are neither available nor affordable. It finds a permanent place in supari and in some pāyasams.

BADAM HALVA

Almond Halva

Makes: 25 servings
Serving size: 75 gms
Calories per serving: 432

INGREDIENTS

Good almonds (mamra) 1 cup or 250 gm
Water 2 cups + 1 tsp
Saffron ¼ tsp + 20 strands
Sugar 1 cup or 225 gm
Ghee 1 cup or 225 gm

Note: If almonds remain in water for too long, the nuts turn brown.

Many are the ways of making badam halva which has always been a staple of weddings in Chennai. However, I have yet to find this delectable sweet made as well as it is in Indira Sivasailam's kitchen. She was always well turned out when she carried this into the kitchen. Whatever she made was also presented in a most appealing way. Her badam halva was well known in her circle and she delighted in making it, packing it into apt containers and distributing it to her family and friends.

METHOD

1. Boil 2 cups of water and pour over the almonds. Cover and soak for 30 minutes. Peel one by one.
2. Grind peeled almonds to a semolina consistency. (Grind in two batches to make it easier.) Remove any large pieces with a spoon and grind again.
3. Crush ¼ tsp saffron in 1 tsp of water with a pestle to make a paste.
4. Place ground almonds in a heavy-bottomed vānali/wok (preferably a heavy-bottomed wide-mouthed deep bronze vessel) over medium heat. Stir continuously for 1 minute, till the almonds release their aroma. Almonds must cook a little, but not change colour.
5. Add sugar at once. Increase the heat slightly and stir continuously, till the almonds and sugar have blended well and thickened to a smooth consistency. This may take roughly 20 to 25 minutes. The halva will start gathering towards the centre of the pan.
6. Add ghee a little at a time, stirring between each addition, till most of the ghee is totally absorbed. A little ghee should float like a thin film over the halva.
7. Add saffron paste, stir continuously for 15 minutes, till it comes out of the pan easily.
8. Mix in half the saffron strands. (If the colour is too pale, powder a few more saffron strands). Sprinkle the rest of the saffron on top.
9. Transfer to a serving dish or a shallow, wide stainless steel/ silver dish/glass and store in a cool place. Scoop out with dessert spoon and serve. Refrigerated halva can stay for a month.

BADAM BURFI Almond Burfi

Makes: 30 servings
Serving size: 75 gms
Calories per serving: 679

INGREDIENTS

Almonds 1 cup
Water 1 cup + ¼ cups
Saffron 20 strands
Sugar 1 cup
Ghee 1 cup + extra for smearing
Plate with a 1-inch rim 1

METHOD

1. Boil 1 cup water and pour over almonds. Cover and soak for 30 minutes. Drain and peel.
2. Grind almonds to a fine, smooth consistency with ¼ cup of water.
3. Mix sugar and ground almonds.
4. Place sugar and almonds mixture in an uruli/heavy-bottomed bronze pan over low heat and stir continuously and gently till the paste starts puffing up. Add a few strands of saffron.
5. Add ghee a little at a time, stirring between each addition, till the ghee is totally absorbed.
6. Smear a plate with ghee.
7. When the mixture develops a floury texture, mix in a few more strands of saffron.
8. Remove from heat and pour evenly onto the plate.
9. Level the surface with a knife and sprinkle a few strands of saffron on top. When cool, cut into 1-inch x 1-inch squares or any other desired shape, and serve.

Variation: Kaju burfi can be prepared in the same way. Soak cashewnuts for about an hour before grinding them.

BADAM PĀL POḶI Almond Milk Poḷi

Makes: 15 servings
Serving size: 75 gms
Calories per serving: 287

INGREDIENTS

Almonds 30
Water 1 cup + 1 tsp
Saffron 1 pinch or 25 strands
Milk 2 cups
Fine semolina 1 cup
Ghee 2 tbsp
Sugar ½ –¾ cup
Cardamom 1, powdered
Ghee and oil mixed for frying 2 cups
White flour for dusting

METHOD

1. Boil 1 cup water and pour over almonds and soak for 30 minutes. Drain and peel.
2. Grind almonds coarsely.
3. Soak 10 saffron strands in a little milk and grind well with pestle and mortar. Mix with ground almonds.
4. Mix semolina with ghee and knead to make a smooth, stiff dough. Let it stand for about 15 minutes.
5. Boil milk in a heavy-bottomed vessel. Add sugar, stir occasionally, till it dissolves.
6. Crush 15 saffron strands in 1 tsp of water with a pestle. Add to boiling milk along with powdered cardamom. Remove milk from heat.
7. Knead semolina dough well. Divide into 12 equal portions and shape into balls.
8. Roll each ball into a thin puri 5-inches in diameter.
9. Take a berry-sized ball of almond paste and spread it evenly over half the poḷi with a spatula. Fold again into half.
10. Spread ¼ tsp of almond paste over the crescent and fold again into a quarter. Seal the edges.
11. Roll out gently by dusting a little flour on both sides, into a triangle.
12. Heat ghee and oil in a vānali/wok. Deep-fry one poḷi at a time over low heat, till light and crisp.
13. Drain poḷi and soak it in the prepared milk.
14. Pour 1 tbsp of milk over each poḷi before serving.

RAVĀ KESARI Saffron Semolina

Makes: 12 servings
Serving size: 75 gms
Calories per serving: 354

INGREDIENTS

Semolina 1 cup
Water 2 ¼ cups + 2 extra tbsp
Saffron 2 pinches or 52 strands
Ghee ½ cup
Sugar 1¼ cups
Cashewnuts 5, broken
Raisins 10
Cardamoms 3, powdered

METHOD

1. Keep a vānali/wok on low heat. Gently toast the semolina for 2 minutes, stirring a few times. The colour should not change. Remove and keep aside.
2. Reserve a few saffron strands. Crush the rest of the saffron in 1 tsp of water with a pestle.
3. Place 2¼ cups of water for boiling.
4. Heat 1 tsp of ghee in a vānali/wok. Fry cashewnuts till they turn golden and raisins till they puff up. Set aside.
5. Add toasted ravā to vānali/wok, sauté once and pour 2 cups of boiling water. Simmer over low heat till it is cooked. If the resultant dough is too thick, add another 2 tbsp of water.
6. Add sugar and stir continuously. Add the rest of the ghee and stir till sugar and semolina are well blended. Add a few strands of saffron.
7. Reduce heat. Mix in saffron paste, cashewnuts, raisins and powdered cardamom.
8. Remove from heat and serve.

Variations:

- *Vermicelli kesari: Can be prepared in the same way, using vermicelli instead of semolina.*
- *Pineapple ravā kesari: Add ½ cup of finely chopped pineapple when the kesari gathers towards the centre. Mix well.*

SURAKĀI BĀSUNDI Bottle Gourd and Milk Sweet

Makes: 6 servings
Serving size: 75 gms
Calories per serving: 105

INGREDIENTS

Bottle gourd (medium) 1
Whole cream milk 1 litre
Sugar ½ cup

METHOD

1. Peel bottle gourd and grate into thin, long shreds.
2. Wash rice and soak in water for about 20 minutes. Drain and grind with 2 tbsp of water to make a fine thick paste.
3. Heat ½ litre milk in a vānali/wok. Add bottle gourd and cook.
4. Add sugar and stir. Remove from heat.

Basumati rice 1 tbsp
Water 2 tbsp
Kewra water[1] 1 tsp
Pistachios 1 tsp, peeled and chopped[2] (optional)

5. Bring to boil the rest of the milk. When it starts boiling, lower heat and add rice paste slowly, stirring simultaneously. Continue to stir milk till it thickens. Add cooked bottle gourd.
6. Remove from heat. Add pandanus/kewra water and mix.

[1] *Kewra water or pandanus water is available in the market.*

[2] *Optional: Garnish with peeled and chopped pistachios.*

GULAB JAMUN

Makes: 60 servings
Serving size: 75 gms
Calories per serving: 654

INGREDIENTS

Mava/Khoya[1] 1 kg
Arrowroot flour ½ cup
White flour/Maida cup
Makhai dana[2] 100 gm
Sugar 2½ kgs
Water ½ cup
Ghee for deep-frying 5 cups

Spices
Nutmeg 1
Mace 2 flakes
Saffron 2 pinches or 52 strands
Rose water 1 tsp–1½ tsp
Cardamoms 10
Saffron for the syrup1–2 pinches

METHOD

1. Pound all the spices except nutmeg. Grate the nutmeg. Mix both together.
2. Crush saffron in a few drops of rose water to make a paste. Mix pounded spices into the paste.
3. Coat each makhai dana with this paste and set aside.
4. Make a sugar syrup of one-thread consistency with ½ cup of water (see Pre-Cooking Processes). Add a few strands of saffron to it.
5. Mix mava with arrowroot and maida in a bowl. Knead to make a smooth dough.
6. Divide dough into 60 portions and roll each with a makhai dana in the centre into a ball (gulab jamun).
7. Heat ghee in a vānali/wok over low heat and fry gulab jamun in batches, till golden brown.
8. Drain and add to sugar syrup. Ensure gulab jamuns are completely covered by the syrup.

Note: The gulab jamun may be sliced in half to reveal its filling, or served whole.

[1] *Mava/khoya is well-evaporated milk and has a dough-like consistency.*

[2] *Makhai dana are tiny sugar balls which resemble popcorn and are available in the market.*

ŚARKARAI PONGAL Sweet Rice with Green Gram Dal

Makes: 4 servings
Serving size: 75 gms
Calories per serving: 188

INGREDIENTS

Any long-grained rice 1 cup
Milk 1½ cups
Water 1½ cups
Green gram dal/Mung dal ¼ cup
Grated jaggery 2 cups
Water ½ cup
Cashewnuts 1 tbsp
Raisins 1 tbsp
Nutmeg 2 gratings
Mace ½-inch piece
Cardamoms 4–5
Saffron 2 pinches

METHOD

1. Break cashewnuts into small bits.
2. Toast mung dal in a vānali/wok lightly over low heat for a minute, tossing all the while; it should not change colour.
3. Powder nutmeg and mace together. Powder cardamoms separately.
4. Dissolve jaggery in ½ cup of water and strain to remove impurities.
5. Heat 1 tsp of ghee in a vānali/wok. Fry cashewnuts over medium heat till golden. Slot out.
6. Fry raisins in a vānali/wok till they puff up. Remove.
7. Boil milk and water in a heavy-bottomed vessel. Wash rice and mung dal and add to boiling milk and water. Cook over medium heat.
8. When rice and dal mixture is cooked well and is soft, add strained jaggery syrup, powdered nutmeg and mace, and cook for 2–3 minutes. Stir often.
9. After 2–3 minutes add 2 tbsp of ghee. Stir. Add fried cashewnuts and raisins and powdered cardamom.
10. Remove from heat and serve.

TIRATTIPĀL Textured Milk Sweet

Makes: 8 servings
Serving size: 75 gms
Calories per serving: 97

INGREDIENTS

Milk 2 litres
Curd 2 tsp, whisked smooth
Grated jaggery ¼ cup
Sugar ¼ cup

METHOD

1. Boil milk in a heavy-bottomed vānali/wok over medium heat. Stir now and then to prevent milk from boiling over or burning at the bottom.
2. When milk has reduced to less than half its original volume, lower heat. Add curd; the milk will split slightly.
3. Add jaggery and sugar and stir now and then till the mixture has a grainy consistency like that of ricotta cheese.
4. Remove from heat and transfer to a serving dish.

Note: Tirattipāl is best when consumed the same day. Leftovers can be refrigerated for another day.

MITHA CHAVAL Sweet Rice

Makes: 30 servings
Serving size: 75 gms
Calories per serving: 370

INGREDIENTS

Basumati rice 2 cups
Cardamoms 20
Almonds (mamra quality) 200 gm
Pistachios 200 gm
Pinenuts 100 gm
Saffron 2 pinches, crushed
Nutmeg ⅓, grated
Mace ½-inch piece
Milk 2 cups
Water 1 cup + 1 tbsp
Ghee 1½ cups
Cloves 15
Sugar 3 cups

METHOD

1. Crush cardamoms by pounding only once with a pestle just to open the ends slightly.
2. Boil 1 cup of water and pour over the almonds. Soak for 30 minutes. Drain and peel. Slice almonds into fine slivers.
3. Shell pistachios. Pour boiling water over them. Set aside for 5–8 minutes. Drain. Slice pistachios into fine slivers.
4. Shell pinenuts, grate nutmeg and break mace into 2 or 3 pieces.
5. Soak rice for 20 minutes and drain.
6. Crush saffron in 1 tbsp of water in a mortar with a pestle.
7. Take milk and water, add pounded cardamom, crushed saffron, nutmeg and mace and bring to a boil. Remove from heat.
8. Heat ghee in a heavy-bottomed vessel.
9. Sauté cloves over low heat for ½ minute.
10. Add drained rice and sauté (do not brown).
11. Pour the boiling milk over the rice.
12. Meanwhile, heat some charcoal pieces till they are red-hot. Spread on an iron tray or in a large deep vānali/wok.
13. Place the heavy-bottomed vessel with rice on the charcoal and cover tightly with a lid, to prevent the steam from escaping. Open the vessel every 2–3 minutes and stir slowly to prevent the milk from sticking to the bottom of the pan.
14. When the rice is tender and the grains are separate, add nuts (reserve a few for decoration). Remove from heat.
15. Boil sugar with ¼ cup of water and make a thick sugar syrup. (If a drop of syrup is put on a plate, it should roll into a ball when handled.)
16. Add sugar syrup to rice. Return vessel to the red-hot charcoal kept on the iron tray/deep vānali/wok. When it starts simmering, cover and place some charcoal on the lid. Remove some charcoal from underneath the vessel. Leave the vessel over heat till the syrup is absorbed.
17. Mix gently so as not to break the rice.
18. Decorate with reserved nuts and serve.

FRUITS IN PLENTY

Fruits play an important role in Indian tradition, poetry and art. Tamil Sangam literature identifies three important fruits of Tamil culture, the mukkani—ma, pāḷa, vāḷai, namely mango, jackfruit and banana. On ceremonial occasions, all or at least one of the three fruits is served and served first. It is believed that eating fruit at the beginning of a meal activates the gastric juices and helps in the proper assimilation of the feast that is to follow.

Fruits have always formed a significant part in the Indian cook's repertoire. Each region in India developed special recipes to accommodate its popular local fruits. They were used not only in sweets, as you would expect, given their natural sweetness, but in a variety of spicy preparations as well. They were added to kuḷambu, rasam, kūtu, gojju and mixed with vegetable(s) as a side dish to rice or as part of the rice dish itself.

Mango is used both in its unripe and ripe forms, taking different avatars according to the area where it is grown. In the south, we have the Māmpaḷa morkuḷambu, while up north its juice is made into aamras. It is used in the signature dishes of Gujarat, like shrikhand and vajeda. Āmras and shrikhand both make perfect accompaniments to puri.

Nendrampaḷam, a variety of banana from the southern state of Kerala, is famously made into banana chips. It is also made into fritters, soaked in sugar syrup, or baked. Being versatile, steamed bananas are consumed at breakfast, while roasted bananas are served with jaggery and used in salads with yoghurt dressing.

Jackfruit is the main ingredient in the Kerala favourite, chakkai prathaman. The popular but complicated dish, koḷukattai, traditionally offered to Lord Vinayaka, is sometimes transformed with a jackfruit filling. It is also used as a filling for appams and for ilai adāis. Jackfruit papads are a tasty Karnataka product which can be stored and toasted when needed.

Pineapple and banana are both part of the sweet dish ravā kesari, made with semolina. Of late, pineapple is also used to make a rasam. Karnataka recipes include a pineapple curry besides using it in some sweets.

Apples grown in Kashmir and Himachal Pradesh lend freshness to salads. A quick apple curry can be made with a seasoning of cloves, cardamom and sugar. Apple chutney makes a delicious accompaniment to roti, as do mango, guava and apple launji.

Dried plums add a flavourful astringency to kofta. Fruit sandesh is an appetizing variant of the Bengali favourite. Wild berries like jojoba (ilaindapaḷam) and wood apple (vilampaḷam) used to be made into chutneys and sweets but they seem to have lost their popularity in recent times.

In Tamil Nadu, nartampaḷam, a special variety of ripe citrus fruit, makes a good gojju and adds a tangy fragrance to a rice dish. Nartampaḷam juice is as refreshing as sweet lime juice and adds a delicate piquancy to a rasam.

MĀLPUVĀ Milk Crêpes

Makes: 15 servings
Serving size: 75 gms
Calories per serving: 499

INGREDIENTS

Milk 2 cups
White flour/Maida 4–5 tbsp
Flour of mot dal/Kal payatham paruppu[1] 2 tsp
Cardamoms 6
Saffron 2–3 pinches
Sugar 1 cup less 1 tbsp or 225 gm
Water 1 tbsp
Ghee for frying 2 cups

Garnish
Finely slivered almonds 1 tbsp

METHOD

1. Place milk in a heavy-bottomed vessel over medium heat and bring to a boil. Continue to boil, stirring continuously, till it is reduced to one-fourth of the original volume. Remove from heat and cool.
2. Sprinkle white flour and mot dal flour into the milk without forming lumps.
3. Powder cardamoms and add to the milk.
4. Crush saffron to a powder.
5. Combine sugar with 1 tbsp of water in another vessel. Boil to make a thin syrup of one-thread consistency (see Pre-Cooking Processes). Remove from heat and add saffron.
6. Place a frying pan over medium heat and add ghee to ½-inch depth.
7. To test, pour a spoonful of batter in the centre and check if it forms a lacy fringe all around and small bubbles appear. The puva should be well under the ghee. If the batter is too thick, add a little more milk and try again. The mālpuvā should not stick to the base.
8. When the mālpuvā rises, flip over till puva is golden brown. Dip it in syrup and drain.
9. Repeat for remaining batter, adding more ghee to the pan as required.
10. Sprinkle with slivered almonds and serve warm.

[1]*Phaseolus trilobatus*

JALEBI

Makes: 12 servings
Serving size: 75 gms
Calories per serving: 735

The traditional way of making jalebis is to make a cone out of a stiff cloth like canvas and to squeeze the batter through the cone tip, shaping the jalebi in the hot ghee. Now, jalebi bags called piping bags, and plastic bottles, both with nozzles, are available in the market.

INGREDIENTS

Jalebi

White flour/Maida 2 cups
Water 1 cup
Apple 1 (for apple variation)
Ghee for deep-frying 2 cups

Sugar syrup

Sugar 1 cup
Water 2–3 cups
Saffron 1 pinch
Rose water 1 tsp
Lime juice 1 drop

METHOD

Sugar syrup

1. Mix sugar with 2–3 cups of water in a heavy-bottomed vessel. Bring to a boil over medium heat. Boil for 2–3 minutes and test for one-thread consistency (see Pre-Cooking Processes).
2. Add saffron, rose water and lime juice and remove from heat.

Jalebi

1. Mix maida with 1 cup of water. It should have a pouring consistency but not like water.
2. Ferment for 3 days in a warm place.
3. Heat ghee for deep frying over medium heat.
4. Fill the piping bag with jalebi batter. Squeeze the jalebi batter out in the hot ghee in a pretzel shape to about 2-inches in diameter.
5. Fry jalebis until golden-brown on both sides.
6. Transfer into the warm syrup.

Variation: Apple Jalebi

1. Peel and core the apple. Slice into ¼-inch thick rings.

2. Dip apple rings in batter and deep-fry in hot ghee over medium heat on both sides, till golden.

3. Dip fried apple jalebi in warm sugar syrup.

4. Remove from syrup and serve.

GAJAR HALVA Carrot Halva

Makes: 15 servings
Serving size: 75 gms
Calories per serving: 192

INGREDIENTS

Carrots 500 gm
Milk 1 litre
Mava/Khoya 100 gm, crumbled
Sugar 250 gm
Ghee ½ cup
Saffron 2 pinches or 50 strands
Cardamom 1

Garnish
Almonds 1 tbsp
Pistachios shelled 1 tbsp
Ghee 2 tbsp

METHOD

1. Pour boiling water over almonds and shelled pistachios. Set aside for 30 minutes. Drain and peel almonds. Slice almonds and pistachios into fine slivers.
2. Powder the cardamom.
3. Peel carrots and grate.
4. Boil milk in a heavy-bottomed vessel over medium heat for about 5 minutes.
5. Add carrots, lower heat and cook, till creamy and soft.
6. Add crumbled mava and sugar, cook till mixture thickens.
7. Add ghee, saffron, powdered cardamom and half the nuts. Gently fold in and remove from heat.
8. Heat 2 tbsp of ghee in a small pan and fry remaining nuts over moderate heat, till golden.
9. Add to the halva.

Note: The halva should be soft and rather moist when removed from heat.

RASAGULLA

Makes: 30–40 servings
Serving size: 75 gms
Calories per serving: 210

INGREDIENTS

Milk 2 litres
Lime juice 2–3 tbsp
Sugar 2 cups
Water[1] 7–8 cups

METHOD

1. Boil milk in a vessel over high heat. Add lime juice while the milk is still boiling. Remove from heat. Wait for the milk to split well, stirring periodically.
2. Keep a colander on top of an empty vessel. Place a muslin cloth in the colander. Pour the split milk over it.
3. When the milk solid is drained well, wash in ice-cold water.
4. Tie the muslin and squeeze out as much whey as possible. Put a weight on it for 5 minutes to remove excess whey but leave the hung cheese slightly moist.
5. Knead the cheese gently, till it forms a smooth dough. Roll into balls.
6. Put the sugar in a pressure cooker with about 7 cups of water. Bring to a boil. As it starts to boil add half of the cheese balls. Close the cooker and place the weight.
7. When the whistling starts, keep for 3 whistles on the same heat and pressure. Do not open. Turn off the heat. Set aside for about 10 minutes.
8. Cool the cooker under running cold water and then open it. Keep the rasagulla in the syrup for 5–10 minutes. Remove the first batch with some of the syrup.
9. Reheat the syrup. If the syrup looks inadequate, add a little more sugar and water. Bring to a boil. Repeat the process. When the second batch is ready, mix with first batch.
10. Serve with a little of the sugar syrup.

[1]*Naturally curdled whey water can also be used.*

BADAM KHEER Almond Kheer

Makes: 7–8 servings
Serving size: 75 gms
Calories per serving: 75

INGREDIENTS

Almonds ½ cup
Milk 1½ litres
Sugar ½ cup
Saffron 1 pinch + 10–15 strands

METHOD

1. Soak almonds for 30 minutes. Drain, peel and grind to a fine paste.
2. Crush saffron in 1 tsp of milk with a pestle.
3. Boil milk in a milk boiler or a deep vessel. When it froths up, remove from heat. Filter and keep aside.
4. Take ground almonds in a heavy-bottomed vessel. Sauté over medium heat for a few seconds, constantly stir in till almond aroma is released. Remove from heat.
5. Add warm milk and keep back on heat and bring to a boil.
6. Remove, mix in saffron paste. Stir well.
7. Sprinkle with saffron strands.
8. Serve chilled or hot.

SHRIKHAND

Makes: 6 servings
Serving size: 75 gms
Calories per serving: 101

INGREDIENTS

Freshly made curd from whole milk 4 cups
Powdered sugar ¾ cup
Saffron ¼ tsp
Rose water 2 drops
Cardamoms 6

Garnish
Slivered pistachios and almonds 2 tbsp
Saffron a few strands

METHOD

1. Powder cardamoms.
2. Soak ¼ tsp of saffron in rose water and grind to make a paste with a pestle.
3. Fold a thick, heavy cotton cloth into 4–5 layers. Spread a piece of thin muslin on top. Spread curd evenly in the centre. Allow all water to drain for about 2 hours. When well drained, the curd solids will come off easily from the cloth. This should be done in a cool place.
4. Transfer all curd to a bowl, using a spatula. Add powdered sugar and whisk till sugar is dissolved and mixture is smooth.
5. Add saffron and powdered cardamoms and mix well.
6. Transfer to a serving dish.
7. Garnish with slivered pistachios and almonds and a few saffron strands.
8. Refrigerate and serve.

SANDESH

Makes: 5 servings
Serving size: 75 gms
Calories per serving: 114

INGREDIENTS

Chena/Freshly made paneer 250–375 gm
Sugar 5 tbsp
Rose water/Kewra water 1 tbsp

METHOD

1. To make chena, see Pre-Cooking Processes.
2. Mix the chena well for 5 minutes and add sugar.
3. Cook over low heat for 10 minutes and then add rose water.
4. Remove from heat and make 10 sandesh of any shape.

Variation: Chena rolls

1. *Take a small ball of chena, knead well and pat into a thin flat circle on a leaf and place one segment of orange, close it like a roll. Arrange in a dish and garnish with a little bit of saffron or ground cardamom.*
2. *Similarly keep a piece of ripe mango and make a roll and garnish with saffron or finely chopped pistachios.*

Note: Sandesh cannot be made with readymade paneer. It has to be made with freshly made paneer.

TIFFIN

Fried Snacks

TIFFIN

'Tipan redi', to use the Tamilized English version of 'Tiffin ready', is a board that we cannot miss when traveling anywhere in Tamil Nadu. The welcoming notice is seen on boards of varying sizes but never followed by the day's promised menu or even one or two names of dishes that would be usually available at the time.

No other state in India seems to have embraced this word as much as Tamil Nadu, a word that, according to the delightful dictionary *Hobson-Jobson*, goes back to at least the year 1807. 'Many persons are in the habit of sitting down to a repast at one o'clock, which is called tiffin, and is in fact an early dinner.' (Cordiner's Ceylon.) In 1810, we have the exact time for tiffin—'The dinner is scarcely touched, as every person eats a hearty meal called tiffin, at 2 o'clock, at home.'

The next year,1811, a graphic picture of life in India for the young Englishwoman—'Gertrude was a little unfortunate in her situation, which was next below Mrs. Fashionist, and who … detailed the delights of India, and the routine of its day; the changing linen, the curry-combing … the idleness, the dissipation, the sleeping and the necessity of sleep, the gay tiffings, were all delightful to her in reciting …'

Finally, in 1832, a captivating extract from the English poet De Quincey's *Casuistry of Roman Meals*: 'Reader! I, as well as Pliny, had an uncle, an East Indian Uncle … everybody has an Indian Uncle … He is not always orientally rich as he is reputed; but he is always orientally munificent. Call upon him at any hour from two till five, he insists on your taking tiffin; and such a tiffin! The English corresponding term is luncheon; but how meager a shadow is the European meal to its glowing Asiatic cousin.'

Picnics on Trains

Tiffin was soon followed by its extension, the 'tiffin box'. Generations of schoolchildren and office-going adults have carried and still carry tiffin boxes to school and to work. Home-cooked food continues to be considered both nutritious and hygienic compared to what one can obtain outside from restaurants or even office 'canteens', yet another 'Indian' word for cafeterias.

Memories of my childhood travels and those of my children are inextricably entwined with memories of delicious food brought to us by friends and aunts leading to great picnics on trains.

When I was a child I looked forward with excitement to our trips to Delhi. Delhi meant northern varieties of mangoes, which we could not taste in Madras, it meant fresh tender peas and cauliflower. All this was mixed up with the anticipation of visiting historical places in and near the capital.

Most of all, the journey meant the added

excitement of meeting my aunt in Nagpur who would visit the traveling contingent with two huge tiffin boxes filled with the most delicious food: pots of rasagullas, homemade almond cookies—everything was unfamilar and tasty and tasted all the better for being eaten on the train.

We would then pass on the tiffin boxes brought by us to my aunt. These would once again be filled up and given to us on our return journey.

Later, when we went to Kodaikanal by train, we were met en route by friends at Dindigul, with a hot breakfast of crisp ravā dosais and spicy gotsu with tomatoes and lentils to go with it, once more in a humungous tiffin box with six tiers. The children loved this picnic on the train and the food was polished off in no time.

It is this love for home-cooked food and the faith that it is both healthier and tastier that has made dabbawallas such an institution in the busy city of Mumbai. The astonishing network of dabbawallas or the tiffin-carriers of Mumbai is a saga that has continued for more than 140 years, since the 1860s.

This fail-proof system collects hundreds of tiffin boxes from homes 20–30 kilometres away and delivers them in offices to the right individuals. In the evening, the process is reversed—the tiffin boxes are collected from offices and delivered back home in far-flung suburbs. This work has now become a management marvel in logistics, drawing the admiration of MBA programmes. Prince Charles was so impressed that he invited the leaders of the dabbawalla association to his wedding. We hear now that this simple but splendid idea of transporting home-cooked food to officegoers has become popular in Cambodia too. We hear of a vegetarian food delivery service there called 'Meat-Free Bento'.

In this age of fast-food kiosks, small Udupi restaurants and street vendors, what is it in the Indian character that insists on a home-cooked meal being delivered to the office for lunch? Hygiene could be a reason, surely economy must be another. Indisputably, taste must be the first and most important reason.

Despite so many continuing changes in the variety and availability of food in the public domain, the Indian's love of homemade tiffin and its receptacle, the tiffin box, continues to this day.

The Tiffin Box as Art

Tiffin boxes come in all materials. Originally made of tin-coated brass in India and Southeast Asia, it is now available in all sizes and shapes in stainless steel. Tiffin boxes in silver were part of the young bride's dower in these countries. Indian brides could also possess tiffin boxes made of lacquer from Cambodia,Thailand and Myanmar. Austria made tiffin boxes of an aluminium alloy that shone like silver with exquisite repoussé work. Czechoslovakia and Germany were famous for their enamel tiffin boxes with the base metal iron covered in lovely bright colours and floral designs.

All over Southeast Asia the tiffin carrier is called a bento box, from the Japanese term. This also comes in a stackable form like the Indian one, and it is made of aluminium or stainless steel. Thais and Japanese continue to take different kinds of food in the bento box.

The unique Indian container has captured the imagination of many an artist. We find paintings featuring the tiffin box and sculptural castings with bunches of tiffin boxes emerging from the solid cast. Pictures featuring rows of tiffin boxes in many striking and colourful ways are found in many an art gallery in India. Vessel merchants delight in hanging tier upon tier of varied tiffin boxes outside their stores to entice buyers.

Iduvatu—Idli

Idli is named after the word used for its making, 'iduvadu' (to make). Now the nationally famous part of the duo idli–vada, with its spicy accompaniment sambar, idli is in many ways the quintessential south Indian dish. All over Tamil Nadu the idli–vada combo is served automatically when you order idli, unless you specifically mention that the vada is not required.

In Karnataka, every road leading to the highway is lined with idli shops. In Madurai, which has been famous for its 'mallippu idlis' (idlis as soft as jasmine) since the 1850s, we can get piping hot idlis even at midnight!

Palayadu, or old cooked rice soaked in water, kept overnight and eaten with salt, green chillies, or salted citrus fruit, was the original fermented breakfast dish. When exactly this was replaced by the idli as the supreme breakfast dish is not known. However, the Kānchipuram idli has been known from very early times as a sacred offering (see Sacred Offerings).

Idlis can be made with other grains like sāmai, a millet variety grown in the hilly areas of southern India and popular upto Maharashtra. Samai idlis are made on days when fasting is undertaken as rice is not consumed during ritual fasts.

Rāgi idlis are popular in Karnataka, palāpaḷa idlis are the favourites in Kerala and coastal Karnataka. Kotte ukadubu ('nut' idlis) are a delicacy of the Mangalore region (see Udupi Recipes). Ravā idli is the easy modern-day version while oats idli is being widely accepted as a healthy choice for diabetics.

Little urchins playing on village roads have been heard singing this song or whistling it, so much do they love the idli!

Idli ettu timben, chutney tottu timben
Pittu pittu timben, idli ettu timben
Nān chutney tottu timben
Sambar pottu timben
Ney vittu timben, idli ettu timben

Idlis? I will eat four and four!
With chutney? A touch to be sure!
And sambar? Do give a generous pour!
Ghee! Do add, and I will eat more!

RICE IDLI

Makes: 25 servings
Serving size: 150 gms
Calories per serving: 204

INGREDIENTS

Parboiled rice 2 cups
Black gram dal/Urad dal ½ cup
Water 1 cup + ½ cup
Salt 2 tsp

METHOD

1. Wash rice and soak in water for 4 hours. Wash urad dal separately and soak in water 3 hours later. Urad dal should soak only for 30 minutes.
2. Drain urad dal and grind first, sprinkling 1 cup of water in parts to make a smooth, fluffy batter (see Pre-Cooking Processes).
3. Drain rice and grind to make a slightly grainy batter with ½ cup of water.
4. Combine both batters in a large container. Add salt and beat or whisk rapidly with a wooden ladle. Taste for salt. Add more if required.
5. Cover batter and let it ferment overnight.
6. Boil water in an idli steamer.
7. Stretch a wet muslin cloth tightly over the depressions of an idli mould. Pour a ladle of batter into each depression. Place the mould in the steamer and steam for 10 minutes.
8. Refrigerate any extra batter and use on the next day or steam all the idlis and freeze by separating them with polythene sheets.

Variations:

- *Samai (a type of millet,* Panicum miliare*) idli: Use it in place of rice. Soak samai for 2–3 hours, grind and proceed as above.*
- *Idli uppuma: Leftover idlis crumbled are seasoned with mustard seeds, black gram dal, dried red chillies, asafoetida powder, curry leaves and idli chilli powder (milagāi podi) to make idli uppuma.*

RAVĀ IDLI Semolina Idli

Makes: 8 servings
Serving size: 150 gms
Calories per serving: 392

INGREDIENTS

Curd, whisked smooth 1½ cups
Water 1 cup
Ghee 2 tbsp
Medium-textured semolina 1½ cups
Salt 1 tsp
Coriander leaves 4–5 stems, chopped
Cut banana leaves or leaf plates or cups[1]

Seasoning
Oil 1 tbsp
Mustard seeds ½ tsp
Cashewnuts 12, broken
Curry leaves 2 sprigs
Green chillies 2, chopped fine

METHOD

1. Whisk curd with 1 cup of water and set aside.
2. Dry roast semolina in a vānali/wok over low heat, without letting it change colour. Remove.
3. Add ghee to vānali/wok. Fry cashewnuts till golden and remove. Splutter mustard seeds, stir in curry leaves and fry for a second.
4. Add seasoning, curd, salt and coriander leaves to semolina and mix well. Add a little water if the consistency is too thick.
5. Cover vānali/wok and set aside for about 30 minutes.
6. Boil water in a steamer.
7. Line an idli mould with cut banana leaves or dried bauhinia leaves. Pour a ladle of batter into the leaf-lined depressions of the mould. Steam for 10–12 minutes.
8. Serve hot with any chutney or milagāi podi.

Variation: Semia ravā idli can be made in the same way. Use 1 cup of vermicelli and ½ cup of semolina.

[1] *Cups made of any leaves in various sizes are available in the market.*

RĀGI IDLI Coracana Idli

Makes: 6–8 servings
Serving size: 150 gms
Calories per serving: 300

INGREDIENTS

Black gram dal/Urad dal ½ cup
Fenugreek seeds ¾ tbsp
Water ½ cup
Rāgi flour 1 cup
Salt 1½ tsp

METHOD

1. Wash urad dal and fenugreek seeds and soak in water for about 2 hours.
2. Drain and grind to make a smooth, fluffy batter with ½ cup of water (see Pre-Cooking Processes).
3. Mix rāgi flour into the batter, add salt and beat or whisk rapidly with a wooden ladle.
4. Cover and set aside to ferment overnight.
5. Boil water in an idli steamer.
6. Stretch a wet muslin cloth tightly over the depressions of an idli mould. Pour a ladle of batter into each depression. Place the mould in the steamer and steam for 10–12 minutes.
7. Serve with coconut chutney (see Chutneys and Tugaiyals).

PALĀPAḶA IDLI Jackfruit Idli

Makes: 8 servings
Serving size: 150 gms
Calories per serving: 279

INGREDIENTS

Raw rice 1 cup
Jackfruit segments (medium) 14
Black pepper powder ¼ tsp
Salt ¾ tsp

METHOD

1. Wash rice and soak it in water for about an hour.
2. Cut jackfruit segments into small even pieces and keep 2 tbsp of the cut fruit aside.
3. Drain rice and grind it with the remaining jackfruit without adding water.
4. Add pepper powder, salt and reserved jackfruit segments. Mix well.
5. Boil water in an idli steamer.
6. Pour batter into cups made of dried bauhinia leaves or banana leaves or on a wet muslin cloth and steam for 10 minutes.
7. Alternatively, stretch a wet muslin cloth tightly over a bread-baking tin. Place the tin in the steamer and steam for about 10 minutes.
8. Slice the idli like bread slices. Cool and serve.

KOḶUKATTAI

Rice Dumplings with Filling of Choice

Makes: 20–22 servings
Serving size: 150 gms
Calories per serving: 176

INGREDIENTS

Rice flour 1½ cups
Water 3 cups
Salt 1 pinch
Oil 1 tsp
Sesame oil 1 tsp
Water 1 tbsp (mixed)
Filling of choice (given after Method)

Koḷukattai, the Tamil word for a glistening dumpling with both sweet and spicy fillings, is descriptive of jelly! From Japan to the south Indian coast, this kind of preparation is popular and known by various names. It is called yakimanchu in Japan, dumplings in China and momos in Southeast Asia. The Sanskrit word 'modak' must be of a later origin than koḷukattai, as steamed preparations have been around south India since antiquity.

In Tamil Nadu koḷukattais are made in various shapes—round, square, crescent and so on. One will know by its very shape what the filling of the koḷukattai will be. The round koḷukattais with a bud on top have a sweet coconut and jaggery filling, while the crescent or shell-shaped one will have a spicy urad dal filling. The squarish koḷukattai with four wings has a spicy sesame filling.

Koḷukattai, offered to Lord Ganesh on festivals, is a tricky dish to prepare, even for the most accomplished cook.

METHOD

Dough

1. Boil 3 cups of water in a heavy-bottomed vessel with salt and oil.
2. When water starts to boil, reduce heat and add rice flour, stirring with a ladle for about 5 minutes. Keep folding well with a spatula often to prevent lumps.
3. Soak a white cloth in water, squeeze out water. Spread the cloth on a plate. Empty the cooked flour on the cloth. Tie it in a bundle and set aside. (This will keep the flour free from lumps). When slightly cool, untie the bundle and knead well.

To assemble the koḷukattai

1. Mix sesame oil with 1 tbsp of water. Smear your palms with this. Take 1½-inch round ball of the dough. Flatten this on the palm making the edges a little thin and the centre a bit thick. By pressing the centre and gathering the edges, make the shape of a crucible.
2. Fill the cup with prepared filling of choice. Seal the cup. One by one, make all the koḷukattais.

3. Place a banana leaf or a muslin cloth on a perforated plate. Arrange a batch of koḷukattais on this and steam for about 7 minutes.
4. To make savoury koḷukattai: make a flat circle on the palm. Keep the filling on one half of the circle, fold over and seal. The edges can be folded in many pretty ways.

Sweet Coconut Filling

Makes: 20–22 servings
Serving size: 150 gms
Calories per serving: 166

INGREDIENTS

Grated jaggery ½ cup
Water 1 tsp
Grated fresh coconut 1 cup
Powdered cardamom ½ tsp
Ghee 1 tsp

METHOD

1. Take jaggery in a vānali/wok, add 1 tsp of water and place over low heat. Stir for a few seconds till jaggery starts to melt.
2. Add coconut and keep stirring, till melted jaggery is fully absorbed and the filling becomes sticky.
3. Add powdered cardamom and ghee and mix well. Cool.
4. Divide into equal portions and use as a filling for sweet koḷukattai.

Savoury Black Gram Dal/Urad Dal Filling

Makes: 20–22 servings
Serving size: 150 gms
Calories per serving: 60

INGREDIENTS

Black gram dal/Urad dal ½ cup
Water ¾ cup
Green chillies 3
Salt ½ tsp

Seasoning
Oil 2 tsp
Asafoetida powder 1 pinch
Mustard seeds 1 tsp
Curry leaves 1 sprig

METHOD

1. Wash dal and soak it in water for about 30 minutes.
2. Drain and grind dal with green chillies, salt and ¾ cup of water to a fine consistency.
3. Steam the ground batter on a perforated plate in a steamer for about 15 minutes. Let cool and crumble.
4. Heat oil in a vānali/wok. Add asafoetida powder and mustard seeds and splutter over medium heat. Stir in curry leaves.
5. Add crumbled dal and sauté for 1–2 minutes.
6. Remove from heat and cool.
7. Divide into equal portions and use as a filling for savoury koḷukattai.

Savoury Sesame-Seed Filling

Makes: 20–22 servings
Serving size: 150 gms
Calories per serving: 95

INGREDIENTS

Sesame seeds ½ cup
Dried red chillies 2
Salt ½ tsp

METHOD

1. Wash sesame seeds and soak in water for about an hour. Rinse seeds, drain and dry.
2. Roast sesame seeds and red chillies in a vānali/wok over low heat, till the seeds change colour slightly.
3. Pound sesame seeds and red chillies to a powder.
4. Add salt and mix well.
5. Divide into equal portions and use as a filling for savoury koḷukattai.

ADAI Banana Leaf Adai

Makes: 6 servings
Serving size: 150 gms
Calories per serving: 393

INGREDIENTS

Rice ½ cup
Water to grind cup
10-inch square banana leaves

Jackfruit-jaggery filling
Jackfruit 4–5 segments, chopped
Ghee 1½ tsp
Grated jaggery 3¼ cups

METHOD

Dough

1. Wash rice and soak it in water for an hour. Drain and grind finely to a thick paste, sprinkling water now and then.
2. Keep six 10-inch square banana leaves ready.

Preparation for jackfruit-jaggery filling

1. Heat ghee in a vānali. Add chopped jackfruit.
2. Lower heat and cook well.
3. Add grated jaggery. Mix well and stir till mixture thickens.
4. Divide jackfruit jam into 6 equal portons.

Preparation of the adai

1. Spread the rice paste with a ladle on the square banana leaves evenly. Place one portion of jackfruit-jaggery on the rice paste on each leaf and fold the leaves into two. Fold the sides over to form a square parcel. Steam for 5 minutes. Ilai adai is ready.

Variation: Alternatively, use sweet coconut filling (see page 189)

MASALA MANI KOḶUKATTAI

Spicy Rice Pearls

If you have excess dough left over after making koḷukattai, it can be used to make this tasty snack.

Makes: 2 servings
Serving size: 150 gms
Calories koḷukattai: 413

INGREDIENTS

Leftover koḷukattai dough ½ cup
Turmeric powder ¼ tsp

Spices for grinding
Dhania/Coriander seeds 1 tsp
Grated fresh coconut 1 tbsp
Dried red chilli 1

Seasoning
Oil 1 tbsp
Mustard seeds ½ tsp
Curry leaves 1 sprig

METHOD

1. Roast coriander seeds, coconut and red chilli in a vānali/wok over medium heat, till aromatic. Grind to make a fine powder.
2. Smear palms with oil and make small berry-sized balls of leftover dough. Steam in a steamer for about 10 minutes.
3. Heat oil in a vānali/wok. Splutter mustard seeds over medium heat. Stir in curry leaves.
4. Mix in ground spice powder and turmeric powder.
5. Add steamed koḷukattai and sauté for 1–2 minutes.

ILAI VADAM Steamed Rice Papers

Makes: 30 servings
Serving size: 150 gms
Calories per serving: 697

INGREDIENTS

Raw rice 500 gm
Water 2½ cups
Salt ¾ tsp + ¼ tsp
Green chillies 5
Jeera/Cumin seeds ¼ tsp
Asafoetida powder ¼ tsp
Banana leaves, cut into hand-sized pieces

METHOD

1. Wash rice and soak in water for about 4 hours.
2. Drain and grind to make a fine batter, using 2½ cups of water. When held between 2 fingers, the batter should be smooth and not grainy.
3. Add ¾ tsp of salt, mix well and ferment overnight.
4. Grind green chillies with ¼ tsp of salt to a fine paste.
5. Mix cumin seeds, asafoetida powder and ground chillies into the fermented batter.
6. Place a piece of banana leaf on the counter. Pour a small ladle of batter in the centre of the leaf. Spread the batter using a circular motion with the back of the ladle till it covers the whole leaf.
7. Boil water in an idli steamer. Fit the perforated plate[1] of an idli cooker.
8. Place the leaf on the plate in the steamer and steam for 1–2 minutes. (The approximate cooking time of one ilai vadam in a steamer is equal to the time taken to spread the batter on the leaf.)
9. Remove leaf from steamer.
10. Serve as it is or peel ilai vadam off the leaf.

Note: Ilai vadams are peeled and dried on a clean sheet. These are stored and can be used throughout the year, eaten both roasted and fried. However, the freshly steamed ones are so tasty that these are specially made as a favourite tiffin.

[1] *The perforated plate for steaming comes with an idli maker and is available in stores.*

SEVAI Rice Vermicelli

Makes: 4 servings
Serving size: 150 gms
Calories per serving: 430

INGREDIENTS

Parboiled rice 2 cups
Water to grind 1 cup
Salt ½ tsp
Coconut or vegetable oil 1 tbsp (do not use sesame oil)

METHOD

1. Wash rice and soak in water for about 4–5 hours.
2. Drain and grind rice with 1 cup of water to make a fine batter of pouring consistency like a dosai batter.
3. Place a heavy-bottomed vessel over low heat. Add 1 teaspoon of cooking oil, pour in the ground batter, stir continuously with a ladle for about 3–4 minutes, so that no lumps are formed.
4. Remove from heat, cool for a few seconds, and with a wet hand make dough into balls to fit the mould of sevai press.
5. Keep a steamer ready filled with enough boiling water. Add dough balls.
6. As dough balls are cooked they rise to the surface.
7. Remove dough balls one by one and press through the mould.
8. Keep a plate below the mould to collect the sevai.
9. Pour a teaspoon of ghee over the sevai and separate the sevai strands with a fork.
10. Serve at room temperature with mor kuḷambu (see 'Kuḷambu/Sambar') and crisp, fried appalam.

MILAGU SEVAI Pepper and Rice Vermicelli

Makes: 4 servings
Serving size: 150 gms
Calories per serving: 438

INGREDIENTS

Ghee and oil mixed 1 tbsp
Black pepper, coarsely powdered 1 tbsp
Jeera/Cumin seeds ½ tbsp
Sevai 2 cups (see recipe for Sevai)
Salt to taste

Seasoning
Mustard seeds ½ tsp
Dried red chilli 1. Curry leaves 1 sprig

METHOD

1. Pound pepper and cumin to a semolina consistency.
2. Place prepared sevai on a plate.
3. Heat ghee–oil mix in a vānali/wok. Splutter mustard seeds, red chilli and curry leaves, powdered pepper, cumin and pour over the sevai.

TENGĀI SEVAI Coconut and Rice Vermicelli

Makes: 4 servings
Serving size: 150 gms
Calories per serving: 537

INGREDIENTS

Sesame oil 2 tbsp
Cooked sevai 2 cups (see Sevai recipe)
Salt to taste

Seasoning
Mustard seeds ½ tsp. Dried red chillies 2
Black gram dal/Urad dal 1 tbsp
Curry leaves 1 sprig
Grated fresh coconut ½ cup
Asafoetida powder ½ tsp

Garnish
Cashewnuts 6–8, broken

METHOD

1. Wash urad dal and soak it in water for about 15 minutes. Drain and set aside.
2. Heat oil in a vānali/wok. Fry cashewnuts over medium heat, till golden-brown. Slot out.
3. Splutter mustard seeds in the same vānali/wok. Add red chillies, soaked dal and stir in curry leaves. Fry till dal turns light golden brown. Add salt and asafoetida.
4. Add grated coconut and fry, till it is aromatic and turns slightly brown.
5. Add sevai. Switch off heat. Mix well with a fork.
6. Garnish with fried cashewnuts and serve.

ELUMICHAMPALA SEVAI Lime and Rice Vermicelli

Makes: 4 servings
Serving size: 150 gms
Calories per serving: 468

INGREDIENTS

Sesame oil 2 tbsp
Cooked sevai 2 cups (see recipe for Sevai)
Lime 1. Salt to taste

Seasoning
Mustard seeds ½ tsp
Black gram dal/Urad dal ½ tsp
Bengal gram dal/Chana dal 1 tsp
Dried red chillies 2
Asafoetida powder tsp
Turmeric powder 1 pinch
Curry leaves 1 sprig

Garnish
Cashewnuts 6–8, broken
Chopped coriander leaves 1 tbsp (optional)

METHOD

1. Heat oil in a vānali/wok. Fry cashewnuts over medium heat, till golden-brown. Slot out and set aside.
2. Splutter mustard seeds in the same vānali/wok. Add the rest of the seasoning and fry till dals turn golden, put off the flame.
3. Add sevai, salt, then add lime juice. Mix well.
4. Garnish with fried cashewnuts and coriander leaves (optional).

RAVĀ DHOKLA Steamed Semolina Dhokla

Makes: 22 servings
Serving size: 150 gms
Calories per serving: 402

INGREDIENTS

Semolina 1 cup
Fresh curd 1 cup, whisked smooth
Salt ¼ tsp
Eno Fruit Salt Powder[1] 1½ tsp
Plates with 1-inch rim 2
Ghee for smearing 2 tbsp

METHOD

1. Whisk semolina with curd and salt and set aside for about an hour.
2. Smear two plates well with ghee on the base and sides.
3. Keep an idli cooker or a steamer ready. Put one greased plate on it and cover, to warm it.
4. Take half the semolina-curd batter and add ¾ tsp of Eno Fruit Salt. Mix quickly and pour on to warm plate. Steam for about 20 minutes.

Seasoning

Oil 2 tsp

Mustard seeds 1 tsp

Asafoetida powder 2 pinches

Green chillies 2, chopped fine

Sugar ¼ tsp

Water 2 tbsp

Curry leaves 1 sprig

Garnish

Coriander leaves 3–4 stems, chopped

5. Remove plate from the steamer and cut the dhokla into 1-inch x 1-inch squares or any other shape. Arrange dhokla on a serving plate.
6. Repeat process with second plate.
7. Heat oil in a vānali/wok. Splutter mustard seeds over medium heat. Add remaining seasoning and fry for a few seconds. Mix in sugar and 2 tbsp of water. Pour evenly on dhokla.
8. Garnish with coriander leaves.

[1] *Eno's Fruit Salt Powder is a popular antacid brand available in the market.*

KHATTA DHOKLA Sour Curd Dhokla

Makes: 4–5 servings

Serving size: 150 gms

Calories per serving: 491

INGREDIENTS

Rice ¾ cup

Black gram dal/Urad dal ¼ cup

Sour curd 1 cup, whisked smooth

Water ½ cup

Bengal gram dal/Chana dal 2 tsp

Fenugreek seeds ½ tsp, lightly crushed

Black pepper powder ½ tsp (optional)

Green chilli paste ½ tsp

Oil 1 tbsp

Salt ½ tsp

Plates with 1-inch rim 2

Red chilli powder ¼ tsp

Jeera/Cumin seeds ½ tsp

Ghee for smearing on plate 1 tbsp

METHOD

1. Wash rice, drain and spread out to dry on a cloth in the shade.
2. Wipe urad dal with a wet cloth and dry.
3. Grind rice and dal separately to make a coarse powder. Mix rice and dal powders well and transfer to a vessel.
4. Whisk the curd with ½ cup of water, till smooth. Add to vessel and mix to make a thick batter of pouring consistency.
5. Ferment in a warm place for 6–8 hours or overnight.
6. Add chana dal, fenugreek seeds, pepper (optional), green chilli paste, oil and salt.
7. Smear the 2 plates well with ghee on the base and sides.
8. Keep an idli cooker or a steamer ready.
9. Pour half the batter on each of the plates to come halfway up the plate, to allow the batter to rise.
10. Mix red chilli powder and cumin seeds and sprinkle over batter.
11. Place the plates in the steamer and steam for 5–7 minutes.
12. Remove plates from the steamer and cool. Sprinkle ghee over the steamed dhoklas. Cut into squares or diamonds. Gently remove them from the plate with a spatula.
13. Serve hot with any chutney.

KUḶAL PUTTU

Steamed Rice Crumble

Makes: 4 servings
Serving size: 150 gms
Calories per serving: 622

INGREDIENTS

Parboiled rice 200 gm
Salt ½ tsp
Water ½ cup
Grated fresh coconut ¼ cup

If you have excess dough left over after making koḷukattai, it can be used to make this tasty snack.

METHOD

1. Wash rice and soak it in water for about 2 hours. Drain thoroughly by spreading on a cloth.
2. Grind rice to a semolina consistency.
3. Mix salt with ½ cup of water and sprinkle gradually into the rice flour. Mix well to a consistency that it can be moulded in your fist, but when you touch it collapses like a sand ball. If flour is too dry add a little more water.
4. Put a fistful of moist flour into the puttu kuḷal (bamboo cylinder). Sprinkle 1½ tsp of grated coconut followed by another fistful of moistened flour. Repeat layering, till you reach the top of the puttu kuḷal.
5. Close with its lid and steam for 7–8 minutes.

Variation: Rāgi Puttu (Steamed Millet Crumble): Mix rāgi flour with half the quantity of parboiled rice flour and follow the process like that of kuḷal puttu.

SWEET PUTTU

Jaggery Rice Crumble

Makes: 10 servings
Serving size: 150 gms
Calories per serving: 1068

INGREDIENTS

Rice 2 cups
Turmeric powder 1 pinch
Water 1 cup
Salt 1 pinch
Ghee 2 tsp
Cashewnuts 6, broken
Grated jaggery 1 cup
Powdered cardamom ½ tsp
Grated fresh coconut 5 tbsp

Rice, in the Indian consciousness, as also in many Southeast Asian countries including Japan, is considered sacred. It symbolizes fertility, and hence a dish made of rice is the central offering in a coming-of-age ritual. The puttu for the ritual is a sweet dish made by steaming moistened rice powder. The rice is slightly dampened, pounded, mixed with a thick jaggery syrup and steamed. It is distributed to all the guests, especially young girls. Oil for an oil bath as well as a fragrant bath powder made with whole mung dal and herbs is also distributed on this occasion.

Puttu is still popular in many villages in Tirunelveli. Several housewives make it on a regular basis for sale.

METHOD

1. Wash rice and soak in water for about 30 minutes. Drain and spread on a cloth to dry in the shade.
2. Grind rice to make a fine powder.
3. Roast rice flour over low heat, till it turns a light brown and sieve twice.
4. Heat 1 cup of water with turmeric powder and salt and cool.
5. Sprinkle the cooled water gradually into the roasted rice flour to make a moist, loose flour. It should not form a dough.
6. Sieve the flour on to a cloth, tie the cloth into a pouch and place it in a steamer for about 10 minutes.
7. Remove from steamer and crumble. There should be no lumps. Set aside to cool. The texture should be fluffy and grainy yet slightly moist.
8. Heat ghee in a vānali/wok. Fry cashewnuts over medium heat, till golden brown. Slot out.
9. Make jaggery syrup to three-thread consistency. (See Pre-Cooking Processes).
10. Pour half the jaggery syrup into a clean vānali/wok. Sprinkle rice flour, stirring continuously. Add remaining jaggery syrup a little at a time and mix well. The end product should be powdery but moist. Mould the puttu in your hand and form a pyramid. After 10 minutes it will crumble.
11. Mix in powdered cardamom, fried cashewnuts and grated coconut.
12. Put the puttu into small containers and distribute/serve.

THE DELECTABLE DOSAI

Some words have their origins in what is known as 'manipravālam' (literally, pearls and corals strung together), a language formed from a combination of Sanskrit and Tamil words. Thus the origin of the popular word dosai is dwiosai, which is also onomatopoeic, mimicking the hissing sound of the batter as it is poured over the hot griddle and once again making the same sound when it is turned over to cook the other side. Dwi and osai mean two sounds.

Outside India, the dosai is called a pancake. This is a misnomer. Some dosais do indeed resemble a pancake, meaning they are round and soft, but there are many others, which look and taste different. This is because dosai is made from a different combination of ingredients. Hence the textures and tastes vary. Ravā dosai made from semolina has a lacy, crêpe-like look and quality and is even made in a different way on the griddle. Neer dosai is extremely fine and soft in texture with a gossamer appearance.

DOSAI

Makes: 30 servings
Serving size: 150 gms
Calories per serving: 330

INGREDIENTS

Parboiled rice 1 cup
Raw rice 1 cup
Water ¾ cup + 1½ cup
Black gram dal/Urad dal ¾ cup
Fenugreek seeds ½ tsp
Salt 1½ tsp
Ghee and oil mix for frying ¼ cup

Notes:

1. While making dosai it is important to regulate the heat.

2. Dosai covers with a handle on top are available in the market.

Guna pātam says:
Dosai: Reduces the anger that arises out of biliousness and wind and phlegm problems.

Sambar Dosai (now made mostly in temples, is called Kovil Dosai): Prepared with asafoetida, pepper, ginger and curry leaves, it will cure disorders caused by phlegm, biliousness and the imbalance of wind.

METHOD

1. Wash both varieties of rice with fenugreek seeds and soak together in water for about 4 hours. Wash dal separately and soak in water 3 hours later. Urad dal should soak for only 30 minutes.
2. Drain dal and grind, sprinkling water now and then with ¾ cup of water to make a smooth, fluffy batter (see Pre-Cooking Processes).
3. Drain rice and grind with 1½ cups of water to make a fine batter.
4. Combine both batters. Add salt and beat or whisk rapidly with a wooden ladle. It should have a thick pouring consistency.
5. Cover and set aside to ferment for 8–12 hours.

To make kal dosai:

1. Keep griddle over medium heat. If the griddle is ready, when a little water is sprinkled, it should sizzle.
2. Smear griddle with oil with a clean cloth rag or a slice of brinjal/raw banana with stalk.
3. Pour a ladle of batter in the centre of the griddle, spread with the back of the ladle to form a thin round shape. Cover dosai with a lid. Open after half a minute, turn over and cook the other side for 2 seconds. Remove dosai. This dosai should be fluffy and soft.
4. After making every dosai, wipe the griddle with the cloth.

To make the more popular crisp dosai/murugal dosai:

1. Prepare the griddle. When hot, smear with oil and spread the batter.
2. Wait for 1 minute. The top will appear well cooked and dry. When the dosai can be lifted easily with the spatula, sprinkle oil around the dosai and all over on top.
3. After a minute turn over and cook for 1 minute. Allow it to turn a golden colour.
4. Remove with a spatula.

MASALA DOSAI Dosai with Potato Filling

Makes: 8 servings
Serving size: 150 gms
Calories per serving: 443

INGREDIENTS

Dosai
Dosai batter (see Pre-Cooking Processes)
Ghee and oil mix for frying ¼ cup

Filling
Potatoes (medium) 3
Onions (medium) 3 (optional)
Salt ¾ tsp
Turmeric 1 pinch
Coriander leaves 2–3 sprigs, chopped
Water 2–3 tbsp

Seasoning
Oil 1 tbsp
Mustard seeds ½ tsp
Green chillies, slit 3–4
Curry leaves 1 sprig

METHOD

Filling

1. Scrub potatoes and boil them in their jackets, till tender. Peel and mash coarsely.
2. Peel and slice onions long and fine.
3. Heat oil in a vānali/wok. Splutter mustard seeds over medium heat. Stir in the green chillies and curry leaves.
4. Add onions and sauté till translucent (optional).
5. Add potatoes, turmeric, salt and coriander leaves and mix well. Pour water and cook for a minute or two and remove from heat.

Assembling the dosai

1. Prepare an iron griddle to cook dosai (see kal dosai).
2. Pour a ladle of batter in the centre of the griddle. Spread with the back of the ladle to form a thin, round shape. Cover dosai.
3. Open after 30 seconds and pour 1 tsp of ghee and oil around the edges and a little all over.
4. When the base is crisp and golden brown, spread 2 tbsp of filling on one half of the dosai. Fold the other half over the filling and serve with chutney.

Note: This dosai is not fried on both sides.

THE FROG TURNS INTO A PRINCE!

Menu cards nowadays flaunt many varieties of uttāppam, the thick, fluffy dosai. Originally, this version may have been created to make the leftover batter more palatable. To spice it up, a smart cook added pepper and cumin seeds or green chillies and curry leaves, made a thick dosai and named it uttāppam perhaps because it was poured like an āppam into hot oil!

Other chefs added onion, coconut, even a dash of jaggery to play on the notes and created new variations. Sometimes tomatoes, raisins, nuts along with white flour are added. Thus, a dish that used leftover batter became a sought-after dish in restaurants!

I must speak of Nandita again and her casual but appealing way with recipes, whipping up dishes in the blink of an eye. One such dish was the ravā–maida dosai, just a cup, with a teaspoon of paneer and a bit of salt in the batter. Spread the batter on a griddle, add finely chopped green chillies and coriander leaves, cover with a lid; when done, spread a teaspoon of curd on the dosai, sprinkle some grated potato (laccha) chips and sev, a few pieces of tomato, fold it and eat at once!

Her innocence and vitality seemed to be part of every dish that she made.

RAVĀ DOSAI Semolina Crêpe

Makes: 15 servings
Serving size: 150 gms
Calories per serving: 361

INGREDIENTS

Fine semolina 1 cup
Rice flour 1 cup
White flour/Maida ½ cup
Water 4–5 cups
Cashewnuts 5–6, sliced fine
Salt ¾ tsp
Ghee and oil mix for frying ¼ cup
Curry leaves 9–10
Green chillies 2–3, chopped fine
Ginger 1-inch piece, chopped fine
Jeera/Cumin seeds 1 tsp (optional)

METHOD

1. Mix semolina, rice flour and maida with 4–5 cups of water. The batter should have a thin pouring consistency. Set aside for about 10 minutes.
2. Add cashewnuts, salt, curry leaves, green chillies, ginger, and cumin seeds to the batter. Mix well.
3. Prepare an iron griddle to cook dosai (see Kal Dosai).
4. Take some batter in a steel cup and pour it evenly over the entire griddle. Lower heat and cook as given for dosai (see Kal Dosai).
5. With this batter you cannot make a perfect circle like an ordinary dosai. Do not attempt to spread the batter. When it is cooked, the surface will appear lacy and golden. Remove and serve.
6. If the batter thickens, you can add more water with a pinch of salt.

PREM PUNJA—DOCTOR, HOMEMAKER, HOSTESS, TEACHER

My collegemate and close friend Prem Punja was my first inspiration to try out new recipes. She not only taught me several dishes but also how to present food in an aesthetic manner. Playing hostess to her husband who was head of a leading multinational company, Prem had to entertain extensively. This made her devise ways to present food in an attractive and appetizing manner.

Prem was one of the kindest, most large-hearted of women. If you asked her for a recipe you would find the dish on your doorstep the very next day. I learned several Mangalorean delicacies such as neer dosai, sanna idli, palāpaḷa idli and Mangalore (basalaikeerai) kuḷambu from her. Whatever she knew she taught people very patiently till they understood completely.

NEER DOSAI Water Crêpe

Makes: 12–15 servings
Serving size: 150 gms
Calories per serving: 370

INGREDIENTS

Raw rice 1 cup
Water 2 cups + ¼ cup
Grated fresh coconut ½
Salt ¾ tsp
Ghee and oil mix for frying ¼ cup

METHOD

1. Wash rice and soak in water for about an hour. Drain and grind to make a fine batter with 2 cups of water.
2. Extract thick coconut milk from grated fresh coconut using ¼ cup of water (see Pre-Cooking Processes). Add to the batter with salt. Mix well.
3. Add extra water, if required, to make a batter of thin, pouring consistency.
4. Neer dosai is usually made on a non-stick pan with a small rim and a matching lid.
5. Pour a ladle of batter into the pan and tilt it around to form an evenly thin layer 7–10 inches in diameter. Cover and let it cook over medium heat for 1–1½ minutes.
6. Once the edges start curling up, remove at once. Turn dosai over a damp bamboo tray. Fold over dosai twice so that a triangle is formed. Serve.
7. Neer dosai must be pure white and soft. The surface will be perforated and appear lacy.

OATS DOSAI

Makes: 8 servings
Serving size: 150 gms
Calories per serving: 340

INGREDIENTS

Black gram dal/Urad dal 1 tbsp
Water 1 tbsp + 1 cup
Whole oats 1 cup
Salt ¼ tsp
Oil 1 tbsp

METHOD

1. Wash dal and soak it in 1 tbsp water for about 20 minutes.
2. Wash and soak oats in 1 cup of water.
3. Grind both together. It should have the consistency of a dosai batter.
4. Add salt, mix well and set aside for 1–2 hours.
5. Prepare an iron griddle to cook dosai (see Kal Dosai).
6. Pour a ladle of batter in the centre of the griddle and cook it on both sides as given for dosai (see Kal Dosai).

RĀGI DOSAI Coracana Crêpe

Makes: 8 servings
Serving size: 150 gms
Calories per serving: 241

INGREDIENTS

Rāgi flour 1 cup
Rice flour 1 tbsp
Okra 4
Water 1 tsp + ½ cup
Salt ¼ tsp
Jeera/Cumin seeds ¼ tsp
Green chillies 1–2, chopped fine
Curry leaves 1 sprig
Ghee and oil mix for frying ¼ cup

METHOD

1. Combine rāgi flour and rice flour.
2. Grind okra in a mixer-grinder with 1 tsp of water and mix into flours.
3. Add salt and ½ cup of water and beat well.
4. Stir in cumin seeds, curry leaves and green chillies.
5. Keep iron griddle on medium heat (see Kal Dosai).
6. Take some batter in a steel cup and pour it and spread quickly over the entire griddle. Lower heat and cook on both sides as given for dosai (see Kal Dosai).
7. With this batter you cannot make a perfect circle like an ordinary dosai. When it is cooked, the surface will be perforated and appear lacy.

TAKKĀLI DOSAI Tomato Dosai

Makes: 10–12 servings
Serving size: 150 gms
Calories per serving: 164

INGREDIENTS

Raw rice 1 cup
Water ½ cup
Tomatoes 2, large and ripe
Dried red chillies 1–2
Salt ½ tsp
Ghee and oil mix for frying ¼ cup

METHOD

1. Wash rice and soak in water for about 2 hours.
2. Deseed tomatoes. Chop tomatoes finely.
3. Drain rice and grind with ½ cup of water to a semolina consistency.
4. Add chopped tomatoes and red chillies and grind further to make a fine paste.
5. Add salt and mix well.
6. Set aside to ferment for about 8 hours.
7. Prepare an iron griddle to cook dosai (see Kal Dosai).
5. Pour a ladle of batter in the centre of the griddle. Spread with the back of the ladle to form a thin, round dosai. Cover with a dosai cover.
6. Open and pour 1 tsp of ghee and oil around the edges and a little in the centre.
7. When the base is cooked, turn over with a spatula and cook for a few seconds. Remove.

Variation: Mogga dosai is made in the same way, using sorghum (jowar) instead of rice.

AVAL DOSAI Beaten Rice Dosai

Makes: 10–12 servings
Serving size: 150 gms
Calories per serving: 282

INGREDIENTS

Raw rice ½ cup
Water ¼ cup + ½ cup
Beaten rice 1 cup
Salt ½ tsp
Ghee and oil mix for frying ¼ cup

METHOD

1. Wash raw rice and soak in water for about an hour.
2. Soak beaten rice in ¼ cup of water for about 20 minutes.
3. Drain raw rice and grind with ½ cup of water to a fine semolina consistency.
4. Add beaten rice to this along with any water not soaked up. Grind further to make a fine batter.
5. Add salt and mix well.
6. Ferment overnight or for about 8 hours.
7. If this dosai is required for breakfast, refrigerate immediately in the morning. Taste for salt and add little more if required.
8. Prepare an iron griddle to cook dosai (see Kal Dosai).
9. Pour a ladle of batter in the centre of the griddle as given for dosai (see Kal Dosai). Cover and cook for about a minute, turn over for a second and flip out.

PESARATTU Green Gram Dal Dosai

Makes: 8–10 servings
Serving size: 150 gms
Calories per serving: 155

INGREDIENTS

Split mung with husk 1 cup
Raw rice 2 tsp
Water 1¾ cups
Green chillies 5, chopped
Ginger 1½-inch piece, chopped
Salt ½ tsp
Ghee and oil mix for frying ¼ cup

METHOD

1. Soak mung with husk, and rice, in water for about 30 minutes.
2. Drain whole mung and rice and grind with green chillies, ginger and salt, gradually adding 1¾ cups of water, to make a grainy batter. (There is no need to ferment the batter.)
3. Prepare an iron griddle to cook dosai (see Kal Dosai).
4. Pour a ladle of batter in the centre of the griddle, spread well and cook on both sides as given for dosai (see Kal Dosai).

ĀPPAM

Āppam is a popular breakfast and tiffin item in south India. This is a dish that is common to all southern states. Each state makes it in a different way. If āppam is to be served at breakfast, soak rice and dal early in the previous afternoon, and grind in the evening. If served for tiffin, it should be soaked early morning and ground in the afternoon. This batter should be slightly more fermented than idli batter.

ĀPPAM–I Rice Hoppers

Makes: 15–20 servings
Serving size: 150 gms
Calories per serving: 197

INGREDIENTS

Raw rice 1½ cups
Black gram dal/Urad dal ½ tbsp
Water 1½ cups
Cooked rice ¾ cup
Yeast ¼ tsp
Salt ½ tsp
Oil for smearing
Sodium bicarbonate 1 pinch

METHOD

1. Wash raw rice and urad dal and soak in water for about 2 hours.
2. Drain and grind rice and dal with 1½ cups of water. Halfway through, add cooked rice and grind to make a fine paste.
3. Prepare yeast[1] and add salt.
4. Cover and set aside to ferment for about 8 hours.
5. Heat an āppam vānali/wok or āppam chatti (āppam pan). Wipe with a cloth puff smeared with oil. Pour a ladle of batter in centre of vānali/wok. Remove vānali/wok from the heat and holding the handles, swirl it so that the batter coats on all sides evenly.
6. If the batter is too thick add some water to give it a pouring consistency. Add a pinch of sodium bicarbonate and mix well.
7. Return to heat. Cover vānali/wok and cook for about 2 minutes. Āppam will come out of vānali/wok easily. Remove.
8. Repeat process with the remaining batter, smearing vānali/wok or āppam chatti with oil each time.

[1] *Preparation of yeast: Add 1 tsp of sugar to water that is warmer than room temperature, add a teaspoon of rice flour and keep in a warm place. The yeast should be added to the batter 1½ hours before making āppams.*

ĀPPAM—II Coconut-flavoured Rice Hoppers

Makes: 10–12 servings
Serving size: 150 gms
Calories per serving: 322

INGREDIENTS

Raw rice 1½ cups
Beaten rice/Poha cup
Black gram dal/Urad dal 1 tbsp
Water 1–1½ cups
Tender coconut water 2 tbsp
Sugar 1 tsp
Salt ½ tsp
Oil for smearing
Sodium bicarbonate ½ tsp only if necessary

METHOD

1. Wash raw rice, beaten rice and urad dal and soak in water for about 2 hours.
2. Drain and grind to make a batter of pouring consistency with 1–1½ cups of water.
3. Add tender coconut water, sugar and salt.
4. Cover and ferment for about 8 hours.
5. If the batter is too thick, add some water to give it a pouring consistency. If āppam is not soft enough add ½ tsp of sodium bicarbonate if necessary.
6. Heat āppam chatti or vānali/wok and make āppams (see Āppam—I recipe).

Variation: Another variety of āppam can be made in the same way by adding 1 tsp white flour/maida and ½ tsp semolina to the batter. Omit tender coconut water.

ĀPPAM—III Rice Hoppers with Parboiled Rice

Makes: 10–12 servings
Serving size: 150 gms
Calories per serving: 283

INGREDIENTS

Parboiled rice 1½ cups
Slightly sour curd ¼ cup
Water for soaking ½ cup
Beaten rice/Poha cup
Water for grinding 1½ cups
Salt ½ tsp
Sugar 1 tsp
Oil for smearing

METHOD

1. Wash parboiled rice and soak in curd whisked with ½ cup of water for about 2 hours.
2. Grind rice with beaten rice to a fine consistency with 1½ cups of water. Do not make batter too thin.
3. Add salt and sugar.
4. Cover and ferment for about 12 hours.
5. If batter is too thick, add some water to give a pouring consistency.
6. Heat āppam chatti or vānali/wok and make āppams (see Āppam—I recipe).

ADAI Mixed Dal Pancake

Makes: 4 servings
Serving size: 150 gms
Calories per serving: 180

INGREDIENTS

Parboiled rice ¼ cup
Raw rice ¼ cup
Red gram dal/Tuvar dal ½ cup
Bengal gram/Chana dal ¼ cup
Black gram dal/Urad dal ¼ cup
Green gram dal/Mung dal 1 tbsp
Grated fresh coconut 3 tbsp (optional)
Dried red chillies 3–4
Asafoetida powder ¼ tsp
Salt 1 tsp
Curry leaves 1 sprig
Ghee and oil mix cup

METHOD

1. Wash both types of rice and soak in water together for about an hour. Wash dals and soak in water separately for about an hour.
2. Drain rice and dals and grind with red chillies to make a coarse batter.
3. If using coconut, add now and grind.
4. Add asafoetida powder, salt and curry leaves and mix well. The batter need not be fermented.
5. Put an adai griddle over medium heat. Pour a ladle of batter in the centre and with the back of the ladle spread the batter into a thick circle. Make a small hole in the centre with the tip of the ladle. Pour 1 tsp of ghee and oil mix around the edges and a little in the hole in the centre.
6. When the edges turn golden brown and the top is cooked, loosen the edges with a spatula and turn it over. Add 1 tsp of oil around the edges and cook the other side, till well roasted.
7. Serve hot with butter, jaggery and any chutney.

Note: As the adai griddle is concave, when ghee is poured, it will automatically go to the centre of the madakku and cook the batter well. Adai can also be made on a dosai griddle.
Variation: Vegetables like amaranth, cabbage, carrot and radish can be grated and added to the adai batter for a change.

SEMIA UPPUMA Vermicelli Uppuma

Makes: 3 servings
Serving size: 150 gms
Calories per serving: 444

INGREDIENTS

Ghee 1 tbsp
Cashewnuts 7–8, broken. Vermicelli 1 cup
Water 2½ cups. Salt ½ tsp

METHOD

1. Heat 1 tbsp of ghee in a vānali/wok over medium heat, fry cashewnuts to a golden colour. Slot out.
2. Keep 2½ cups of water boiling in a vessel.
3. Add vermicelli to vānali/wok and fry to a light golden colour. Pour 2 cups of the boiling water on to the vermicelli, add salt, stir, and cook till it is done.

Seasoning
Ghee and oil mix 2 tbsp
Mustard seeds ½ tsp
Black gram dal/Urad dal 1 tsp
Dried red chilli 1
Green chillies 2–3, chopped fine
Ginger ½-inch piece, chopped fine
Curry leaves 1 sprig

Garnish
Chopped coriander leaves 1 tbsp (optional)

4. Lower heat. Test if it is well done (vermicelli should not stick together). If necessary add a few tablespoons of water and cook.
5. Garnish with coriander leaves and serve.

RAVĀ UPPUMA Softly Cooked Semolina with Spice

Makes: 3 servings
Serving size: 150 gms
Calories per serving: 366

INGREDIENTS

Semolina 1 cup
Water 3 cups
Ghee 2 tbsp
Lime juice ½ lime (optional)
Salt 1 tsp

Seasoning
Oil 1 tbsp
Mustard seeds 1 tsp
Black gram dal/Urad dal 1 tsp
Green chillies, chopped fine 2–3
Ginger, crushed ¼-inch piece
Asafoetida powder ½ tsp
Curry leaves 1 sprig
Cashewnuts 6, broken

Garnish
Lime juice ½ lime (optional)
Chopped coriander leaves 1 tbsp

METHOD

1. Toast semolina lightly in a vānali/wok over low heat. It should not change colour. Cool.
2. Keep 3 cups of water boiling in vessel.
3. Heat 1 tsp of ghee in a vānali/wok. Fry cashewnuts and slot out.
4. In the same vānali/wok take 1 tbsp of oil. Splutter mustard seeds over medium heat. Add remaining seasoning and fry for 30 seconds.
5. Add the boiling water to vānali/wok, add salt, and gently pour in semolina, stirring to avoid lumps.
6. Cook over medium heat, till all the liquid is absorbed. Cook over low heat for another minute. If the uppuma seems a little dry add a few tablespoons of water and cook for 30 seconds.
7. Add remaining ghee and stir to blend. Remove from heat. Cover for a few minutes.
8. Squeeze lime juice on the uppuma and fold well. Garnish with coriander leaves.
9. The uppuma should be soft.

Note: If semolina is of a very fine variety, reduce quantity of water.

RAVĀ PONGAL Semolina Pongal

Makes: 8 servings
Serving size: 150 gms
Calories per serving: 680

INGREDIENTS

Green gram dal/Mung dal ½ cup
Water 3 cups + 2 cups
Ghee ¾ cup
Cashewnuts 8, broken
Ginger 1-inch piece, chopped fine
Whole black pepper 1 tsp
Jeera/Cumin seeds 2 tsp
Asafoetida powder 1 pinch
Curry leaves 1 sprig
Semolina 1¼ cups
Salt ½ tsp

METHOD

1. Toast semolina in a vānali/wok without changing its colour. Keep aside.
2. Wash mung dal and cook in 3 cups of water till three-fourths done. Remove vessel from heat.
3. Heat 1 tbsp of ghee in a vānali/wok. Fry cashewnuts over medium heat, till golden. Slot out.
4. Add rest of seasoning to vānali/wok and sauté for about a minute.
5. Add 2 cups of water and bring to boil. Lower heat.
6. When water boils, add semolina gradually and stir simultaneously so as to avoid lumps. Add mung dal and simmer till pongal is cooked.
7. Mix in salt.
8. Add remaining ghee to cooked pongal and stir, till well blended. The pongal should be moist and soft.
9. Add fried cashewnuts to pongal.
10. Remove from heat and serve hot with chutney, pickle, or gojju.

KAMALA ORANGE AVAL UPPUMA

Orange-flavoured Beaten Rice Uppuma

Makes: 2 servings
Serving size: 150 gms
Calories per serving: 287

INGREDIENTS

Beaten rice 1 cup
Tender shelled green peas ½ cup
Salt ¼ tsp
Orange juice from a loose-jacket orange ½ fruit

METHOD

1. Soak beaten rice in water, till ready to use.
2. Heat ghee–oil mix in a vānali/wok. Sauté cumin seeds over medium heat. Add remaining seasoning and fry for 30 seconds.
3. Add green peas and sauté, till tender.
4. Drain beaten rice and add to pan with salt. Sauté for a few minutes.

Seasoning

Ghee and oil mix 1 tbsp

Jeera/Cumin seeds 1 pinch

Cloves 2

Whole green chillies 2, pricked with a fork

Cardamom 1, crushed

Garnish

Shredded orange from 1–2 peeled segments

Chopped coriander leaves 1 tbsp

5. Switch off heat, add orange juice and toss well.
6. Garnish with shredded orange segments and coriander leaves and serve.

MORKUḶ Savoury Buttermilk Mousse

Makes: 4–5 servings

Serving size: 150 gms

Calories per serving: 391

INGREDIENTS

Raw rice 1 cup

Water 2 cups + 4½ cups

Sour curd 1 cup, whisked smooth

Salt 1 tsp

Mormilagai[1] 2–3

Oil ½ tsp

Seasoning

Sesame oil 2½ tbsp

Dried red chillies 4

Mustard seeds ½ tsp

Black gram dal/Urad dal 1 tsp

Asafoetida powder ½ tsp

Green chillies 2

Curry leaves 2 sprigs

METHOD

1. Wash rice and soak in water for about an hour. Drain and grind to a fine consistency with 2 cups of water.
2. Whisk curd with 4½ cups of water, till smooth. Add salt.
3. Mix rice batter with whisked curd and beat well.
4. Heat oil in a big-sized vānali/wok. Splutter red chillies and mustard seeds over medium heat. Add remaining seasoning and fry, till dal turns golden brown.
5. Lower heat. Slowly pour in rice batter, stirring to prevent lumps.
6. Cook over medium heat, stirring often, till it is well cooked to the consistency of thick porridge and has a glaze.
7. Fry mormilgai in ½ tbsp oil over medium heat.
8. Add fried mormilgai to morkuḷ, mix well and serve hot.

Note: Kuḷ is an ancient Tamil word in use from 2 BCE for a porridge-like dish.

Variation: Morkali is a similar dish made with rice flour and curd (proportion 1:2) using only red chillies. It is cooked to a solid consistency, unlike morkuḷ, and can be cut into pieces and served.

[1] *Mormilagai are sun-dried green chillies which are previously soaked in curd and salt.*

FRIED SNACKS

Hot vadais just off the fire is a favourite with both adults and children. Here is a little children's ditty sung out enticingly to attract them.

Shuda shuda vadai shuda shuda vadai
Tattu mele ondru rendu shuda shuda vadai
Chinna chinna pappa sikramai vā vā
Shuda shuda vadai shuda shuda vadai

Hot hot vadai, hot hot vadai
On a plate one or two hot hot vadai
Come come little child, come soon little child,
Hot hot vadai, hot hot vadai

VADAI

Vadai is always round, slightly flattened and made from rice/dals in differ ent combinations. The word vadai derives from the word 'vattam', meaning round. Vadais when made with a hole in the centre resemble the Western doughnut. Vadais also have puffed centres but may vary in texture.

The batter for a vadai should be fluffy and well-aerated. Usually, a plantain leaf is used to make the vadai and to pat the batter. Sometimes, a piece of fine wet cloth can be used. The batter is slid into the oil gently to prevent splattering or breaking up the dough. The number of vadais in a batch will depend upon the size of the vānali used. Always mix the salt in the batter before making a batch of vadais. Salt tends to loosen the batter, so do not add salt to the batter at once.

MEDU VADAI Black Gram Dal Vadai

Makes: 16 servings
Serving size: 100 gms
Calories per serving: 1479

INGREDIENTS

Black gram dal/Urad dal 1 cup
Salt ¼ tsp
Green chillies 2–3, chopped fine
Ginger ½-inch piece, chopped fine
Curry leaves 1 sprig
Banana leaves or 12-inch muslin cloth pieces 2–3
Oil for deep-frying 2 cups

METHOD

1. Wash urad dal and soak in water for about 30 minutes.
2. Drain and grind dal to make a smooth thick batter. The water absorbed by dal while soaking is enough for grinding. If batter is thick, sprinkle a few drops of ice water now and then.
3. Add green chillies, ginger and curry leaves to the batter.
4. Keep a bowl of water ready to dip your finger in as you shape the vadais.
5. Keep oil for deep-frying in a vānali/wok over medium heat.
6. Add salt to enough dough to make a batch of 5–6 vadais.
7. Keep banana leaves ready. Place a lime-size ball of batter on a leaf and pack into 2-inch diameter 1-cm thick circles. Make a hole in the centre with the finger or with the end of the spoon. Invert this on to the wet forefingers of the other hand and slide in gently into hot oil. Fry for a minute and turn over. Remove after 1 minute. Make 4 or 5 vadais in the same way. See the vānali/wok is not overcrowded.

KEERAI VADAI Leafy Vadai

Makes: 16 servings
Serving size: 40 gms
Calories per serving: 110

INGREDIENTS

Black gram dal/Urad dal 1 cup
Methi leaves 50 gm
Cabbage 50 gm
Amaranth 100 gm
Oil
Banana Leaves
Chillies
Rice Flour 2 tbsp

METHOD

1. For amaranth—discard stalk and root and chop the leaves finely.
2. Grind ¾ cup of soaked and drained urad dal finely by sprinkling water. When fluffy add ¼ reserved dal and grind for 30 seconds.
3. Mix the chopped vegetables, chillies and 2 tsp of rice flour and salt in vadai batter and fry as given for medu vadai.

Note: If the batter is very thick, test it by frying one vadai. If the vadai is not light and fluffy, add a little water to batter. Do not add too much. If it is too watery, add a little rice flour. Vadai batter if left for too long absorbs more oil while frying. Use up vadai batter as quickly as possible.

TAYIR VADAI Black Gram Dal Vadai in Spiced Curd

Makes: 16 servings
Serving size: 100 gms
Calories per serving: 645

INGREDIENTS

Curd 2 cups, whisked smooth
Grated fresh coconut 2 tbsp
Green chilli 1
Salt ½ tsp
Medu vadai 16 (see Medu Vadai)

Seasoning
Oil 2 tsp
Mustard seeds ½ tsp
Curry leaves 1 sprig

Garnish
Chopped coriander leaves 2 tbsp

METHOD

1. Beat the curd and place in a bowl.
2. Grind coconut, green chilli and salt not too finely. Add to curd and mix well. Keep aside.
3. As soon as you remove a batch of vadais from the oil, drop them in warm water and remove immediately. Press gently between two slotted ladles to remove excess water. Add to curd.
4. When vadais absorb the curd and become soft, transfer to a plate and arrange neatly. Leftover curd on the plate should be poured over the vadais.
5. Heat oil in a vānali/wok. Splutter mustard seeds over medium heat. Stir in curry leaves. Pour evenly over the tayir vadais.
6. Garnish with coriander leaves.

Notes: Garnish with very thinly grated carrot (quarter of a carrot) along with coriander leaves. During the summer, mix 1 cup of milk with 1 cup of curd, to prevent vadai from turning sour.

ĀMAI VADAI Bengal Gram Dal Vadai

Makes: 15 servings
Serving size: 100 gms
Calories per serving: 1024

INGREDIENTS

Bengal gram dal/Chana dal 1 cup
Dried red chillies 2–3
Green chilli 1. Ginger ½-inch piece
Curry leaves 1 sprig
Asafoetida powder 1 pinch
Salt ¾ tsp
Banana leaves or 10-inch square muslin cloth pieces 2–3
Oil for deep-frying 2 cups

METHOD

1. Chop green chilli and ginger finely.
2. Wash chana dal and soak in water for about 2 hours. Drain. Reserving 1 tbsp of the dal, grind remaining dal and red chillies coarsely.
3. Add reserved dal, green chillies, ginger, curry leaves and asafoetida powder. Add salt to batter.
4. Shape the vadai and fry (see Medu Vadai). Turn over till both sides are golden. Do not make a hole in the centre of the vadai.
5. Make all the vadais in batches within a short time after the salt has been added to batter.

Note: This vadai is called masal vadai when onion is chopped fine and added to batter.

VAḶAIPŪ VADAI Banana Flower Vadai

Makes: 7 servings
Serving size: 100 gms
Calories per serving: 2545

INGREDIENTS

Banana flower 1½ cup, cut
Curd 1 tbsp
Bengal gram dal/Chana dal ¼ cup
Ginger 1 tsp
Green chilli 1
Salt ¼ tsp
Oil for deep-frying 2 cups
Banana leaf pieces 6-inch square 2–3

METHOD

1. Chop green chilli finely and ginger into fine juliennes.
2. Prepare banana flower (see Pre-Cooking Processes). Chop fine and immerse in water mixed with 1 tbsp of curd.
3. Wash chana dal, soak in water for about 30 minutes. Drain and grind coarsely without water.
4. Add chopped banana flower, green chilli, ginger and salt. Mix well.
5. Shape the vadai without a hole and fry as given for medu vadai (see Medu Vadai).

JAVVARISI VADAI Sago Vadai

Makes: 12–15 servings
Serving size: 100 gms
Calories per serving: 1210

INGREDIENTS

Sago 1 cup
Potato (medium) 1
Ginger ½-inch piece, finely chopped
Green chillies 2, finely chopped
Coriander leaves 3–4 sprigs, chopped
Lime juice ½ tsp
Peanuts, pounded coarsely cup
Salt ½ tsp
Oil for deep-frying 2 cups

METHOD

1. Wash sago and soak in enough water to cover ½-inch above sago for about 30 minutes. Drain excess water. Do not squeeze.
2. Scrub potato and boil with jacket, till tender. Peel and mash coarsely.
3. Combine sago with potato, cut ginger, chopped green chillies and chopped coriander leaves, lime juice, pounded peanuts and salt. Mix well to form a dough without mashing the potatoes further.
4. Divide into 12–15 equal portions. Shape with lightly oiled hands into rolls, round patties or into rectangles (4-inch x 2-inch) and place them on a very lightly oiled plate.
5. Put half the oil in a vānali/wok over medium heat. When hot, drop vadai gently one by one and deep-fry, till golden brown. Add more oil as required. Drain vadais well.
6. Serve hot with any chutney.

MYSORE VADAI

Makes: 20 servings
Serving size: 100 gms
Calories per serving: 1070

INGREDIENTS

Parboiled rice 1 cup
Red gram dal/Tuvar dal ½ cup
Dried red chillies 2. Ginger 1-inch piece
Salt ½ tsp
Curry leaves 2 sprigs
Chopped coriander leaves 2 tbsp
Oil for deep-frying 2 cups
Banana leaf pieces 2–3

METHOD

1. Wash rice and tuvar dal and soak together in water for about 2 hours. Drain and grind coarsely with red chillies and ginger.
2. Add salt, cut curry leaves and coriander leaves. Mix well.
3. Flatten vadai on a leaf or muslin cloth without making a hole. Fry as given for medu vadai (see Medu Vadai).

KORA VADAI Green Gram Dal Vadai

Makes: 16 servings
Serving size: 100 gms
Calories per serving: 1018

INGREDIENTS

Green gram dal/Mung dal ½ cup
Water 1 tbsp
Dhania/Coriander seeds ½ tsp, coarsely pounded
Jeera/Cumin seeds ½ tsp
Red chilli powder ½ tsp
Asafoetida powder ¼ tsp
Ginger ½-inch piece, crushed
Green chillies 2
Wholewheat flour 2 tsp
Salt ½ tsp
Coriander leaves chopped 1 tbsp
Muslin cloth 7 x 5-inches
Oil for deep-frying 2 cups

METHOD

1. Chop fine the green chillies and ginger.
2. Wash mung dal and soak in water for about 20 minutes. Drain and grind such that it is fine yet grainy to the touch with 1 tbsp of water.
3. Mix all ingredients, except salt.
4. Keep oil in a vānali/wok over medium heat.
5. Lower heat. Add salt to dough. Take a small lime-size ball, flatten it thin, and slide it into the oil. Make 3 or 4 and drop them in oil. With a slotted ladle splash hot oil over the vadais. These will puff up like little puris. Turn over and remove.
6. Serve hot.

MUNDIRI PARUPPU VADAI Cashewnut Vadai

Makes: 18 servings
Serving size: 100 gms
Calories per serving: 1168

INGREDIENTS

Cashewnuts 250 gm
Rice flour ½ cup
Bengal gram flour/Besan 2 tbsp
Green chillies (long) 2
Ginger ½-inch piece
Coriander leaves 2 stems
Salt ¾ tsp
Cotton/Cheese cloth 6-inch square
Oil for deep-frying 2 cups

METHOD

1. Chop fine green chillies, ginger and coriander leaves.
2. Soak cashewnuts in water for about 2 hours. Drain and grind coarsely.
3. Mix rice flour and besan with ground cashewnuts.
4. Add green chillies, ginger, coriander leaves and salt. Mix well. Divide into equal portions.
5. Take a portion of vadai dough and flatten it on a piece of damp thin cotton/cheese cloth into a 2-inch disc. Gently remove from the cloth and fry in batches of 4 vadais until golden.

PUḶUNGAL ARISI VADAI Parboiled Rice Vadai

Makes: 8–10 servings
Serving size: 30 gms
Calories per serving: 46

INGREDIENTS

Uncooked parboiled rice ½ cup
Curd ½ cup
Fresh grated coconut 3 tbsp
Coriander leaves 3 tbsp
Green chillies 2
Asafoetida 1 tsp
Salt to taste
Cooking oil for frying ½ cup

METHOD

1. Soak the boiled rice in curd overnight or for 8 hours.
2. Using a thin cloth or a tea strainer, allow the soaked rice to drain the yoghurt. This should take 2 hours.
3. Grind coconut, green chilies, salt and asafoetida to a fine paste. Do not add water. Add the drained yoghurt from the rice.
4. Add the drained rice and grind to a fine paste. Use the drained curd for moisture. Do not add water.
5. Check for salt.
6. The consistency of the batter must be like that of soft butter.
7. Divide the dough into 8–10 equal sized balls, flatten them on a banana leaf like thin discs (around 4 cm diameter). Do not flatten the edges.
8. Deep fry the flattened vadais in hot oil until it puffs up like puris.
9. Serve hot with milagāi podi or as is.

VAḶAIKKAI BAJJI Plantain Bajji

Makes: 18 servings
Serving size: 100 gms
Calories per serving: 1203

INGREDIENTS

Plantain 2

Batter
Bengal gram dal/Chana dal 1 cup
Black gram dal/Urad dal ¼ cup
Red gram dal/Tuvar dal ¼ cup
Green gram dal/Mung dal 3 tbsp
Rice 1 tbsp. Salt ¾ tsp
Asafoetida powder ¼ tsp
Oil for deep-frying 2 cups

METHOD

1. Peel plantain and cut into two. Cut the two halves into lengthwise pieces. These will be rectangular.
2. Grind all dals with rice to make a fine powder.
3. Mix rice–dals powder with salt and asafoetida. Gradually add 1–1¼ cups of water to make a dipping batter.
4. Heat oil in a vānali/wok on medium heat.
5. Dip sliced plantain in the batter and coat well.
6. Deep-fry bajji in batches.
7. Serve hot with any chutney.

Variation: Potato peeled and cut into wafers can be made in the same way.

Note: This is a traditional bajji, which will keep for several days.

VEGETABLE PAKODA

Vegetable Fritters

Makes: 2–3 servings
Serving size: 100 gms
Calories per serving: 1164

INGREDIENTS

Bengal gram flour/Besan 1 cup
Water ¼ cup
Fenugreek leaves 3 tbsp, chopped
Carrot, beans, cauliflower, pālak and cabbage 1 cup
Green chillies 4, finely chopped
Ginger 1½-inch piece, finely chopped
Dried pomegranate seeds 1 tsp
Salt ½ tsp. Oil for deep-frying 2 cups

Use a combination of carrots, French beans, cauliflower, cabbage and a few pālak leaves. Chop carrot, beans and cauliflower into small bits. Chop cabbage and pālak very fine.

METHOD

1. Cut carrot, beans, and cauliflower into small bits; chop cabbage and pālak fine.
2. Cut ginger and green chillies to fine pieces.
3. Mix flour, water, vegetables, ginger, green chillies and dried pomegranate seeds with salt into a thick batter.
4. Heat oil in a vānali/wok over medium heat.
5. Take batter in 4 fingers and deep fry in hot oil. This will make a 4-inch long pakoda. When half cooked, remove, cool, break into 2 or 3 pieces and keep aside. When needed, fry again till crisp and serve.

NEER MOR BONDA Green Gram Dal Bonda in Buttermilk

Makes: 25 servings
Serving size: 100 gms
Calories per serving: 471

INGREDIENTS

Green gram dal/Mung dal ½ cup
Green chilli 1
Ginger ¼-inch
Salt ¼ tsp
Very sour curd 2 tbsp
Cold water 4 cups
Oil for deep-frying 1 cup

Seasoning for the water
Jeera/Cumin seeds ¼ tsp
Curry leaves 1 sprig
Salt 2 pinches

METHOD

1. Soak mung dal for 30 minutes.
2. Drain and grind with green chilli and ginger to a fine batter.
3. Keep oil for deep-frying in a small vānali/wok over medium heat. Add salt to batter and mix. Make 4–5 cherry-sized balls and drop into oil. When they puff up, turn over. Remove immediately. Drop into cold water.
4. Take 2 cups of soaked water, add curd and blend with 2 pinches of salt to make a thin buttermilk.
5. Keep oil in a vānali/wok over medium heat. Splutter cumin seeds and curry leaves. Pour over buttermilk.
6. Drop the bondas into buttermilk.
7. Serve bondas with buttermilk in bowls.

PATTĀNI BACHKA[1] Green Pea Bachka

Makes: 2–3 servings
Serving size: 100 gms
Calories per serving: 1007

INGREDIENTS

Bengal gram flour/Besan ½ cup
Rice powder 2 tbsp
Salt ½ tsp
Chopped coriander leaves 1 tbsp
Green chilli ½ tsp, chopped fine
Shelled, fresh tender green peas 1 cup
Oil for deep-frying 2 cups

METHOD

1. Combine all ingredients, except green peas. Gradually add ¼ cup of water to make a batter of pouring consistency. Crush green peas lightly and add to batter.
2. Keep a flat frying pan on medium heat and pour oil to 1-inch depth.
3. When oil is hot, pour a ladle of batter into pan. Spread to 4–5 inches round. Splash hot oil in the pan over the bachka 2 or 3 times till it is well done.
4. Remove and serve hot.
5. Repeat for the remaining batter, adding oil to the pan as required.

[1] *Bachka when fried resembles a honeycomb.*

MAKAI VADAI Corn Patties

Makes: 4–5 servings
Serving size: 100 gms
Calories per serving: 163

INGREDIENTS

Cooked rice ½ cup
Tender corncobs 5
White flour/Maida 2 tbsp
Semolina 1 tbsp
Coriander leaves 1 tbsp
Green chillies 2–3
Fresh curd 2 tbsp, whisked smooth
Salt ½ tsp
Oil 2 tsp
Leaves of corncobs to wrap the patties 20

METHOD

1. Chop green chillies and coriander leaves finely.
2. Grate the corn kernels and set aside.
3. Mix the grated corn with remaining ingredients.
4. Smear some oil on the corn leaves.
5. Spread a little mixture on each leaf and fold it over to form a triangle.
6. Put an iron griddle over medium heat. Smear with a little oil. When hot, place 2 or 3 corn leaf parcels fastened with a toothpick on the griddle and roast for 5 minutes, till light brown spots appear on top. Repeat till the filling is over.
7. Remove and serve as parcels.
8. Serve hot with curd/cucumber pacchadi (see Pacchadis/Salads on Page 69).

TÉNKUḶAL AND MANOPPU

Crisp Salty Snacks Resembling Jalebis

Makes: 20–22 servings
Serving size: 100 gms
Calories per serving: 1166

INGREDIENTS

Rice flour 1 cup
Black gram dal flour ¾ cup minus 1 level tbsp
Salt ¾ tsp
Ghee 1 tbsp
Cumin seeds 1 tsp
Asafoetida powder tsp
Refined oil for frying 2 cups

METHOD

1. Mix asafoetida powder and salt in a cup of water.
2. Sieve rice flour and black gram dal flour together. Add cumin seeds and ghee and mix. Knead well into a firm dough by adding water little by little.
3. The dough should not be sticky to handle.
4. Heat oil in a vānali.
5. Insert the ténkuḷal filter in the slot of the press (the ténkuḷal disc has 3 circular punches).
6. Take big fistful of dough into the cylinder of ténkuḷal press and by making circular motion squeeze the dough to form 3-inch circles. Make 3 or 4 ténkuḷals. Reduce the heat to moderate after a minute. Turn the ténkuḷals to the other side and fry till sizzling subsides. Remove from oil and drain well.
7. Continue process with rest of dough.
8. Store in an airtight container. Shelf-life: 7–10 days.

Variation: Manoppu is made in the same way: substitute black gram dal flour with green gram/mung dal flour. A filter with star-shaped perforation is used for this.

RECIPES FROM OTHER REGIONS

REGIONAL CUISINE

It used to be said that one could understand India if one were to think of it as another Europe, for that was the only way that we could comprehend the immense diversity of the country. This diversity can be seen in the variety of cuisines seen in the different states that make up the union of India, in the cuisines of the various communities within those states.

Each regional vegetarian cuisine in India has its own special list of dishes. Many communities in Tamil Nadu are wholly vegetarian while other groups are strictly vegetarian on special days.

The list of regional recipes is long and extensive. I present those recipes that fall within the ambit of this book.

RECIPES FROM THE RĀJAPĀLAYAM RAJU FAMILIES

The Rājapālayam Rajas or Rajus are Telugu-speaking Kshatriyas who settled down in the county of Palayapalayam in the Tamil country during the time of the Vijayanagara kings, as early as 1483. With the conquest of Madurai, many of these warriors served under Chokkanatha Nayaka, and their valourous deeds were appreciated and rewarded by the king. More Rajas migrated from Andhra, near Vijayawada, in the mid-seventeenth century and settled down in Pudupalayam near Rājapālayam.

Traditionally deeply devout and cultured, the Rajas follow all religious rituals with great fervour and faith and are emotionally connected to many great temples in south India. Countless temples are being supported by their generosity and donations. They hold extensive annadānams during festivals at these temples and support many charitable and social causes.

My good friend Smt.Sudarsanamma Ramasubramanya Raja is a devout and pious person whose time is fully devoted to charitable activities like Sanskrit and Veda pathśālas, schools, orphanages, housing for tribals and most importantly, annadānam, the food offering to the needy on a daily basis. Yet she runs an immaculate and efficient kitchen in her home turning out many delicacies as a matter of course. An expert in the entire repertoire of Tamilian cuisine, the exciting twirl she gives common south Indian recipes makes her cooking unrivalled. I obtained many of the recipes in this section from her.

The Rājapālayam cuisine is a blend of the spiciness of Andhra cuisine with many Tamilian flavours. Their kuḷambus and gojjus have an interesting twist. Their pickles are unrivalled, most delectably their ennai māngāi and kadarankai urugai, virtual masterpieces.

The following three recipes make a combo. The starch of the millet is made tasty by the addition of the tangy citrus fruit-amaranth stew and the tomato salsa. This is a signature combo of the Rājapālayam Rajas.

RĀGI/KEPPAI URUNDAI Coracana Balls

Makes: 4 servings
Serving size: 100 gms
Calories per serving: 139

INGREDIENTS

Rāgi powder (Coracana powder) 1 cup
Black gram dal/Urad dal ½ cup
Salt Pinch
Tomato salsa

METHOD

1. Boil 1 cup of water in a vessel over high heat. Lower heat to medium and add rāgi powder gradually, stirring once or twice with a wooden ladle.
2. After a few minutes mixture will foam up.
3. Switch off heat and stir well so that no lumps are formed.
4. While still warm, wet your hands and make even-sized balls. Drop them into a bowl of cold water.
5. Cook urad dal to a soft consistency and mash. Add a pinch of salt.
6. Make tomato salsa.

Serve rāgi balls with urad dal and tomato salsa (see Takkāli Sutta Gojju below*).*

TAKKĀLI SUTTA GOJJU Tomato Salsa

Makes: 4 servings
Serving size: 100 gms
Calories per serving: 28

INGREDIENTS

Tomatoes 4 large
Green chillies 2
Dried red chillies 2
Dried citrus (dried nārtankāi) 1-inch (available in groceries in south India)
Curry leaves 1 sprig
Salt ½ tsp
Tamarind water ½ tsp (see Pre-Cooking Processes)

METHOD

1. Roast tomatoes on a gas flame over medium heat. Keep turning, till they are well roasted and peel is charred. Sprinkle with cold water and let them cool. Remove charred peel.
2. Roast green chillies over red-hot charcoal. Turn them a few times, till the skin starts splitting. Remove chillies from embers and wipe them. Cool and slice fine.
3. Roast red chillies on a griddle, till they turn dark and aromatic. Do not let them burn.
4. Mash tomatoes, green and red chillies and dried citrus with a wooden masher.
5. Add curry leaves and salt.
6. Add tamarind juice if you want it tarter.
7. Mix in a little water if the consistency is too thick.

NĀRTANKĀI–MULAIKEERAI MASIYAL

Citrus—Amaranth

Makes: 4 servings
Serving size: 100 gms
Calories per serving: 81

INGREDIENTS

Amaranth 2 bunches (100 stems to a bunch)
Salt ½ tsp
Dried citrus fruit (Nārtangai)[1] 1½-inch piece
Green chillies 4, chopped fine

Seasoning
Sesame oil 1 tbsp
Mustard seeds ½ tsp
Dried red chillies 2–3
Jeera/Cumin seeds ¼ tsp
Curry leaves 1 sprig
Tomato 1 large, deseeded and chopped

METHOD

1. Remove and discard thick stems of amaranth. Wash leaves and tender stems well. Chop fine.
2. Boil 2 tbsp of water in a vessel over medium heat. Add amaranth and salt and cook, till amaranth is tender. Add citrus fruit and green chillies and cook for a few minutes longer. Remove from heat and mash.
3. Heat oil in a vānali/wok over medium heat and splutter mustard seeds. Add remaining seasoning in the order given and then the tomato. Sauté for 1–2 minutes.
4. Cool and grind to make a fine paste. Add to cooked amaranth and simmer for about 2 minutes.
5. Remove from heat and serve.

[1] *Called nārtankāi in Tamil, its botanical name is* Citrus jhambhiri *and it is widely available all over south India from November to March. It is salted and dried and this version is available in grocery stores and prepared annually by many families at home.*

TENGĀI TAKKĀLI GOJJU Tender Coconut in Tomato Gravy

Makes: 4 servings
Serving size: 100 gms
Calories per serving: 254

INGREDIENTS

Tender coconut 1, medium sized
Tomatoes 4
Salt ½ tsp

Seasoning
Oil 2 tsp
Mustard seeds ½ tsp
Black gram dal/Urad dal ½ tsp
Green chillies 4, slit
Curry leaves 1 sprig

Spice Powders
Red chilli powder ¼ tsp
Sambar powder ½ –1 tsp (see Podis and Readymade Powders)
Turmeric powder ¼ tsp

METHOD

1. Scoop out tender coconut cream and chop into bite-size pieces (1½-inches).
2. Deseed tomatoes and cut fine.
3. Heat oil in a vānali/wok over medium heat. Splutter mustard seeds, sauté urad dal for ½ minute, stir in green chillies and curry leaves.
4. Add tender coconut, blend in spice powders and sauté for about 2 minutes.
5. Mix in tomatoes and salt and sauté for about 2 minutes more.
6. Serve hot.

RASAM WITHOUT DAL

Makes: 4 servings
Serving size: 100 gms
Calories per serving: 52

INGREDIENTS

Tomatoes 6
Turmeric powder ¼ tsp
Salt 1 tsp
Tamarind 1 berry-sized piece (optional)

Spice powder
Oil 2 tsp
Dried red chillies 2–3
Dhania/Coriander seeds 2 tsp
Bengal gram dal/Chana dal 4 tsp
Jeera/Cumin seeds 1 tsp
Whole black pepper 1 tsp
Asafoetida powder 1 pinch

Seasoning
Ghee 1 tsp
Mustard seeds ½ tsp
Curry leaves 1 sprig

METHOD

1. Blanch tomatoes (see Pre-Cooking Processes), peel and purée. Add turmeric powder and salt.
2. Heat oil in a vānali/wok. Fry spices over medium heat, till dal turns golden brown. Cool and grind to make a coarse powder.
3. Heat ghee in a heavy-bottomed vessel. Splutter mustard seeds over medium heat. Stir in curry leaves.
4. Pour in tomato purée and bring to a boil.
5. Stir in ground spice powder and boil for about 3 minutes.
6. Add enough water to make 4–5 cups of rasam and taste.
7. If more tartness is required, add a small berry-sized piece of tamarind to rasam and boil for about a minute.
8. Continue boiling, till rasam foams up and rises to the brim. Remove from heat.

RECIPES FROM TONDAIMANDALAM REGION

Speaking of groups that still follow the strict principles of a pure vegetarian ethos, we have to mention the Tondaimandalam Mudaliars, also called Pettai Mudaliars or Śaiva Vellālars, a prosperous community of landowners since the time of the Pallavas. The Pallava kings had given them the right to clear forests and establish habitations. This conferred on them the title of 'kādu vettiyar'. Once called Talavāi Mudaliars being foremost in battle, these accomplished men had the right to choose kings and to coronate them. They have also been in the forefront of politics from British times and had held high offices in the East India Company, giving rise to the saying, 'pettai mudal kottai varai' 'from community to the fort', meaning Fort St. George, the seat of the Tamil Nadu government.

Being a pious people, they worshipped at and patronized the temples where they settled. They are closely associated with important temples in and around Kānchipuram. Earliest and best known in this community is Tiru Kacchi Nambigal (twelfth century CE) who served the Lord at Sri Varadarāja Perumāl temple in Kānchipuram and who was believed to have conversed with the deity directly.

Tondaimandalam Mudaliars are patrons of the arts and run many charitable institutions. Being agriculturists, Pongal is their chief festival and is celebrated on a grand scale even today.

The vegetarian recipes of Tondaimandalam Mudaliars add a different dimension to vegetarian cuisine.

TENGĀIPAL TIRATTIPĀL Coconut Milk Halva

Makes: 15 servings
Serving size: 100 gms
Calories per serving: 471

INGREDIENTS

Coconuts 2
Cow's milk 2 litres
Sugar ¾ kg
Ghee 1 tbsp

METHOD

1. Extract milk from the coconuts twice (see Pre-Cooking Processes). Total extract should be 2 cups.
2. Place a heavy-bottomed vessel over medium heat. Add coconut milk and cow's milk and bring to a boil. Lower heat, simmer for about 20 minutes, stirring often to prevent milk from boiling over or burning at the bottom.
3. When milk has thickened, add sugar. Stir and mix well.
4. Continue to simmer over low heat, till milk thickens a little more. Add ghee and stir well.
5. When mixture reaches a semi-solid consistency and is still moist, remove vessel from heat and transfer to a serving dish.

TENGĀI PUTTU KALI Coconut Rice Kali

Makes: 8 servings
Serving size: 100 gms
Calories per serving: 357

INGREDIENTS

Parboiled rice 250 gm
Water to grind ½ cup
Sago 2 tbsp
Coconut ½
Jaggery 250 gm
Cardamoms 3
Ghee 2 tbsp + extra for greasing
Cashewnuts 10
Water to cook dough 1 cup
Plate with a 1-inch rim 1

METHOD

1. Wash rice and soak in water for about an hour. Drain and grind to make a fine batter with ½ cup of water.
2. Extract coconut milk (see Pre-Cooking Processes). Keep the thick and thin milk separate.
3. Grate cashewnuts into bits. Powder cardamoms.
4. Heat 1 tbsp of ghee in a vānali/wok. Fry cashewnuts over medium heat, till golden. Slot out.
5. Place 1 cup of water in a vessel and bring to a boil. Add thin coconut milk.
6. Add rice batter with sago, cook for 6 minutes and test if the dough is cooked, if not, simmer till dough is cooked. Stir frequently, to prevent lumps. Add 1 tbsp of ghee and stir.
7. Add jaggery and thick coconut milk.
8. Cook, till mixture leaves sides of vessel. Add powdered cardamoms and cashewnuts and turn off heat.
9. Grease a plate and spread prepared mixture evenly over it. Cool.
10. Cut into cubes or scoop out kali and serve.

PUTTARASI KALI[1] Sweet Black Rice Halva

Makes: 8 servings
Serving size: 100 gms
Calories per serving: 414

INGREDIENTS

Black rice (Burma arisi/puttarasi) 1 cup
Grated fresh coconut from 2 large coconuts
Sugar/grated jaggery 2 cups
Ghee 2 tbsp
Cardamoms 4

METHOD

1. Wash rice, drain well and dry in the shade. Grind to make a fine powder.
2. Powder cardamoms.
3. Extract milk twice from coconuts (see Pre-Cooking Processes). Keep aside.
4. Place a heavy-bottomed wide vānali/wok over high heat with ½ cup of water. Bring to a boil and add sugar/jaggery. Make a syrup of one-thread consistency (see Pre-Cooking Processes). If using jaggery, strain the syrup.
5. Mix rice flour with the thin coconut milk and stir, till the batter has a smooth pouring consistency.
6. Pour batter into hot sugar/jaggery syrup gradually, stirring all the while so that no lumps are formed.
7. Place vessel over medium heat and boil, till the batter is well cooked to a thick porridge.
8. Stir in the thick coconut milk and transfer to a stainless steel bowl which fits into a pressure cooker.
9. Pour 1 cup of water into the cooker. Place bowl on a trivet in the cooker. Close cooker and pressure-cook for 5–6 minutes after it reaches full pressure.
10. Allow pressure to fall and remove bowl from cooker. Transfer contents of bowl into a vānali/wok.
11. Place vānali/wok over low heat. Add ghee and powdered cardamoms. Stir and mix well. Transfer to a wide-mouthed stainless steel canister.
12. Serve warm.

[1] *The kali is like a sticky dough. It will stay fresh for up to 2 days at room temperature and 4–5 days in the refrigerator. Warm before serving.*

KADAMBA ŪRUKĀI Mixed Vegetable Pickle

Makes: about 1¼ kg servings
Serving size: 100 gms
Calories per serving: 145

INGREDIENTS

Tender chow-chow 1
Tender French beans 12
Potato 1, medium
Tender, very thin drumsticks 6
Bitter gourd 1
Yam 50 gm, peeled
Carrot 1, large
Cluster beans 15
Lime juice from 30–32 limes 2¾ cups
Salt 200 gm

Seasoning

Fenugreek seeds 2 tsp
Asafoetida powder ½ tsp
Red chilli powder ½ cup
Green chillies 20
Ginger 3x2-inch
Mustard seeds 2 tsp
Turmeric powder 2 tsp
Sesame oil ¾ cup

METHOD

1. Cut all vegetables into very thin matchstick-sized pieces.
2. Parboil each vegetable separately. Use the same water filtering after each vegetable is boiled. Vegetables should not be over cooked. Drain and spread out on a sterile white cloth and dry well in shade.
3. Slit green chillies and julienne ginger, set aside.
4. Heat a little sesame oil in a vānali/wok. Fry fenugreek seeds and asafoetida powder over medium heat. Grind to make a fine powder.
5. Strain lime juice in a steel vessel. Add salt and bring to a boil. Remove from heat. Cool and strain.
6. Mix green chillies, ginger, red chilli powder, fenugreek-asafoetida powder and lime juice with vegetables.
7. Heat remaining oil in a wok. Splutter mustard seeds over medium heat, stir in the turmeric powder, pour over pickle.
8. Store in clean, dry airtight jars for up to 3–4 months in the refrigerator or a week at room temperature.

Note: It is important that only tender vegetables are used for this pickle.

KONGUNĀDU RECIPES

Kongunādu, the region spread out around the Javvaji area, originally became the home of Andhra chieftains of the Vijayanagara kingdom. Nayak chieftains followed soon after, hence the presence of a large Telugu speaking population called Kammavārs in that region.

The Kammavars had been excellent warriors under the Chola kings. They, in fact, trace their lineage as far back as the time of the Mahabharata. Basically non-vegetarian, they practice vegetarianism for most days of the month. This has perhaps made them evolve a distinct vegetarian cuisine.

The recipes of Kongunādu have the flavour of three climatic zones. They use a variety of produce from these three regions—the plains, the forests and the mountains. The word 'kongu' means pollen and honey indicating a land full of flowers. The hills and the forests yielded honey and wild mangoes, the plains gave millets and a less glutinous wheat.

A variety of millets are grown in the area and lend themselves to tasty dosais like sorghum dosai (mogga dosai) and similar dishes made from bajri, kambu and rāgi. Their pickles are also slightly different in the mixture of spices they use. They present interesting variations of some of the common pickles that are to be found in the South.

PĀL VADAI Rice and Milk Vadai

Makes: 4 servings
Serving size: 100 gms
Calories per serving: 1110

INGREDIENTS

Parboiled rice 1 cup
Coconut ½, medium sized
Salt ½ tsp
Milk for grinding ½ cup + a few tbsp if needed
Banana leaves 4-inches square 2–3 pieces
Oil for deep-frying 2 cups

METHOD

1. Wash rice and soak in water for about 2 hours.
2. Grate coconut, taking care not to scrape the brown husk.
3. Drain rice and grind with coconut and salt to make a thick batter with ½ cup of milk, almost like a dough.
4. Divide batter into 16 portions and shape into balls. Place the balls on a lightly greased banana leaf and flatten with your fingers into 3-inch round puri.
5. Heat oil in a vānali/wok. Fry one vadai at a time over medium heat. t should puff up like a puri. Turn over and immediately remove. The colour of the puri should be creamy white and not golden. Drain and serve.

Variation: Puli Vadai–Method is the same. Grind coconut with cumin seeds ½ tsp, dried red chillies 5, curry leaves, tamarind 1 ½ packed tbsp, and salt ½ tsp. Fry vadais in the same manner.

PALUTHA PĀVAKĀI TOKKU Ripe Bitter Gourd Chutney

Makes: 4 servings
Serving size: 100 gms
Calories per serving: 757

INGREDIENTS

Ripe bitter gourd 150 gm
Oil 1 tbsp. Salt 1 tsp
Tamarind 15 gm

For Frying
Oil 3 tbsp
Dhania/Coriander seeds 80 gm
Black gram dal/Urad dal 80 gm
Bengal gram dal/Chana dal 80 gm
Dried red chillies 8
Curry leaves 1 sprig

METHOD

1. Wash ripe bitter gourd, drain thoroughly and cut into small pieces.
2. Heat 1 tbsp of oil in a vānali/wok. Fry gourd over medium heat.
3. Add salt and sauté, till water evaporates. Remove gourd from vānali/wok.
4. Heat oil in a vānali/wok. Add each ingredient for frying and fry separately. Remove and cool.
5. Grind fried ingredients to a coarse powder.
6. Add tamarind and bitter gourd grind further to make a chutney.

MILAGĀI IDLI Chilli-Flavoured Idli

Makes: about 35 servings
Serving size: 100 gms
Calories per serving: 323

INGREDIENTS

Batter
Parboiled rice 2 cups
Water 1 cup
Black gram dal/Urad dal 1 cup
Water ¾ cup
Sesame oil for frying 1½ tsp
Dried red chillies 6
Asafoetida powder ½ tsp
Sesame oil ½ cup

Seasoning
Sesame oil 1 tbsp
Mustard seeds 1 tbsp
Black gram dal/Urad dal 2 tbsp
Curry leaves 2 sprigs. Salt ½ tsp

METHOD

1. Wash rice and urad dal and soak in water separately for about 2 hours.
2. Heat 1 tsp of oil in a vānali/wok. Fry red chillies and asafoetida over medium heat, for 1 minute. Grind to make a coarse powder.
3. Drain urad dal and grind first to make a smooth, fluffy batter with ¾ cups of water. Grind as for idli (see Pre-Cooking Processes).
4. Drain rice and grind to make a slightly grainy, coarse batter with 1 cup of water.
5. Combine both batters in a large container. Add salt and stir with a wooden spatula.
6. Add ground red chillies-asafoetida powder and mix well.
7. Stir in ½ cup of sesame oil and set aside to ferment for 8–12 hours.
8. Heat 1 tbsp of sesame oil in a vānali/wok. Splutter mustard seeds over medium heat. Add urad dal and fry, till golden. Stir in curry leaves and pour on the batter.
9. Cook the idlis as per the Idli recipe.

MOR VADU MĀNGĀI Tender Mangoes in Buttermilk Pickle

Makes: ¾–1 kg servings
Serving size: 100 gms
Calories per serving: 67

INGREDIENTS

Tender mangoes 1½ kg
Curd, whisked smooth 6 cups. Salt 1 cup

Spice Powder
Dried red chillies 250 gm
Whole dried turmeric stick ½
Mustard seeds, powdered 1 tbsp

METHOD

1. Wash mangoes, drain and dry thoroughly in a kitchen towel.
2. Cut mangoes into quarters, removing seeds.
3. Beat curd with ½ cup of ice-cold water, till smooth and set aside.
4. Grind spice powder ingredients to a fine consistency. Stir in salt.
5. Mix ground spices with whisked curd.
6. Add cut mangoes and mix well.
7. Store in clean, dry airtight jars in the refrigerator for up to 6 months.

VADU MĀNGĀI

Tender Mango Pickle

Makess: 1–1¾ kgs servings
Serving size: 100 gms
Calories per serving: 48

INGREDIENTS

Tender mangoes 4 kg
Castor oil 2 tbsp
Mustard seeds, powdered 2 tbsp
Turmeric powder 2 tbsp
Red chilli powder 375 gm
Salt 500 gm

Tender mangoes (known as vadu) are baby mangoes varying 1-inch to 2½-inch. If some of the mangoes are too big remove them.

METHOD

1. Wash mangoes, drain and spread on a cloth to remove excess moisture.
2. Spread mangoes in a large shallow stainless steel basin and drip 2 tbsp of castor oil over mangoes. Mix with hands, turning mangoes over and over so that they are coated with oil.
3. Remove ½ cup of the measured salt and chilli powder and set aside.
4. Put half the mangoes in a stainless steel/ceramic container. Mix half of mustard powder, turmeric powder and chilli powder. Cover with 1 cup of salt.
5. Repeat process with rest of the mangoes. Add to the first batch.
6. Place a stainless steel lid or wooden plate directly on the pickle. Place a clean heavy weight on top of the lid.
7. On the third day, shake the mangoes well. The mangoes would by then have let the juices out. If there is too much juice, add reserved salt and chilli powder and shake again.
8. Shake daily for a week.
9. Store in clean, dry jars. This, when carefully handled, will have a shelf life of a year.

Note: This pickle is made in all south Indian states of Karnataka, Andhra Pradesh, Telagana, Tamil Nadu, and Kerala. The spices may vary a little.

KĀRA VADU MĀNGĀI Spicy Tender Mangoes

Makes: about 3 kg servings
Serving size: 100 gms
Calories per serving: 411

INGREDIENTS

Tender mangoes 2 kg, large
Salt as required
Sesame oil 3½ cups

Spices
Dried red chillies 500 gm
Dhania/Coriander seeds 125 gm
Jeera/Cumin seeds 125 gm
Asafoetida powder 1 tsp

METHOD

1. Wash tender mangoes, drain and dry thoroughly in a kitchen towel.
2. Slit mangoes into quarters, lengthwise from the top without separating the pieces.
3. Dry the spices in the sun and grind to a fine powder.
4. Measure spices in a cup measure.
5. Measure out twice the amount of salt and mix with ground spices.
6. Stuff mangoes with this powder.
7. Place mangoes in a large plate, with the cut portion facing upwards. Set aside, till the next day. Heat sesame oil and pour it over mangoes. Keep for 3 days.
8. Transfer mangoes to a clean, dry airtight jar.

Note: Shelf life of this pickle when refrigerated is 1 month.

UDUPI RECIPES

All of us are familiar with Udupi cuisine as we have patronized, at one time or another, the trademark Udupi hotels that are to be found in every corner of India. Udupi cuisine has become synonymous with good and easily available vegetarian food.

The origins of this cuisine can be traced to the Krishna temple at Udupi,Karnataka. The Krishna temple at Udupi was established by Madhvacharya himself who also set up eight maths which would rotate the management of the temple every two years. The daily temple feeding at the Krishna temple is a tradition that goes back several centuries. Everyone who comes to the temple regardless of caste or creed is fed. On normal days, between 5,000 and 7,000 people are fed, the number going up to 15,000 on festive days.

The priests of the temple who also doubled as cooks and servitors are all drawn from 100 villages around Udupi and are known as Sivahalli brahmins. The temple hosts the heads of the other maths during festival and commemorative days. As a mark of respect and hospitality the incumbent acharya would desire to serve a fine feast comprising very many courses of sweets and vegetables to his honoured guests. This was a challenge to the cooks in charge of the kitchen and very often they would rise to the occasion by preparing several variations of everyday dishes.

The Sivahalli Brahmins innovated with all that grew in the tropical rain region where they lived. They constantly experimented with different spices for rasam or diverse ways of making vegetable dishes, sweets or tiffin. It is this constant experimentation that has made Udupi cuisine a hallmark of excellence. We can recognize Udupi cuisine in the generous use of coconut, jaggery and coconut oil.

KĀYA RASA Gravied Vegetables

Makes: 4 servings
Serving size: 100 gms
Calories per serving: 209

INGREDIENTS

Bitter gourd 2 or Okra 10
Oil ½ cup (if required)
Tamarind 12 gm
Water 1 cup
Grated jaggery ¼ cup
Turmeric powder 3 pinches
Salt ½ tsp

Spice powder
Oil 2 tsp
Dried red chillies 6–8
Fenugreek seeds 1 tsp
Black gram dal/Urad dal 2 tsp
Bengal gram/Chana dal 1 tsp

Seasoning
Oil 3 tsp
Mustard seeds 1 tsp
Dried red chillies 3

METHOD

1. Cut bitter gourd/okra into thin round pieces, pan fry in oil and keep aside.
2. Extract tamarind juice using 1 cup of water (see Pre-Cooking Processes).
3. Heat oil in a vānali/wok. Add red chillies and fenugreek seeds; when fenugreek starts turning brown, lower heat, add dals and fry. Grind to a powder.
4. Mix tamarind juice, jaggery, salt, turmeric powder, ground spice powder and vegetable in a vessel. Boil for 10–12 minutes over medium heat.
5. Heat oil in wok. Splutter mustard seeds over medium heat. Add red chillies and sauté.
6. Pour seasoning over kāya rasa and serve.

ANNĀSI PAḶA KARI Pineapple Kari

Makes: 4 servings
Serving size: 100 gms
Calories per serving: 133

INGREDIENTS

Pineapple 250 gm
Jaggery 50 gm
Salt 2 pinch

Seasoning
Oil 2 tsp. Mustard seeds 1 tsp
Black gram dal/Urad dal 1 tsp
Dried red chillies 5–6
Asafoetida powder 1 pinch
Curry leaves 1 sprig

METHOD

1. Cut pineapple into 2-inch cubes.
2. Heat oil in a vānali/wok, splutter mustard seeds, add urad dal, fry till light brown, add red chillies and fry.
3. Lower heat, add asafoetida, curry leaves and grated jaggery, stir well, add pineapple cubes. Turn the pineapple cubes a few times to mix with jaggery.
4. Add two pinches of salt, cover and cook with lid on, simmer 20 to 25 minutes, stir once or twice. The pineapple should be firm and glisten. Serve.

KOTTE KADUBU (IDLI) Steamed Rice Cake

Makes: 6 servings
Serving size: 100 gms
Calories per serving: 198

INGREDIENTS

Rice 2 cups
Water 1–1½ cups
Black gram dal/Urad dal 1 cup
Water ¾ cup
Salt to taste
Jackfruit leaves 50–60

METHOD

1. Wash rice and urad dal and soak them separately in water for about 2 hours.
2. Drain rice and grind to a coarse consistency with 1 to 1½ cups of water.
3. Drain dal and grind to a smooth batter with ¾ cup of water.
4. Combine both batters in a large container. Add salt and mix well. Ferment overnight.
5. Pin 4 jackfruit leaves together with the help of small sticks to make pyramid-shaped cups with a small opening at the top.
6. Pour batter into the leaf cups and steam for about 10 minutes, till cooked through.

Variations:

- *The rice can be coarsely ground in a mill, to a semolina consistency, washed and added to the dal batter.*
- *You can steam the idli in steel tumblers, lightly greased with ghee.*

PADIPE SĀSMI Red Spinach with Mustard

Makes: 10 servings
Serving size: 100 gms
Calories per serving: 135

INGREDIENTS

Red pālak, chopped 4 cups
Water 1 cup

For grinding
Tamarind 5 gm
Grated coconut 1 tbsp
Mustard seeds 1 tsp
Dried red chillies 3
Salt ½ tsp

Seasoning
Oil 2 tsp
Mustard seeds 1 tsp
Dried red chillies 2

METHOD

1. Wash red pālak, remove stalks, chop.
2. Cook red pālak with 1 cup of water in a vessel over medium heat, till tender.
3. Grind tamarind, grated coconut, spices and salt to a fine consistency.
4. Add spice paste to the pālak and boil for 5 minutes. The mixture should not be too thick nor watery.
5. Heat oil in a vānali/wok. Splutter mustard seeds and red chillies over medium heat. Pour seasoning over pālak.

Variation: Peeled and grated beetroot can be cooked in the same way. 1 cup thick sour buttermilk should be added to beetroot and spice paste instead of tamarind.

GOLBAJE Mangalore Bonda

Makes: 3–4 servings
Serving size: 100 gms
Calories per serving: 266

INGREDIENTS

White flour/Maida 3 cups
Green chillies 3, chopped fine
Sugar 1 tsp
Chopped coriander leaves ¼ cup
Salt ½ tsp
Sour curd, whisked ¾ cup
Water ¼ cup
Oil for deep-frying 2 cups

METHOD

1. Combine all the dry ingredients in a bowl.
2. Add ¼ cup of water to the curd and whisk well.
3. Add whisked curd to bowl, blend with maida to make a smooth batter, a little thicker than idli batter. If required add a little additional water.
4. Heat oil in a vānali/wok. Gently drop lime-sized balls of batter into the oil and fry till golden brown.
5. Drain well and serve hot with any chutney. This should always be served hot.

PARADI PĀYASAM Turmeric-flavoured Rice Pearl Pāyasam

Makes: 4 servings
Serving size: 100 gms
Calories per serving: 258

INGREDIENTS

Rice ½ cup
Water 1 cup + 1½ cups
Salt 1 pinch
White flour/Maida 1 tbsp
Whole turmeric leaves 1–2
Grated jaggery ½ cup
Thick coconut milk 1 cup (see Pre-Cooking Processes)
Cardamoms, powdered 4

METHOD

1. Wash rice and soak in water for about an hour.
2. Drain rice and grind with a pinch salt to make a fine batter with 1 cup of water, a little thinner than idli batter consistency. Add maida to batter and mix till well blended.
3. Cut turmeric leaves into 4 large pieces.
4. Cook jaggery with 1½ cups of water in a heavy-bottomed pan, till dissolved.
5. When it starts to boil pass the rice batter through a perforated plate (used to make boondi[1]) into the jaggery syrup.
6. When boondis are cooked, add coconut milk and powdered cardamoms. Mix well and remove from heat.
7. Add turmeric leaves to the pāyasam and cover for about 5 minutes.
8. Remove turmeric leaves and discard and serve.

[1] *Perforated filter plates to make boondies (batter drops) are available in stores.*

BAJJAMBADE Bondas in Chutney

Makes: 8 servings
Serving size: 100 gms
Calories per serving: 429

INGREDIENTS

Ambade
Black gram dal/Urad dal 2 cups
Bengal gram dal/Chana dal ½ cup
Water 1½ cups
Salt 1 tsp. Oil for frying 2 cups

Bajji
Grated coconut 1 cup. Mustard seeds 2 tsp
Red chillies 10. Tamarind 7 gm
Jaggery 15 gm. Green chillies 2 chopped
Asafoetida 1 pinch. Curry leaves 3–4
Salt ½ tsp

METHOD

Ambade
1. Soak both dals together in water for an hour, drain and grind to a fine thick paste. Add salt and mix well.
2. Make lemon-size dumplings and deep fry in oil till golden brown.

Bajji
1. Grind coconut, mustard seeds, red chillies, tamarind, jaggery, and salt to a thin batter.
2. Add asafoetida, curry leaves and green chillies. Keep on medium heat and bring to boil.
3. Remove from heat.
4. Add fried ambade in bajji. Serve after half an hour.

KASHMIR

Gar firdaus bar rue zameen ast
Hameen asto, hameen asto, hameen ast
(If there be a paradise on earth,
it is this, it is this, it is this)
—Amir Khusrau

Every visitor to Kashmir will vouch for the truth of this statement. The towering snow-capped mountains, the lordly chinar trees, the pristine lakes and grassy slopes, the balmy weather, the grace of its inhabitants are all part of the Kashmir dream.

Kashmiri vegetarian cuisine has evolved based on the vegetables and greens available there. Haaq (collard greens) and nadru (lotus stem) are two extremely popular vegetables that are used in iconic Kashmiri dishes. Originally a part of the Kashmiri boatmen's daily fare, nadru quickly gained favour and is a widely used ingredient in the Kashmir kitchen. Nadru is boiled, fried and steamed, and used in combination with other vegetables in a variety of dishes.

Haaq and nadru are so deeply embedded in the Kashmiri psyche that it is not surprising that the preparations using these vegetables, Karam Haaq and Nadru Yakhni, have become sacred offerings in Kashmir.

KARAM HAAQ

Collard Greens

Servings: 3–4
Calories per serving: 128

For Kashmiris, Karam Haaq is a vegetable for every meal, every season. This leafy green was not known outside of Kashmir, except in Punjabi cuisine. As collard greens and kale became superfoods in US for their health benefits, these greens have become more popular Indian kitchens in the last decade.

INGREDIENTS

Haaq 500 gm
Water 1 litre/5 cups
Smoked mustard oil ½ cup
Asafoetida powder 1 pinch
Red or green pepper 1 whole, seeds removed
Baking soda ½ tsp
Salt 1 tsp

METHOD

1. Smoke the mustard oil and keep it aside. (See 'Cooking with Mustard Oil')
2. Wash and clean the haaq leaves under tap water.
3. Put a pan on the stove, on high flame, and pour in 5 glasses of water.
4. Add the smoked oil, asafoetida powder, pepper and baking soda. Cover with a lid.
5. Check after 10 to 15 minutes. Once it comes to a boil, keep on high flame for another 5 minutes.
6. Now gradually add the haaq leaves and let them soak well.
7. Add salt and reduce the flame to cook till tender for about 30 minutes.
8. Serve with boiled rice.

Variations: Large variety colocasia, breadfruit and jackfruit can be cooked in the same way.

DUM ĀLU

Slow-Cooked Potatoes

Servings: 4
Calories per serving: 236

Dum Ālu or Ālu Dum is a signature dish of Kashmiri cuisine. Lighter and more distinctly flavourful than its Punjabi version, this delightful potato dish is now a popular pan-Indian recipe. In Kashmir, Ālu Dum is an absolute essential for every auspicious occasion.

INGREDIENTS

Potatoes 500 gm (ideally 2-inches long, medium, even-sized)
Mustard oil 1 cup
Salt 1 tsp + 1½–2 tsp
Almonds 5–6, blanched
Water 2½ cups
Thick curd, beaten 1 cup

Seasoning
Ghee ¼ cup
Mustrd oil 1 tbsp
Jeera/Cumin seeds 1 tsp
Asafoetida ½ tsp
Ginger 1-inch piece, grated
Cloves 6
Cardamoms 2
Red chilli powder 1½ tsp
Dhania/Coriander powder 3 tsp
Water 1 tsp
Dried ginger ½-inch piece
Fennel seeds ¾ tsp
Garam masala 1 tsp
Tej patta 1
Ghee 1 tsp
Saffron paste from 1 pinch saffron + 1 tsp water

METHOD

1. Scrub potatoes and boil in their jackets for about 30 minutes. Peel potatoes and prick all over with a fork.
2. Grind almonds with a little water, mix with curd and keep aside.
3. Pound fennel seeds and dried ginger and keep aside.
4. Take reheated mustard oil in a vānali/wok. Deep fry potatoes over medium heat. When they are half-fried, mix 1 tsp of salt with 1 tbsp of water and sprinkle over potatoes. Continue frying for about 2 minutes longer. Drain and remove from pan.
5. Heat a mix of 1 tbsp of oil with ¼ cup of ghee in pan. Sauté cumin seeds, asafoetida powder, grated ginger for a few seconds.
6. Add cloves, crushed cardamom, chilli and coriander powders mixed with 1 tsp of water.
7. Add potatoes, salt and 2–1/2 cups of water. Add garam masala and tej patta to almond-curd mix and add to pan. Boil for 2–3 minutes. Cover and place some red-hot charcoal pieces on lid. Cook over low heat for about 10 minutes. Check once or twice to see that curd remains moist.
8. Add saffron paste, pounded fennel seeds and dried ginger to potatoes.
9. Transfer to a serving dish and serve.

Variation: Large colocasia, breadfruit and jackfruit can be cooked in the same way.

HIMACHAL PRADESH

Himachal Pradesh, as the name suggests, consists of hilly terrain with only the lower slopes offering vegetables. This has given rise to two different kinds of cuisines in that the food of the upper slopes use more grains while vegetables are the staple of the cuisine of the lower Himalayas. Yoghurt based curries are a distinctive feature of Himachali cuisine and always find a place on festival days.

Whole communities in Himachal Pradesh like the Soods of the Kangra valley are vegetarians. The Himachali Dham, a traditional feast, akin to the Tamil Nadu kalyana sappadu (wedding feast) has a specific set of specific dishes. The Dham includes, rice, mung dal (green gram), a madra of rājma (red kidney beans in yoghurt) or chickpeas, khatta (a tamarind sauce) and many desserts. Dham is usually cooked by a particular sect of Brahmin chefs.

MADRA Tasty Curd Gravy with Chickpeas

Servings: 8
Calories per serving: 123

INGREDIENTS

Chickpeas, soaked for 10–12 hours 100 gm
Full fat curd (not too sour) 1 kg
Cloves 4
Fenugreek/Methi seeds ½ tsp
Jeera/Cumin seeds ½ tsp
Asafoetida 2 pinches
Coriander powder 1 tsp
Red chilli powder ½ tsp
Cardamoms 2 crushed
Turmeric powder ¼ tsp
Saffron 2 big pinches
Salt 1 tsp
Boiling water 1 cup
Sugar 1 tsp

METHOD

1. Beat the curd until it's smooth. Keep aside.
2. Soak cloves, fenugreek seeds, cumin seeds and asafoetida in 2 tbsp water for 1 hour.
3. Drain the soaked chickpeas and cook till soft.
4. Place a heavy bottom vessel on fire.
5. Add ghee. When melted, add the asafoetida water with its contents—cloves, fenugreek seeds and cumin seeds. Fry for a minute.
6. Add the beaten curd and 1 tsp salt. Keep stirring constantly on a low to medium heat till the curd becomes grainy.
7. Add all the powders, crushed cardamom, and some of the saffron.
8. When the curd reduces to half, add 1 cup boiling water and the sugar. Switch off the flame. Do not allow it to boil.
9. Add the remaining saffron.

Note: Gucci (morel) can be used instead of chickpeas in the above recipe, otherwise preparation is the same. It is served with rice.

TELIA MAH

Whole Black Gram/Urad Dal with Mustard Oil

Servings: 8
Calories per serving: 196

INGREDIENTS

Black gram/urad dal 425 gm
Rājma 125 gm
Ginger, coarsely ground 1 tsp
Turmeric, a pinch
Salt to taste
Dry ginger powder 1 tsp
Jeera/Cumin seeds 1 tsp
Fenugreek/Methi seeds ½ tsp
Coriander powder 1 tsp
Chilli powder ½ tsp
Garam masala powder ½ tsp
Asafoetida, a pinch
Mustard oil 1 tbsp
Ghee ¾ tbsp

Red beans or rājma is a popular bean variety used in Himachali cuisine. Telia Mah is a recipe found in Kashmiri and Punjabi cuisines as well. Ingredients and method of preparation are similar in all, the variation occurring only in the proportion of black gram dal and red beans.

METHOD

1. Wash dal and rājma. Place together in a cooker with sufficient water roughly 4 times the volume of dal and rājma, along with mustard oil, ginger paste, turmeric, salt and dried ginger powder.
2. Boil under pressure for 15 minutes. Release pressure.
3. Place an ordinary lid on cooker and simmer dal on very low heat for another 10–15 minutes or till it acquires the right consistency. If necessary, a little hot water may be added at this stage.
4. Just before serving, bring dal to boil once again.
5. In another pan, heat ghee. Add cumin seeds, fenugreek seeds, coriander powder, chili powder, garam masala and asafoetida. Fry lightly and pour over the dal.

RAJASTHAN

For a state that is largely desert, Rajasthani cuisine has spread the whole length and breadth of India, and justly so. Using the cereals and vegetation of an arid land, this cuisine offers us several distinctive, flavourful dishes. The same dishes are also the sacred offerings at many of the well-known Krishna and Devi temples of the state.

The quintessential representation of Rajasthani cuisine is undoubtedly the Dal Bāti Churma trio. This iconic dish combines two or more cooked dals that are eaten with bāti—a ball of kneaded flour that is baked and soaked in ghee. This dish is usually eaten in the colder season and is combined with a sweet crumble called churma. Traditionally dal, bāti and churma are served together.

A well-known story attributes the custom of baked bāti to the soldiers of the Rana of Mewar in the 17th century. The soldiers would leave the bātis under a thin layer of sand before leaving for the battlefield. On their return, they would find the balls of dough finely baked. The bātis were then soaked in ghee and consumed. The combination of the grainy whole wheat flour, semolina and ghee made the bāti an ideal food for the winter months months yielding considerable warmth and staving off hunger.

DAL BAATI CHURMA—The King of Rajasthani Cuisine

Dal with Kneaded Flour Balls and Crumble

Servings: 3–4
Calories per serving: 240

INGREDIENTS

Baati

Wheat flour 2 cups
Semolina 1 tbsp
Ghee 2 tbsp
Salt to taste

Dal

Green gram with skin /Dhuli moong dal ½ cup
Bengal gram dal/Chana dal 1 tbsp
Water 1 cup
Ghee 1 tbsp
Garam masala ½ tsp
Red chilli powder 1 tsp
Turmeric powder ¼ tsp
Coriander powder ½ tsp
Lime ½
Coriander leaves, chopped 1 tsp
Ginger ½-inch piece, grated
Cumin seeds ½ tsp

Churma

Wheat flour 200 gm
Ghee 400 gm
Khoya/Mawa 100 gm
Sugar 200 gm (grounded)
Soaked almond 50 gm
Cardamom 4 small
Cinnamon 1-inch piece

METHOD

Bāti

1. Mix the wheat flour, semolina, salt and ghee. Knead into a very stiff dough with warm water.
2. Shape into lime-sized balls.
3. Heat a gas tandoor or oven and roast dough balls on low heat till the outer cover is brown and crusty.
4. Break open the baked rounds of dough and pour some fresh ghee on the halves.
5. Traditionally, it is served soaked in hot ghee.

Dal

1. Wash both dals together. Add 1 cup of water and a pinch of turmeric powder and cook it well. Remove from fire.
2. Mix all the spices in ½ cup of water to make a thin paste.
3. Add ghee in a pan and heat. Splutter mustard and cumin seeds. Add ginger and the spice paste.
4. Fry for a minute, then mix in the boiled dal.
5. Add remaining water, salt and stir well. Bring to a boil.
6. Add lime juice and garnish with chopped coriander.

Churma

1. Melt 150 gm of ghee and mix it in wheat flour. Make a stiff dough using very little water.
2. Make about 15–20 balls with the dough.
3. Heat the rest of the ghee in a wok.
4. Fry the dough rounds on low flame till they become golden brown.
5. Churn the cooked dough rounds in a grinder after they cool down.
6. Mix khoya.
7. Heat 1 tbsp ghee in a wok. Add cardamom seeds and the cinnamon stick. Add the above mixture of wheat flour and khoya. Fry for a minute.
8. When it cools down, add sugar and finely chopped almonds. Mix well and serve.

KER SANGAR KA SAG—Desert Glory

Dal with Kneaded Flour Balls and Crumble

Servings: 3–4
Calories per serving: 737

INGREDIENTS

Mustard oil 2 tsp
Fenugreek seeds 1 tsp
Anise 1 tsp
Dried sangar[1] 200 gm
Ker[2] 25 gm
Dried lotus stems 10
Dried dates 8 (hard ones)
Babul seeds[3] 15 gm

Powders
Turmeric powder 1 tsp
Dhania/coriander powder 2 tbsp
Dried mango powder/amchur 30 gm
Rajastahni/Kashmiri red chilli powder 30 gm
Mustard powder 1 tsp
Dried ginger powder 1 tsp
Salt 2 tsp

Seasoning
Mustard oil 200 gm
Asafoetida ½ tsp
Fenugreek seeds ¼ tsp
Kalonji/nigella 2 pinches
Dried fruits/powdered kachri 4–5 dried (optional)

METHOD

1. Remove stones from dates and cut them into quarters. Soak overnight with sangar, ker, and dried lotus stems.
2. Heat 2 tsps of the mustard oil (see Pre-Cooking Processes) on medium heat.
3. Fry fenugreek seeds and anise in oil and powder. Keep aside.
4. Boil and peel the outer covering of babul seeds. Keep aside.
5. Drain the water from the soaked ingredients. Take fresh water and pressure-cook all the desert fruits for 2 whistles.
6. Remove from the pressure-cooker, drain water, but retaining 1 tbsp of water.
7. Mix all the powders together with salt.
8. Mix babul seeds with sangar and other boiled ingredients.
9. Take rest of the oil in a vānali, add the asafoetida, fenugreek seeds and kalonji, remove from heat. Cool and grind these to a crisp powder.
10. Add boiled ingredients and the mixed powders slowly, turning well for a minute or less.
11. Finally add the fried and powdered fenugreek, anise, and kachri. Store it in a closed container and serve after a few hours. It tastes best the next day.

[1] *Prosopisia cineraria beans*
[2] *Cappari deciduas*
[3] *Accacia arabica seeds*

PANIPHAL KHICHDI

Khichdi with Water Chestnuts

Servings: 6

Calories per serving: 726

The seasonal water chestnuts known as singhada/paniphal have inspired the creations of many delicacies. This recipe, inspired by the Sheherwali[1] cuisine is an amalgamation of rich flavours, yet simple to prepare. Choose paniphal which are fresh and tender.

INGREDIENTS

Long-grained rice (such as basmati) 1 cup
Peeled paniphal/Water chestnuts 2 cups
Ghee 5–6 tbsp
Almonds 20
Milk or water ½ cup

Curd Mixture

Fresh curd ½ cup
Besan 1 tsp
Salt
Chilli powder 2 tsp chilli powder
Sugar 1 tsp

Tempering

Mustard seeds ½ tsp
Jeera/Cumin seeds ½ tsp
Fenugreek/methi seeds ½ tsp
Asdafoetida, a pinch
Cinnamon stick ½-inch
Green cardamoms 4
Cloves 4

Final flavours

Garam masala ½ tsp

METHOD

1. Wash and soak rice for about 30 minutes. Strain and set aside. Cook the rice, making sure each grain of the cooked rice remains separate. Spread on a plate, fluff it up and allow to cool.
2. Wash and quarter the paniphals. Sauté in 1 tbsp ghee for 5 minutes and keep aside.
3. Blanch the almonds, peel and grind into a fine paste with ½ cup milk or water. Set aside.
4. For the curd mixture, beat the curd and besan with salt, chili powder and sugar in a bowl. Set aside.
5. For the tempering, heat 1 tbsp ghee in a wok and add mustard, cumin, fenugreek seeds, asafoetida, cinnamon sticks, cardamom and cloves. Sauté for 8–10 seconds. Add the curd mixture and allow to cook for a few minutes. At this point, check the consistency. If it has become very thick, add 2–3 tbsp water.
6. Add the sautéed paniphal, cooked rice, garam masala and 3–4 tbsp ghee. Mix well, serve hot.

Note: The consistency of this dish is pasty. If required, add more hot milk or water and cook for a couple of minutes.

[1] *Not many are aware of the distinctive Sheherwali cuisine originating in the Bengali sheher (town) of Murshidabad that is a blend of many influences. It is the cuisine of a Rajasthani Jain community who migrated to Bengal 300 years ago. They brought with them their love of ghee and milk and added more vegetables to their preparations under the Bengali influence, since vegetables were not easily available year-round in their native arid zone. To this was added the rich delectable ingredients of Nawabi cuisine like a diversity of nuts, saffron, rose water and kewra water. The result is a unique blend of tastes and methods of preparation.*

PUNJAB

As a predominantly agrarian society, Punjabi cuisine lays importance on its many wheat and corn preparations, and a variety of greens. The beautiful mustard fields of Punjab have also yielded its most quintessential dish, the sarson ka saag. This dish is traditionally served with makki di roti to use the Punjabi term.

Makki di roti or makki ki roti is made of maize flour and pairs divinely with sarason ka saag.

Punjabi cuisine is justifiably famous for its hunger-appeasing rotis, naans and parathas. Khara or khada pershad is a sweet preparation made of wheat flour and sugar. This is the customary prasad or sacred offering that is served to the congregation after prayers to the Granth.

The langars, the free communal kitchens attached to gurudwaras are well known for their hospitality to every pilgrim who visits. Breakfast, lunch, tea and dinner are served to all who come. The food is considered the prasad of the guru.

SARSON KA SAAG—Green Song of Punjab

Mustard Greens Curry

Servings: 4
Calories per serving: 250

INGREDIENTS

Sarson ka saag/ Mustard greens 600 gm
Bathua saag/Chenopodium album 200 gm
Pālak/Spinach 200 gm
Ginger 2-inches piece
Green chillies 2 green
Coriander powder 1 tbsp
Red chilli powder 1 tbsp (optional)
Salt 2 tsp
Hot water
Makki ka atta/Maize flour

Seasoning
Mustard seeds 1 tsp
Dried red chillies 2
Asafoetida ¼ tsp
Ghee 200 gm

METHOD

1. Wash and clean green leafy vegetables well.
2. Chop the above including the stems as they add juice and flavour to the dish.
3. Chop ginger into small pieces.
4. Take a deep wok, put the greens and ginger in it and add hot boiling water with salt.
5. Once the greens start boiling, add all the dried spices, mix and cover the lid. Cook on medium low flame.
6. Mash the greens using a steel masher or mathni (wooden churner) well to a paste.
7. After 30 min, add ¾ tbsp makki ka atta in the greens and mix well. Ensure that there are no lumps of maize flour in the greens.
8. Greens will take approximately 45 minutes to 1 hour to cook properly and to reach the correct consistency.
9. Heat 2 tbsp fresh ghee in the pan. When hot, add 1 tsp mustard seeds, 2 dried red chilies, and asafoetida. Sauté for a few seconds, then add the cooked saag (greens).
10. Mix everything well and let the saag cook for 5 minutes.

MAKKI KI ROTI Maize Flour Roti

Servings: 8 rotis
Calories per serving: 482

INGREDIENTS

Makki ka atta/Maize flour 500 gm
Salt to taste
Water, as required knead into a soft dough

METHOD

1. Knead the corn flour dough with salt and water.
2. The dough is made for 2 rotis at a time as this gives softer rotis.
3. Makki ka atta should not be mixed with wheat flour.
4. Put the iron griddle on gas on medium heat.
5. Take parchment paper or butter paper on rolling board, start spreading small amount of kneaded corn flour dough using hands. Make roti (flat bread) of 4-inch diameter and ½ cm thickness. Moisten hands while spreading the dough.
6. Now place the rolled out dough on the griddle and cook. Once dark spots appear on one side, flip it, and cook the other side.
7. Now using tongs, pick up the roti and cook on direct heat.
8. Spread ghee on the roti.
9. Serve hot saag topped with a generous amount of white butter.

Notes:

- *Do not pressure cook the saag, it has to be cooked and mashed together to get the correct consistency.*
- *If possible cook saag and roti on a chulha (earthen stove) or charcoal stove to get that authentic flavour.*
- *Corn flour is little tricky to handle so ensure to use butter paper or parchment paper to spread it, using hands.*
- *Proportion of greens: Bathua (*Chenopodium album*) and pālak (spinach) will be ⅓ the quantity of sarson ka saag (mustard greens).*

ĀLU PARANTHA

Servings: 4
Calories per serving: 254

INGREDIENTS

For dough
Wheat flour 250 gms
Water as required for kneading

For filling
Potatoes 3, medium sized
Green chilli 2
Ginger 2 tsp, finely chopped
Ajwain ½ tsp
Jeera/Cumin seeds ½ tsp
Garam masala a pinch
Anardana 1 tsp
(coarsely ground dry pomegranate seeds)
Coriander leaves 2 tsp, finely chopped
Salt as required
Ghee for cooking

Paranthas, layered rotis made of atta or whole wheat flour, have their origin in Peshawar in present-day Pakistan, flowing into the Punjab region. Stuffed paranthas (or parathas) were a later innovation. Of all stuffed paranthas—mooli or raddish, paneer, cauliflower, mixed vegetables—ālu parantha or paratha with potato filling reigns supreme.

A beloved breakfast dish in the whole of northen India around New Delhi and Punjab, it's delectable taste has won over the whole of India. Best of all, the ālu parantha requires no side dish. It is a true winner with just the accompaniments of curds and pickle.

METHOD

1. To prepare the dough, take a large bowl and sieve the flour in it. Make a well in the centre. Add water and mix it well with your fingers. Knead the mixture to prepare a smooth soft dough. Cover it and keep it aside for 20–30 minutes.
2. To make the stuffing for the parantha, boil and mash the potatoes in a bowl. Combine finely chopped green chillies with mashed potato. Add ginger, coriander leaves, garam masala, ajwain, cumin and anardana in the mixture. Sprinkle salt and mix the ingredients with a spoon.
3. Take a medium sized ball dough. Roll and flatten it. Dust with some flour and roll it in a circle of about 5-inches in diameter.
4. Place the potato stuffing in the center, keeping about 2-inches space from the sides.
5. Pleat the edges bringing them to the centre. Join the pleats together and make sure the filling is not seen.
6. Press the pleats at the centre. Sprinkle some flour and roll the parantha to about 6-inches diameter.
7. Place the parantha on a hot tawa and cook. When the parantha is half cooked, flip it and smear some ghee.
8. Flip again and spear some ghee on this side too.
9. Cook till both sides turn crispy and golden brown in colour. Once done, serve hot with butter and yoghurt.

RAJMA Red Beans Dal

Servings: 4
Calories per serving: 308

INGREDIENTS

Red rajma 500 gm
Tomatoes 2
Peppercorns 2–3
Ginger paste 1 tsp
Chilli powder 1 tsp
Turmeric powder 1 tsp
Jeera/Cumin seeds ½ tsp
Garam masala 1 tsp
Oil/ghee 1 tbsp

METHOD

1. Soak the rajma overnight.
2. The next day, throw away the water after taking out the rajma.
3. Keep a fairly big vessel on fire. Boil 4 cups of water. When it comes to boil, add the beans, ginger, peppercorns and cook the beans till it is completely soft.
4. Make a smooth puree of the 2 tomatoes and keep aside.
5. Heat oil in a pan and sizzle the cumin seeds. Then, add the tomato puree, chili powder, turmeric powder and salt. Sauté the masala until it turns thick and leaves the side of the pan.
6. Add the boiled rajma along with the stock to this masala and simmer for about 20 minutes.
7. Mash some soft cooked rajma with little water and add it to the simmering gravy. This thickens the gravy and makes it creamier.
8. Add a little water if the gravy is too thick.
9. Add the garam masala and cover. Cook for a few minutes and turn off the heat.

Note: Onion and garlic are optional

KADA PRASAD—Guru's Grace

Wheat Flour Halva

Serves: 4–6
Calories per serving: 1338

INGREDIENTS

Wheat flour 1 cup
Sugar 1 cup
Ghee ¾ to 1 cup
Water 1½ cups

METHOD

1. Mix the sugar and water in a vessel. Place on low heat till the sugar melts.
2. Heat ghee in a vānali/wok, add the wheat flour.
3. Saute the wheat flour till it becomes fragrant.
4. Add sugar-water mixture to the wheat flour and mix well. Cook to a halva consistency.

GUJARAT

Gujarati cuisine is a vegetarian's delight. A wide array of vegetables is cooked with distinctive Gujarati spices and seasonings, in a myriad ways. Undhiyo, a delectable sātvik preparation of many vegetables is an important sacred offering in Gujarat.

So also is Lapsi and Kansar, both of which are broken wheat desserts. Kansar, also known as Ormu, is cooked on all auspicious occasions. It is an indispensable part of a wedding menu for it is the first spoonful of this delicacy that is partaken of by the newly wedded couple.

Lapsi is a sacred offering, always cooked on festive days like Akshaya Tritiya, Navaratri and Deepavali. Like Kansar, it finds an important place for many other auspicious occasions.

KANSAR

Servings: 4
Calories per serving: 520

INGREDIENTS

Broken wheat 1 cup broken
Jaggery cut fine ½ cup
Ghee ⅓ cup
Water 2 cups

Garnishing
Hot ghee, as required
¼ cup powdered sugar (optional)

METHOD

1. Mix the ghee and the broken wheat well in a plate.
2. In a in a vānali/wok, melt jaggery in boiling water on a medium flame. Strain and boil again. Gradually, add the ghee-wheat mixture. Gently stir as it starts to boil. See that no lumps are formed.
3. Lower the flame. Place a griddle over it. Keep the in a vānali/wok on it. Cook till the wheat grains are tender, 10 minutes approximately. Switch off the gas. Stir gently.
4. Sprinkle hot ghee and powdered sugar at the time of serving.

Note: To pressure cook, in a pressure cooker, mix the ghee, broken wheat, jaggery and waterand cook for 3 whistles. Garnish and serve hot.

UNDHIYU Vegetable Medley

Servings: 6–7
Calories per serving: 162

INGREDIENTS

Surti papdi (*dolichos lablab*) 500 gm
Tender small brinjals 250 gm
Small potatoes 500 gm
Sweet potatoes 500 gm
Surti purple yam (ratalu kand) 500 gm
Peas ½ cup
Ripe bananas[1] 3
Chilly-ginger paste 3 long green chillies + 2-inch piece of ginger, made into a paste
Green chillies 2, slit
Coriander 1 bunch, finely chopped
Coconut 1, grated
Garam masala 1 tsp
Asafoetida 1 tsp
Ajwain, a pinch
Water 110 ml
Salt 2 tsp
Soda, a pinch

Muthia

Methi ½ bunch
Bhakri flour ½ cup
Red chilli powder ¼ tsp
Turmeric powder ¼ tsp
Asafoetida ¼ tsp
Salt ½ tsp
Sugar ½ tsp
Oil to deep fry

[1] *Any flavourful banana like Rasathali/Poovan/Rajapuri*

METHOD

1. In a wide pan, heat oil, add ajwain, asafoetida and then the papdi. Add 110ml water and a pinch of soda (optional). Then add the slit green chillies.
2. Mix the finely chopped coriander, grated coconut, ginger/chili paste, sugar, garam masala and salt to taste. This is the green masala.
3. In a small pan, add heat the ghee and saute half cup peas. Add a pinch of soda (optional). Let it cool.Take the pea mixture and add to the green masala.
4. Stuff the above masala into the slits of the potatoes, brinjals and bananas.
5. Layer all the vegetables except the bananas over the papdi along with the remaining peas.
6. Do not stir. Put it on low heat and cover to cook. It will take about 330 minutes to cook.
7. When all the vegetables are almost done, add muthia and banana on top. Cover and cook for another 5–7 minutes.

Prepping the Muthia and Vegetables

Muthia

1. Mix ½ bunch of finely chopped methi with ½ cup of bhakri flour.
2. Add salt, red chilli powder, turmeric powder, asafoetida, sugar and oil.
3. Knead dough and make small oval shaped balls and deep fry.

Vegetables

Surti papdi/dolichos beans: Remove the fibrous strings on its sides. Then break each bean with your hands.
Brinjals: Make a criss-cross cut at the bottom of the brinjals and cut only the stalks, keeping the calyx intact.
Yam and Sweet potato: Peel, dice into 2-inch cubes and slit them halfway.
Potatoes: Peel the potatoes and make slits.
Bananas: Cut the bananas into 2-inch pieces with the skin. Slit each piece halfway.
Peas: Crush the peas coarsely and keep aside.

LAPSI

Servings: 10–12
Calories per serving: 203

INGREDIENTS

Broken wheat 500 gm
Jaggery cut fine 500 gm
Ghee 300 gm
Water 6 cups, boiled

Garnish
1 tsp cardamom, coarsely powdered
3 tbsp almonds, in slivers
For kesari lapsi: 1 tsp saffron paste

METHOD

1. On a low flame, in a vessel, melt jaggery in 2 cups of water. Strain to remove impurities. Keep aside.
2. Place a vānali/wok on low heat. Melt ghee. Add broken wheat. Stir continuously till it becomes light golden brown in colour.
3. Add the remaining boiled water. Boil on a high flame till the wheat is cooked.
4. Reduce heat. Add the jaggery water and stir. Cook till the water is absorbed and the ghee separates.
5. Garnish and serve hot. Some people like to serve boiled channa with this.

Notes:

- *If the lapsi becomes too dry, add extra warm water.*
- *For kesari lapsi: add the saffron paste after adding jaggery water.*

BĀSUNDI Creamy Layers

Servings: 3
Calories per serving: 462

INGREDIENTS

Milk 1 litre
Sugar ¼–½ cup
Lime juice 1 tsp
Saffron paste (optional)
Cardamom powder
Almond and pistachio (slivers)

METHOD

1. Boil milk in a thick bottomed vessel on low heat.
2. As the milk thickens, scrape layers of cream formed in the milk, mix this with the milk and stir gently.
3. Boil the milk till it is reduced to nearly half the quantity.
4. For a granular textured bāsundi, add lime juice. Mix well.
5. Remove vessel from the fire and cool. Add sugar, saffron paste and cardamom powder.
6. Garnish with almond and pistachio slivers.

ASSAM

The rich textile and craft tradition of Assam extends to its cuisine built on the many exotic greens found in the region. Along with this, sesame, the oldest known seed, first cultivated in the Indian subcontinent 5500 years ago, is a vital part of the Assam New Year (Bihu) platter. The dishes that are the sacred offerings in Assam are the til pitha and the dekhia saag. Boot-moong, a preparation of soaked moong dal (green gram) and black chickpeas with rice, ground coconut, salt, sugar and grated ginger, is almost always the sacred offering on many ritual occasions. It is a special offering to the goddesses Kali and Lakshmi.

In Assam, Magh Bihu or Bhogali Bihu, literally the festival of feasting, coincides with the harvest festival celebrated in the other states of India in the middle of January. Just as in Tamil Nadu, the festivities extend over three to four days.

The traditional Assamese bhogali bihu platter comprises of an assortment of pithas like til pitha, ghila pitha, laru, sitol pitha and so on. Of these different sweet preparations, til pitha is considered to be the quintessential component of the Assamese bihu platter. Til pitha is a sweet dry rice pancake which is totally oil free, prepared from a type of glutinous rice called bora saul in Assam, a unique variety available in Assam, Northeast India and Bangladesh. It is made by rolling ground rice in sesame seeds, sweetened and flavoured with jaggery. It is usually served with tea.

Dekhia saag is an interesting dish—a favourite in Assam, but not a sacred offering.

TIL PITHA Sweet Rice Rolls

Servings: 15 pieces
Calories per serving: 630

INGREDIENTS

Bor daan/Glutinous rice 3 cups
Jaggery 200 gm
Black sesame seeds 150 gm
Water as required

METHOD

1. In a big bowl, soak the rice in around 6 cups of water for 6–7 hours. Wash and drain the excess water by letting the water dry over a newspaper or muslin cloth for around 30 minutes.
2. Make sure that the water is not completely dried. Do not leave the rice to dry in the sun or below the fan. Keep it in a cool and dry place.
3. Now grind it in a mixer grinder to get a fine powder. Traditionally the rice is pounded in a Ural or Dheki as known in Assamese. Ural is a stone grinder (see page xxvii)
4. Make sure the grinder does not become too hot or else the stickiness of the glutinous rice will reduce and the pithas will fall apart. Keep the powder in a bowl covered with a wet muslin cloth until use.
5. Dry roast the sesame seeds in a pan for 3–4 minutes. Grind it into a coarse powder. Chop the jaggery fine. Mix the sesame seeds and jaggery. Set aside.
6. Heat an iron tawa and spread the semi-wet rice flour over it to the size of roti, patting it with the back of your hand.
7. Place the stuffing in the middle.
8. As soon as the rice flour gets firm, fold its sides to form a roll and cover the filling. Turn it over and heat lightly before taking it off from the fire.
9. Make the rest of the pithas in the same way. When done the pithas will be crunchy.
10. Serve with a cup of tea or coffee.

Note: You can store these pithas for 10–12 days in an air-tight container. Handle the pithas with utmost care or else they may break and fall apart.

BENGAL

'Delicious' is the word that naturally comes to mind when Bengali milk sweets are mentioned. But it is the dish of many vegetables, lamda, that takes pride of place as the sacred offering to Devi. Sukta/shukto, also a multi-vegetable dish, is always found on a celebratory menu like weddings and birthdays.

SHUKTO

Mélange of Vegetables

Servings: 2–3 persons
Calories per serving: 183

INGREDIENTS

Bitter gourd 2 or 3, green and firm
Sweet potato 1, medium
Beans (dolichos/lablab/French) 3
Potato 1 big
Ghee 4 tbsp
Methi seeds/Fenugreek 1 tsp
Curry leaves 6
Water 425 ml
Jeera/Cumin seeds 1 tsp
Mustard seeds 1 tsp
Ginger 2 tsp, grated
Green chillies 1 or 2, seeded and minced
Turmeric powder ½ tsp
Coriander 2 tsp
Fennel seeds ¾ tsp
Asfoetida ½ tsp
Yoghurt 250 ml
Salt 2 tsp

Shukto is usually made with several types of vegetables. It derives its distinctive flavour from one vegetable in particular, which is bitter gourd, also known as karela.

METHOD

1. Remove the seeds from the bitter gourd and cut them into 2-inch pieces. Cut all the vegetables into 2-inch pieces. Potatoes and sweet potatoes should be peeled.
2. Heat 2 tbsp of ghee over medium-high heat in a large saucepan. Fry the fenugreek seeds for 30 seconds, then add the cut vegetables. Add the curry leaves and stir-fry the vegetables for 5 minutes, turning them gently with a wooden spoon. Now pour in the water, cover the pan, and allow to cook over medium heat for 10 minutes.
3. In the meantime, use a mortar and pestle or a small blender to grind together the cumin seeds, mustard seeds, grated ginger, minced chillies, turmeric powder, and a few drops of water, to make a smooth masala paste. Heat the remaining tablespoon of ghee or oil in a small saucepan and stir-fry the masala paste for a minute or two.
4. Then, add the fennel powder, ground coriander, and asafoetida. Stir for a few seconds. Pour the remaining water into the seasonings and bring to a boil for 1 minute. Empty the liquid masala into the cooking vegetables and continue cooking over medium heat for 15 to 20 minutes, stirring every now and then, until the vegetables are barely tender.
5. Lift the lid and fold in the yogurt and salt. Stir and toss gently to mix the spices and sauce evenly with the vegetables. Simmer for a few minutes uncovered, then serve as a main dish with rice or an Indian bread.

Notes:

- *Sukto is to Bengal as avial is to Kerala.*
- *Several vegetables like ridge gourd, raw banana, white radish and carrot can also be added to the dish.*
- *If you like, you can add sada pakoras or bhajas immediately after the yoghurt is added, but not later, as they need a few minutes of simmering to absorb some of the sauce and blend with the other ingredients.*

LAMDA

Mixed Vegetables

Servings: 6–8
Calories per serving: 182

INGREDIENTS

Mixed vegetables 1 kg
Ghee 2 tbsp
Salt to taste

Panchphoran masala
Fennel seeds ½ tsp
Nigella seeds ½ tsp
Fenugreek/Methi seeds ½ tsp
Mustard seeds ½ tsp
Jeera/Cumin seeds ½ tsp

Seasoning
Cinammon sticks ½-inch
Jeera/Cumin seeds ½ tsp
Cloves 1
Cardamoms 3, crushed
Grated fresh coconut 2 tbsp
Cashewnuts 10, broken
Seedless raisins 8–10
Green chillies 2–3, chopped fine
Ginger 1-inch, chopped fine
Sugar 1 pinch

Several vegetables like potatoes, peas, cauliflower, cabbage, wax gourd (parval), green plantain, white radish, plantain stem, red pumpkin, brinjal, broad beans and whole leaves of spinach can be used for this recipe. Cauliflower was not used in the earlier days as a sacred offering but with Westernization, it has been introduced in the recipe.

METHOD

1. Cut cauliflower into small florets, cabbage into ½-inch leaves.
2. Heat ghee in a large heavy-bottomed vānali. Splutter panch phoran, add seasoning and fry for about a minute.
3. Add radish first and sauté for a few minutes. Then add other vegetables one by one, according to the time required for cooking. Green leaves and cabbage may be added after about 10 minutes and sautéed for about a few minutes.
4. Add salt. Sprinkle water a couple of times and cover vānali with a lid with rim. Pour some water onto the lid. Lower heat and cook, till vegetables are mostly tender.
5. Add a pinch of sugar to blend the flavours. Shake vānali periodically, or stir vegetables gently with a wooden ladle.
6. Open vānali and cook, till vegetables are tender.
7. Serve with luchi puri.

Notes:

- *Luchi is puri made with white flour/maida.*
- *Do not use watery vegetables like cucumber, white pumpkin, ridge gourd etc for this dish.*

KERALA

The Kerala sādhya (banquet), like the Tamil Nadu kalyāna sāppadu (wedding feast), has a set menu and is served for all auspicious occasions. The sādhya is most importantly linked with the Onam festival of Kerala. Typically, twenty-four to sixty-four dishes are served for a sādhya.

Even non-Keralites are familiar with some of the dishes served at a sādhya like kālan, olan, pulisseri, etc. What takes pride of place in any feast is the sweet dish, usually a pāyasam.

About Pāl Pāyasam

Ada pradhaman, a rice-and-jaggery preparation, has long held pride of place in the Kerala sādhya. Originally made with jaggery and coconut milk, it was altered when milk became abundant, and became pāl (milk) ada pradhaman. The person who transformed it and became the by-word for its excellence was Kannan Swamy of Thrissur, a chef celebrated for his culinary skills. Kannan Swamy came from a long line of excellent chefs, chief being his grandfather, Sri Vellappaya Krishna Iyer.

Krishna Iyer began his culinary career catering to the foremost Namboodiri Illams, households of the Namboodri Brahmins in Kerala. At the height of his fame, dates for important events were set only after confirming his availability! Krishna Iyer and his team of professionals catered to functions where upto one lakh guests was common.

Sri Krishna Iyer was greatly responsible for the supreme position that pālada pradhaman holds today in any sadhya. The much-loved pālada pradhaman is a delectable preparation created by boiling sheets of boiled rice paste in milk and sugar for a long time in brass vessels called cherakkus. The heavy metal cherakkus with their thick bases make it possible to reduce milk to a lovely creamy consistency without fear of the milk getting overheated or burnt. In modern kitchens, pressure cookers are used to get the right consistency and hue.

PĀLADAI PRATHAMAN The Ultimate Pāyasam

Servings: 10
Calories per serving: 262

INGREDIENTS

For Ada

Rice flour 1 cup
Sugar 2 tsp
Coconut oil 2 tsp
Banana leaf strips, 8-inch wide 12
Water 2–2½ cups

For Pāyasam

Cow's milk 10 cups
Sugar 2½ cups

METHOD

Ada

1. Mix rice flour with 2 tsp of sugar and 2 tsp of coconut oil in a bowl. Gradually add 2–2 ½ cups of water and stir to make a semi-thick batter.
2. Cut banana leaf in the middle into 2 pieces. Remove the thick central portion of the leaf. Cut these half portions into 1-foot-long pieces.
3. Dip these leaves in boiling water for a second to make them pliable.
4. Spread rice flour batter on the soft banana leaves with the back of a ladle evenly.
5. Roll leaves tight and tie with strings made of banana leaf fibres so that the batter does not leak out.
6. Bring 3 litres of water to a full boil. Drop leaf rolls in the water. Boil for about 20 min till the batter in the rolls turns translucent and the leaves start floating. Remove leaf rolls from the boiling water and place them in cold water.
7. Untie the rolls, remove the cooked ada (dough) from the leaves and chop them into small flaky pieces. Set aside.

Pāyasam

1. Boil milk in an uruli/heavy-bottomed bronze pan.
2. Add sugar and stir continuously over medium heat till milk has a thick creamy colour, which is the pāyasam.
3. Add ada pieces and keep stirring for 10–15 minutes. (Take a ladle of the pradhaman out and see if the adai floats. If it settles down, it needs to cook more)
4. Remove from heat and serve.

Note:

- *If required, cashewnuts can be broken and fried in ghee till golden brown and added to the pāyasam.*
- *Ready-made ada is available in the market.*
- *Slow cooking imparts immense flavor and aroma to the pāyasam.*
- *Ensure the adai is cooked perfectly. Overcooking will result in the ada getting stuck at the bottom of the vessel and will get burnt.*

KURUKKU KĀLAN

Glossy Rich Curry

Servings: 4–5

Calories per serving: 246

INGREDIENTS

Elephant yam 2 small pieces (1.5–2 cm)
Long raw banana (cut into
5–7 quarter pieces) ¼
Curd 1 litre
Coconut ¾
Jeera/Cumin seeds 5 gm
Green chillies 2
Black pepper powder 20 gm
Water 1 cup
Turmeric powder 1 tsp
Fenugree seeds, roasted and powdered 1 tsp
Salt to taste

Seasoning

Coconut oil 1 tsp
Mustard seeds 1 tsp
Curry leaves 1 sprig

Kalan is an inimitable part of the sadhya. Kurrukku kalan is a specialty of Sri Krishna Iyer of Thrissur. The dish has to be slow cooked and may take well over 45 minutes.

METHOD

1. Cut the elephant yam and the raw banana into small pieces.
2. Grate ¾ th of a coconut, grind it with cumin seeds and green chillies. Set it aside.
3. Soak black pepper powder in a cup of water. Strain it twice.
4. Take a heavy bottomed vessel, cook the vegetables with the pepper water.
5. Add turmeric powder and salt to the vegetables.
6. When the vegetables are cooked and the water is reduced, add the curd. Stir till the mixture thickens.
7. Remove from fire and add the ground coconut paste. Mix well.
8. Add the roasted and powdered fenugreek seeds to the kalan.
9. Heat a tsp of oil and splutter the mustard seeds and curry leaves. Pour this over the kalan.

Mampazha Kalan

A tasty variation of kalan is the mampazha kalan. Five small mangoes are peeled, cut and boiled along with the seed, on a low flame. Black pepper powder is not used for this dish. Instead, add red chilli powder along with turmeric while boiling the mangoes.

Usually, Chandrakaran, a small, fibrous and flavourful mango variety, is used in the mampazha kalan. Chandrakaran grows plentifully in the Thrissur region, and is used also for the pickle māvadu preparation. Any small mango variety can be used in this recipe.

THE INEFFABLE BETEL LEAF EXPERIENCE

Many Indian traditions connected to food have their origins in the science of Ayurveda. So is the practice of chewing paan, the consumption of betel leaf with areca nut and slaked lime after a meal. This works as a digestive and helps to counter excessive eating or any other adverse effects of indigestion.

Though this sounds simple enough, the elaborate preparations before the betel leaf is consumed, the different varieties of betel leaf and areca nuts, besides the other accompaniments to the making of a paan, places this Indian custom at par with the Japanese tea ceremony!

The greatest classical Indian danseuse of the twentieth century, Bālasaraswati, once explained to me the correct way to prepare the betel leaf and the areca nut. She demonstrated with elegant movements how the betel leaf is first taken, cleaned with water, then wiped on a clean cloth, the ends of the leaf broken off; how the slaked lime mixed with coconut water is smeared on the back of the leaf, then a sharp slice with the hand to pull out the central nerve cutting the leaf into two, a deft shaping of the leaf into a cone and the gentle placing of it into the mouth.

Then, and only then, is the areca nut taken and warmed between the palms of the two hands and popped into the mouth. If the essence of food could be conjured up magically through choreographic movement, Bālasaraswati made it come alive for me.

The twelfth-century CE poet philosopher, Sri Vedanta Desikan, an austere man, set out in his treatise on *Discipline of Food* the several precautions to be taken in the use of the betel leaf. His very first injunction is that the betel leaf should be taken first, followed by the areca nut. Both should not be placed in the mouth at the same time. Nor should one drink water while chewing on the betel leaf. Everyone who has made this mistake will vouch for the danger of choking on the leaf.

The renowned teacher also lays down the rule that one should not take the betel leaf during times of sorrow. This might be because that the betel leaf and areca nut together stand as witness in everything auspicious or sacred.

The popular usage of betel leaf, which is pan-Indian in character, gave rise to some beautiful artifacts to hold the betel leaf and the accompaniments that make the ubiquitous paan a post dinner finale.

Down South, in Tamil Nadu, men carried a small rectangular box made of brass, silver and later stainless steel, according to each one's taste and affordability. It was called the vettrilai chellam or the darling betel leaf box!

Wealthy men would tote around boxes shaped like peacocks or mangoes whose metal stomachs would hold all that the man or woman needed for the delectable digestive.

North India had many more additions to the paandaan, there being several different kinds of areca nut, sugared and silvered, chuna (slaked lime), gum katechu spices, copra, grated almonds, saffron, musk and dried dates.

Gulkand, a glutinous sweet mixture of rose petals and sugar was and is an important part of Indian paan. The need to accommodate so many ingredients made the north Indian paandaan an even more elaborate affair, more creative and more aesthetic.

No poets' or intellectuals' meet was complete without several paans being consumed. Salons and dinners had their best conversations after the meal, probably inspired by the consumption of paan. I once met a famous paanwallah in Lucknow who was considered to be the last word in making pan. It would be a misnomer to call him just a paanwallah–he was more than that. He was a poet and loved to recite verses. What is more, he would flatly refuse to sell the paan unless one appreciated his shayiri (poetry).

Both in the North and the South, it was the woman who prepared the paan at home for family and guests. Many of them were very imaginative in preparing differently shaped pans using as many as 10 to 15 ingredients.

The nutcracker was used to cut the areca nut fresh. This gave rise to beautiful nutcrackers of various shapes and sizes which are still to be found in many a collector's home.

The two most valued betel leaf varieties are the rāsi and the raveśi leaves. The word raveśi deriving from the Sanskrit root word lava or ravā meaning very tiny or tender, places the raveśi betel leaf on the highest plane of quality amongst betel leaves. The maghai leaf from Varanasi alone could be said to supersede the raveśi. Pre-eminent in the South is the peppery kamār betel leaf, dark green and small with an intense pungency.

It is believed that the betel nut has traces of something akin to strychnine, which has the property of constricting the stomach and which gives a sense of fullness after a meal. This is perhaps what makes it addictive to users.

THE 'GIDDY' BEEDĀ

As children, while visiting Delhi, we used to look forward to making a trip to the great exhibitions that used to take place there. What was most exciting about these trips was the shaven ice with syrup that enticed us. Another rare treat was the beedā in the paan shops, the ones with silver foil were for a rupee and the ones with gold foil-wrapped around them were for two rupees. Children were not allowed to eat betel leaf at home as it was considered to thicken the tongue and mutilate speech.

Hence, we would make a beeline to the paan shop as soon as we entered the exhibition grounds. Once, munching the beedā and enjoying every mouthwatering moment, we suddenly felt the blood rushing to our heads, the tips of our ears turning red and getting dizzy. There was a great ruckus, we were forced to down water in quantities, made to sit down and rest, and probably given a lecture in the bargain on being greedy for things unsuitable for our age.

What could it be? We learnt later that it was a beedā with fine zardā (tobacco) packed in it which the shopkeeper had given us children by mistake. Tobacco was sometimes wrapped into the paan to give one that final 'lift'. It was soaked in rose essence and saffron and called zardā 101 or zardā 1001. This kind of paan was much sought after.

CHUTNEYS AND TUGAIYALS

CHUTNEYS AND TUGAIYALS

There is a subtle difference between chutneys and tugaiyals. Though some chutneys use tamarind, it is mandatory in a tugaiyal. Chutneys also tend to have fewer spices and more fresh ingredients like green chillies, ginger and coriander leaves. Both chutneys and tugaiyals are well ground, and neither should be like a fine paste.

APPLE CHUTNEY

Makes: 4 servings
Serving size: 20 gms
Calories per serving: 57

INGREDIENTS

Green apple (preferably Granny Smith or any sour apple) 1
Coriander leaves 1 cup, chopped
Green chillies 1–2
Jeera/Cumin seeds ¼ tsp
Salt to taste
Sugar 1 pinch

METHOD

1. Peel the apple and discard the core. Chop apple coarsely.
2. Chop coriander leaves, green chilllies and crush cumin seeds coarsely. Grind all ingredients to the consistency of chutney.
3. Taste and add salt as required. Add a pinch of sugar.

KOTTAMALLI CHUTNEY Coriander Leaf Chutney

Makes: 6 servings
Serving size: 20 gms
Calories per serving: 44

INGREDIENTS

Chopped coriander leaves, with tender stalks 2 cups
Green chillies 6
Tamarind ¾ tbsp
Salt to taste
Water 2 tsp

METHOD

1. Grind all ingredients together smoothly sprinkling 2 tsp of water.

Variations: Use a combination of coriander leaves and mint leaves or use only mint leaves to make mint chutney.

KADALAIMAVU CHUTNEY Bengal Gram Flour Chutney

Makes: 4 servings
Serving size: 20 gms
Calories per serving: 46

INGREDIENTS

Thick curd ½ cup, whisked smooth
Water 1 cup
Bengal gram flour/Besan ½ cup
Turmeric powder ¼ tsp
Asafoetida powder ¼ tsp
Salt to taste

Seasoning
Oil 2 tsp
Mustard seeds 1 tsp
Green chillies 5, chopped fine
Curry leaves 1 sprig

METHOD

1. Mix curd with 1 cup of water and beat vigorously to remove all lumps.
2. Mix besan into the curd to make a smooth paste.
3. Add turmeric powder, asafoetida powder and salt.
4. Heat oil in a vānali/wok. Splutter mustard seeds over medium heat. Stir in green chillies and curry leaves.
5. Add besan, mix and cook, till it becomes slightly thick.

Note: This is a simple chutney/sauce, easy to make, and goes well with ravā (semolina) dosai.

CARROT TUGAIYAL

Makes: 4 servings
Serving size: 20 gms
Calories per serving: 22

INGREDIENTS

Carrots 250 gm
Oil 1 tsp
Tamarind ½ tbsp
Salt to taste
Water 1 tsp

Seasoning
Oil 2 tsp
Dried red chillies 3–4
Black gram dal/Urad dal 1 tbsp

METHOD

1. Peel carrots, grate and set aside.
2. Heat oil in a vānali/wok. Fry red chillies and urad dal over medium heat, till dal turns golden brown. Set aside.
3. Add 1 tsp of oil to vānali/wok. Sauté carrots over medium heat, till cooked.
4. Grind tamarind, salt and fried seasoning coarsely with a teaspoon of water. Add carrots and grind not too fine.
5. Taste and add more salt if required.

TENGĀI CHUTNEY Coconut Chutney

Makes: 4 servings
Serving size: 20 gms
Calories per serving: 48

INGREDIENTS

Bengal gram dal/Chana dal 1 tbsp
Grated fresh coconut 1 cup
Green chillies 4–5
Ginger ½-inch piece
Tamarind ½ tsp
Salt to taste. Water ¼ cup

Seasoning
Oil 2 tsp
Mustard seeds ½ tsp
Black gram dal/Urad dal 1 tsp (optional)
Asafoetida powder ¼ tsp
Curry leaves 1 sprig

METHOD

1. Roast chana dal lightly in a vānali/wok over medium heat, till aromatic.
2. Coarsely grind roasted dal with coconut, green chillies, tamarind and ginger, with ¼ cup of water.
3. Taste and add salt.
4. Heat oil in a vānali/wok. Splutter mustard seeds over medium heat. Add remaining seasoning and fry for a few seconds.
5. Pour contents of vānali/wok over chutney.

Variation: Roasted, puffed Bengal gram dal (pottukadalai) may be substituted for Bengal gram dal. This need not be fried.

VERKADALAI CHUTNEY Peanut Chutney

Makes: 3–4 servings
Serving size: 20 gms
Calories per serving: 63

INGREDIENTS

Roasted peanuts 2 tbsp
Dried red chillies 3, roasted
Jeera/Cumin seeds 1 tsp, roasted
Ginger 1-inch piece
Lime juice 3 drops
or
Tamarind 1 packed tsp
Salt ¼ tsp
Water 2 tbsp

METHOD

1. Grind all the ingredients, except lime juice and salt, but not to a paste.
2. Mix in lime juice if more tang is needed, and salt.

DOSAIKĀI TUGAIYAL Melon Cucumber Tugaiyal

Makes: 2–3 servings
Serving size: 20 gms
Calories per serving: 38

INGREDIENTS

Dosaikāi (melon cucumber) 1
Oil 2 tsp + 1 tsp
Black gram dal/Urad dal 2 tbsp
Dried red chillies 2–4
Green chillies 2
Curry leaves 1 sprig
Asafoetida powder 1 pinch
Tamarind 1 packed tsp
Mustard seeds ¼ tsp
Grated jaggery 1 pinch
Salt to taste
Water 1–2 tsp

METHOD

1. Peel dosaikai and dice small.
2. Heat 2 tsp of oil in a vānali/wok. Fry urad dal over medium heat, till golden.
3. Add red and green chillies, curry leaves and asafoetida powder. Stir and remove from heat.
4. Grind fried ingredients with tamarind and 2 tbsp of diced dosakai to make a coarse paste. Set aside.
5. Heat 1 tsp of oil in a vānali/wok. Splutter mustard seeds.
6. Add remaining dosaikāi and sauté well. Sprinkle a little water and cook, till dosaikāi is tender.
7. Mix in ground spices and cook, till oil separates.
8. Stir in jaggery and salt to taste.

ORANGE TOLI TUGAIYAL Orange Peel Tugaiyal

Makes: 4 servings
Serving size: 20 gms
Calories per serving: 43

INGREDIENTS

Peel of loose-jacket orange 1 cup
Sesame oil ½ tbsp + ½ tbsp
Dried red chillies 2, broken
Asafoetida powder ¼ tsp
Mustard seeds ½ tsp
Tamarind 1 packed tsp
Salt ½ tsp
Water 1–2 tsp

METHOD

1. Scrape and discard white pith of orange peel completely. Chop the peel finely.
2. Heat ½ tbsp oil in a vānali/wok. Add red chillies, asafoetida powder and orange peel and sauté over medium heat for about a minute. Add salt and remove from heat. Cool.
3. Grind orange peel, fried ingredients, and tamarind not too fine. (It should not become a mushy paste.)
4. Splutter mustard seeds in remaining oil over medium heat. Pour on tugaiyal.

PACHAI MILAGĀI CHUTNEY Green Chilli Chutney

Makes: 6 servings
Serving size: 20 gms
Calories per serving: 23

INGREDIENTS

Green chillies 6
Roasted peanuts 2 tbsp
Coriander leaves 1 cup, chopped
Ginger 1-inch thin slice
Sugar 1 tsp
Strained juice of 1 lime
or
Strained tamarind juice 1 tsp
Salt to taste
Water 2 tsp

METHOD

1. Grind all ingredients together, except lime or tamarind juice, with water.
2. Mix in lime or tamarind juice.
3. Taste and add salt.

PEERKANKĀI TUGAIYAL Ridge Gourd Chutney

Makes: 4 servings
Serving size: 20 gms
Calories per serving: 46

INGREDIENTS

Ridge gourd 1

For grinding
Sesame oil 1 tbsp
Dried red chillies 3–4
Bengal gram dal/Chana dal 1 tsp
Black gram dal/Urad dal 1 tbsp
Asafoetida powder 1 pinch
Tamarind 1 packed tsp

METHOD

1. Scrape ridge gourd and chop fine.
2. Heat oil in a vānali/wok. Add red chillies and chana dal and fry over medium heat, till dal turns golden brown. Set aside.
3. Add Urad dal and asafoetida powder to the vanali and fry till golden. Set aside.
4. Add ridge gourd and tamarind, and saute till tender.
5. Grind red chillies and chana dal with salt to a fine paste. Add ridge gourd and grind coarsely.
6. Finally add black gram dal and grind.

Variations: Add coriander leaves while grinding at the end.
Use tomato instead of tamarind.

Chow-chow tugaiyal: One medium size chow-chow peeled and grated can be made into tugaiyal. It can be seasoned with mustard seeds and curry leaves.

PARUPPU TUGAIYAL Red Gram Dal Tugaiyal

Makes: 4 servings
Serving size: 20 gms
Calories per serving: 71

INGREDIENTS

Oil 2 tsp
Red gram dal/Tuvar dal ½ cup
Dried red chillies 1–2
Tamarind ½ tsp
Salt ½ tsp
Water 1 tbsp

METHOD

1. Heat oil in a vānali/wok. Fry tuvar dal over medium heat, till golden.
2. Add red chillies and fry. Cool.
3. Grind fried dal and red chillies, tamarind and salt, with 1 tbsp of water.

Note: This is usually made to go with tamarind kuḷambu, (without dal), also as an alternative to coconut tugaiyal, where diet restrictions are followed.

KATRIKĀI TUGAIYAL Brinjal Tugaiyal

Makes: 4 servings
Serving size: 20 gms
Calories per serving: 28

INGREDIENTS

Brinjal (large variety) 1
Oil ½ tsp
Tamarind ¾ tbsp
Salt to taste

To grind
Black gram dal/Urad dal 1 tbsp
Dried red chillies 5
Asafoetida powder 1 tsp

Seasoning
Oil 2 tsp
Mustard seeds 1 tsp
Green chilli 1
Curry leaves 1 sprig

METHOD

1. Brush brinjal with oil and roast it on a gas stove over low heat. Keep turning, till brinjal is well roasted and peel is charred. Pierce with a fork to ensure that brinjal is cooked through. Remove charred peel and mash pulp well with a fork. Set aside.
2. Finely cut red chillies.
3. Heat oil in a vānali/wok over medium heat. Fry urad dal and red chillies for 3 seconds. Cool.
4. Grind brinjal, tamarind, dal, red chillies, asafoetida and salt well, but not into a puree.
5. Heat oil in a vānali/wok over medium heat. Splutter mustard seeds, add green chilli and curry leaves, sauté for a few seconds and pour over tugaiyal.

KARIVEPPILAI TUGAIYAL Curry Leaf Tugaiyal

Makes: 4–5 servings

Serving size: 20 gms

Calories per serving: 51

INGREDIENTS

Fresh curry leaves 4 cups
Oil 1 tbsp
Dried red chillies 7–8
Asafoetida powder 1 pinch
Black gram dal/Urad dal 2 tsp
Tamarind 1 packed tbsp
Salt 1 tsp
Water 2 tbsp

METHOD

1. Remove stems from curry leaves and discard. Wash leaves and pat dry.
2. Heat oil in a vānali/wok. Add red chillies and fry over medium heat till aromatic. Add asafoetida and tamarind. Turn over once and remove from vānali/wok.
3. Add curry leaves to a vānali/wok and sauté for a minute till raw smell disappears. Keep aside. In the same pan, fry urad dal till golden.
4. Grind red chillies, asafoetida powder, tamarind and salt in a grinder.
5. Add urad dal to tugaiyal and grind.
6. Add curry leaves and blend well, but not to a paste.

Variation: Kottumalli tugaiyal–4 bunches of coriander leaves and tender stems can be made in to tugaiyal in the same way.

TENGĀI TUGAIYAL Coconut Tugaiyal

Makes: 4–5 servings

Serving size: 20 gms

Calories per serving: 68

INGREDIENTS

Oil 1 tbsp
Black gram dal/Urad dal 3 tsp
Dried red chillies 6–7
Asafoetida powder 1 pinch
Grated fresh coconut 1
Salt 1 tsp
Tamarind 1 packed tsp
Water 2–3 tbsp

METHOD

1. Heat oil in a vānali/wok. Fry red chillies over medium heat. Remove.
2. Add urad dal and fry till golden. Add asafoetida powder and remove from heat.
3. Grind grated coconut with salt, tamarind and fried ingredients, but not too fine.

PICKLES

CHUTNEYS AND TUGAIYALS

Mango and lime are perhaps the most common fruits that are pickled in India. They form an essential part of Indian cuisine in their many variations all over India. Apart from these two favourites there are numerous other pickles, using almost all the fruits, vegetables and berries that are available in the different regions of the country. The spices used and the methods of pickling vary according to the region giving us the ultimate in a tasty miscellany.

A verse from a circa 3 CE poem, the *Perumpanatrupadai* describes a common scene on the roads of the time:

Nadaka magalir ādukalat edutha
Vīsivīn inniyum kaduppak kayiru pinaithu
Kādivaita kalanudai mukin
Perumpanatrupadai
(Verses 55–56)

Pickles were so popular that 'large jars of pickles were often transported on carts and when seen from a distance these jars resembled Indian drums'. Many of these gigantic jars were imported from Myanmar.

Tender mango pickles have been part of the south Indian menu since ancient times. The thought of having the pickle was so inviting that people would want to have their mid-day meal once again.

Varthai varthaiyai alaikkum
Vadu māngāi chotrai alaikkum

Words invite (other) words
Tender mango (pickle) invites more food

A very popular form of relish is made out of nārtankāi (citrus jambhiri), a strongly flavoured citrus/lime variety. The whole fruit is cut spirally, salted and dried in the sun. This can be stored for years and improves with age. This goes extraordinarily well with rice and curds, which is a staple lunch in Tamil Nadu.

A story explains the important place of the nārtankāi relish in practice. A village woman was in the custom of sending curd and rice (possibly very watery curd) and one spiral of this relish every day with her husband as his mid-day meal after his hard work in the fields. As she had a plentiful supply of this relish, she could continue to send this lunch for a long time till the day arrived when she found only half a spiral right at the bottom of the pot. That evening, her husband berated her for not sending enough rice for his meal. It was not the quantity of rice that was wanting that day but the paucity of the nārtankāi relish!

Making fresh pickles at home is a long and tedious process. It is not possible for many. A wide variety of pickles from across India are now available on supermarket shelves. These are quite popular.

In days past, and even today in some south Indian homes, pickles were preserved for up to a year in large ceramic jars. Preparing the jars and filling them with the pickle is a special process.

The jars are thoroughly washed, dried and placed in the sun for a few hours. When the pickle is ready, a large piece of burning charcoal is put on a metal plate and a pinch of asafoetida is sprinkled on top. When it starts smoking, the jar is inverted over the charcoal, so that its mouth covers the charcoal. After 3–4 minutes, the jar is set on its base and filled with the pickle. The top is levelled and a layer of oil, ⅛-inch–¼-inch deep is spread over the pickle.

The mouth of the jar is covered with a piece of sterile white muslin cloth, which is tied with a clean string around the neck. The pickle is cooled after sterilizing it by placing it over a flame for 3 minutes. It is stirred every fortnight with a long flat ladle.

When stored in this manner, pickles last well for over a year. Today, with nuclear families being the norm, pickles need not be made in large quantities.

MĀHALI KIḶANGU URUKĀI Swallow Root Pickle

Makes: 250 gm
Serving size: 5 gms
Calories per serving: 4

INGREDIENTS

Mustard seeds 1 tsp
Dried red chilli 1
Salt 1 tbsp
Thick curd 1 cup, whisked smooth
Swallow/Mahali roots 250 gm

METHOD

1. Grind mustard seeds, red chilli and salt together without water and add to the curd. Whisk till well blended.
2. Wash mahali roots and peel them. Cut them lengthwise, remove hard vein in the centre and slice into half-moons.
3. Add to curd and mix well.
4. Store in a clean, dry airtight jar for up to a year.

Note: The botanical name for swallow root is Decalepis hamiltonii. It has medicinal properties. It has a delectable vanilla flavour.

MANJAL, INJI, MĀNGĀINJI URUKĀI

Fresh Turmeric, Ginger, Mango Ginger Pickle

Makes: 650 gm
Serving size: 5 gms
Calories per serving: 17

INGREDIENTS

Fresh turmeric 200 gm
Fresh mango ginger 100 gm
Ginger 50 gm
Green chillies 100 gm
Mustard oil ½ cup (see Pre-Cooking Processes)
Lime juice ½ cup

Spices
Mustard seeds 2 tbsp, powdered
Fenugreek seeds 1 tbsp
Aniseed 1 tbsp
Kalonji/Nigella seeds ½ tbsp
Asafoetida powder ½ tsp
Salt 2 tbsp

METHOD

1. Cut fresh turmeric, mango ginger, ginger and green chillies lengthwise like matchsticks.
2. Mix spices and salt and spread over cut roots.
3. Heat mustard oil and pour hot oil over prepared root pieces.
4. Cool and transfer to a clean, dry jar.
5. Cover with a cloth and sun-dry for 4–5 days in the mornings for an hour.

Note: Refrigerated, this pickle will last for almost a year.

MUḶU ELUMICHAI URUKĀI Whole Lime Pickle

Makes: 500 gm
Serving size: 5 gms
Calories per serving: 14

INGREDIENTS

Well-ripened limes 12
Fenugreek seeds 2 tbsp
Turmeric powder 1 tsp
Red chilli powder 100 gm
Asafoetida powder 1 tsp
Salt ¼ the weight of limes
Oil ½ cup
Mustard seeds 2 tsp

METHOD

1. Weigh limes and take a fourth of their weight in salt.
2. Slit lime vertically into quarters, keeping them intact at the base.
3. Toast fenugreek seeds in a dry vānali/wok till they turn dark brown. Remove from heat, add turmeric powder. Powder together.
4. Mix fenugreek and turmeric powders, red chilli powder, asafoetida powder and salt. Add 1 tbsp of oil to the spice mix.
5. Pack spice mix into limes.
6. Arrange limes upright in a jar. Keep overnight.
7. The next day, heat ¼ cup of oil, and splutter mustard seeds. Cool and pour over the limes.
8. Taste for salt, add a little more if necessary.
9. Keep jar in the morning sun (between 9 a.m. and 11 a.m.) for 2 days.
10. Pickle has to be turned well after 2–3 days.
11. It will be ready to use after 2–3 weeks. Keeps for a year.

NEER ELUMICHANKĀI Salted Lime Pickle

Makes: 500 gm
Serving size: 5 gms
Calories per serving: 5

INGREDIENTS

Limes 12
Tender ginger 50 gm
Green chillies 10, slit
Salt ¼ the weight of limes

Seasoning
Sesame oil 2 tbsp. Mustard seeds 1 tsp
Turmeric powder 1 tsp
Asafoetida powder ¼ tsp

METHOD

1. Parboil whole limes. Slit vertically into 8 segments, keeping them intact at the base.
2. Cut ginger into thin round slices.
3. Combine lime, ginger, green chillies and salt in a bowl. Set aside for 2–3 days, stirring every day.
4. Heat oil in a vānali/wok. Splutter mustard seeds over medium heat. Remove from heat, then add turmeric and asafoetida powders and add them to the lime. Mix well.
5. Refrigerated, it will keep for a month.

KARA MĀNGĀI Fenugreek Mango Pickle

Makes: 4–5 servings
Serving size: 5 gms
Calories per serving: 14

INGREDIENTS

Sour mango (large) 1 or (medium-sized) 2
Salt 1 tbsp
Red chilli powder 3 tbsp
Sesame oil 1 tbsp
Fenugreek seeds 1 tsp
Asafoetida powder 1 tsp

Seasoning
Sesame oil 1 cup
Mustard seeds 2 tsp

METHOD

1. Wash mango and dry thoroughly. Finely chop.
2. Mix mango with salt and chilli powder and set aside for about 30 minutes.
3. Heat 1 tbsp of oil in a vānali/wok. Fry fenugreek seeds and asafoetida powder over medium heat, till golden brown. Cool and grind to a fine powder. Add to the cut mango and mix till well blended.
4. Heat 1 cup of oil in a vānali/wok. Splutter mustard seeds over medium heat. Pour contents of vānali/wok over mango and stir well.
5. Let it cool completely and store in a clean, dry, airtight jar for up to 2 months in the refrigerator.

Note: This pickle is made fresh and served at feasts. The remainder can be refrigerated and used for a few more weeks.

MĀNGĀI THOKKU Grated Mango Chutney

Makes: 2 kgs
Serving size: 5 gms
Calories per serving: 6

INGREDIENTS

Mango 2 kgs
Fenugreek seeds 4 tbsp
Sesame oil ½ cup
Mustard seeds 2 tsp
Asafoetida powder 2 tsp
Turmeric powder 2 tsp
Red chilli powder 3 tbsp
Crystal salt 4 tbsp

METHOD

1. Wash mangoes, drain and dry thoroughly. Peel mangoes and grate.
2. Roast fenugreek seeds in a vānali/wok over medium heat, till deep brown. Cool and grind to make a fine powder.
3. Heat oil in a vānali/wok. Splutter mustard seeds over medium heat. Add asafoetida powder.
4. Pan fry mangoes, salt, turmeric powder, chilli powder and powdered fenugreek together.
5. Turn contents often to prevent pulp from sticking to the bottom. Cook till grated mango has shrivelled and oil separates, then add red chilli powder and mix well. Remove from heat.
6. Cool. Do not cover.
7. Store in a clean jar. Refrigerate.

TITTIPU MĀNGĀI URUKĀI Sweet Mango Pickle

Makes: 3 kgs
Serving size: 5 gms
Calories per serving: 11

INGREDIENTS

Raw mangoes 2½ kgs
Salt 250 gm
Fenugreek seeds 30 gm
Whole dried turmeric stick 1
Asafoetida powder 50 gm
Grated jaggery or sugar 60 gm
Red chilli powder 200 gm
Oil 2 cups
Mustard seeds 30 gm
Curry leaves 2 sprigs

Note: If using jaggery, make a thick syrup of jaggery and mix with mango pickle.

METHOD

1. Wash mangoes, drain and dry thoroughly. Cut mangoes into cubes with the skin.
2. Place mangoes with salt in a wide-mouthed jar. Set aside for 3 days. Water would have oozed from the mixture.
3. On the fourth day, remove mangoes from the water. Reserve water.
4. Dry mangoes in the sun for a day.
5. Add red chilli powder and sugar to the reserved water.
6. Roast fenugreek seeds, turmeric stick and asafoetida powder in a vānali/wok over medium heat. Cool and grind to make a fine powder.
7. Heat oil in a vānali/wok. Splutter mustard seeds over medium heat. Stir in curry leaves and add to the mango water along with ground spice powder.
8. When the spiced mango water is cool, add dried mango pieces and mix well.
9. Store in a clean, dry airtight jar for upto a year.

INJI THOKKU Ginger Chutney

Makes: 225 gm
Serving size: 5 gms
Calories per serving: 27

INGREDIENTS

Tender ginger 100 gm, grated
Dried red chillies 12–15
Tamarind 1½ packed tbsp
Crystal salt ¼ cup
Grated jaggery 100 gm

Seasoning
Sesame oil ¼ cup. Mustard seeds 1 tsp
Asafoetida powder 1 tsp

METHOD

1. Grind ginger, red chillies, tamarind and salt, with very little water, into a paste. Mix in jaggery.
2. Heat oil in a vānali/wok. Splutter mustard seeds over medium heat. Stir in asafoetida powder.
3. Add ground paste and cook over low heat, till well blended.
4. Cool and store in refrigerator. This will keep for a few weeks.

TAKKĀLI THOKKU Tomato Chutney

Makes: 250 gm
Serving size: 5 gms
Calories per serving: 5

INGREDIENTS

Firm, red tomatoes 250 gm
Grated jaggery 1 tsp
Salt ¾ tsp
Red chilli powder 2–3 tsp

Seasoning
Oil 1 tbsp
Mustard seeds ½ tsp
Dried red chillies 2
Asafoetida powder 1½ tsp
Curry leaves 1 sprig

METHOD

1. Mash tomatoes.
2. Heat oil in a vānali/wok. Splutter seasoning over medium heat. Add mashed tomatoes and simmer.
3. When it starts bubbling, add grated jaggery and salt.
4. Cook for 10 minutes, add red chilli powder and cook for further 5–10 minutes.
5. Remove and cool. Store in a clean jar.
6. Refrigerated, this will keep for 15 to 20 days.

PACHAI MILAGĀI THOKKU Green Chilli Chutney

Makes: 1.8 kgs
Serving size: 5 gms
Calories per serving: 4

INGREDIENTS

Green chillies 1 kg
Coriander leaves 400 gm, chopped
Ginger 100 gm
Tamarind 250 gm
Salt 350 gm
Sesame oil 300 ml
Fenugreek seeds 1 tbsp
Mustard seeds 1¾ tsp
Asafoetida powder 1½ tsp
Grated jaggery 50 gm

METHOD

1. Wash green chillies, drain and dry thoroughly.
2. Remove and discard roots and thick stems from coriander leaves. Wash leaves and stalks well. Drain and chop.
3. Grind green chillies, coriander, ginger, tamarind and salt to make a paste without adding water.
4. Heat oil in a vānali/wok. Splutter mustard seeds over medium heat. Lower heat, then add fenugreek and fry till it turns deep brown.
5. Add ground paste and asafoetida powder and sauté till oil separates.
6. Add jaggery, melt and blend with the green chilli paste.
7. Cool and store in a clean, dry airtight jar for up to 10–12 days in the refrigerator.

Note: This chutney is usually made fresh for a feast or a party. Half the quantity can be made and refrigerated for home use.

PODIS Readymade Powders

SAMBAR POWDER

Makes: Approx. 1½ kgs
Serving size: 5 gms
Calories per serving: 15

INGREDIENTS

Dhania/Coriander seeds 750 gm
Bengal gram dal/Chana dal 250 gm
Red gram dal/Tuvar dal 125 gm
Black gram dal/Urad dal 5 tbsp
Fenugreek/Methi seeds 4½ tbsp
Whole black pepper 2½ tbsp
Turmeric sticks 4
Curry leaves 2 sprigs
Oil 1 tbsp
Dried red chillies 250 gm

METHOD

1. Dry roast each ingredient, except red chillies, separately in a vānali/wok over medium heat till aromatic, and dals till golden.
2. Heat oil and fry red chillies over medium heat.
3. Grind all ingredients together to make a fine powder.
4. Store in a clean, dry and airtight container.

Variation: Sun-dry all ingredients in the shade for one day and grind to make a fine powder.

VARUTHARACHA SAMBAR POWDER

Makes: Approx. 800 gm
Serving size: 5 gms
Calories per serving: 15

INGREDIENTS

Red gram/Green gram 285 gm
Sesame oil 1 tbsp
Dry red chillies 200 gm
Bengal gram dal/Chana dal 85 gm
Dhania/Coriander seeds 475 gm
Whole black pepper 30 gm
Fenugreek/Methi seeds 85 gm
Turmeric 6 sticks

METHOD

1. Dry roast all the ingredients separately in a vānali/kadāi.
2. Grind each ingredient except the chilly into a nice powder.
3. In a vānali, add 1 tbsp sesame oil, fry the chillies and grind it.
4. Mix everything well and store in an airtight container.

RASAM POWDER

Makes: Approx. 800 gm
Serving size: 5 gms
Calories per serving: 17

INGREDIENTS

Dhania/Coriander seeds 375 gm
Green gram dal/Red gram dal 100 gm
Dried red chillies 80 gm
Bengal gram dal/Chana dal 75 gm
Whole black pepper 60 gm
Jeera/Cumin seeds 65 gm
Fenugreek seeds/Methi seeds 2 tsp

METHOD

1. Roast each ingredient separately over low heat. The colour should not change.
2. Cool. Grind all ingredients together coarsely— it should feel like semolina to the touch.
3. Store in a clean, dry and airtight container.

Variation: Sun-dry all ingredients in the shade and grind coarsely.

MYSORE RASAM POWDER

Makes: Approx. 1 kg
Serving size: 5 gms
Calories per serving: 20

INGREDIENTS

Dry red chillies 350 gm
Dhania/Coriander seeds 400 gm
Black pepper 120 gm
Fenugreek/Methi seeds 130 gm
Jeera/Cumin seeds 55 gm
Mustard seeds 20 gm
Asafoetida 2 tbsp
Cinnamon stick 1½-inch stick
Curry leaves 2 sprigs
Sesame oil 1 tbsp
Ghee 1 tbsp

METHOD

1. Fry the pepper in 1 tbsp ghee. Keep aside.
2. In 1 tbsp sesame oil, fry the asafoetida.
3. Heat an iron pan, and toast the rest of the ingredients separately till the aroma comes out.
4. Cool the spices. Grind them into a coarse powder.
5. Sieve and mix everything well.
6. Store in an airtight container.

Note: If coconut is used, the rasam powder may lose flavour soon; instead 1 tsp copra can be fried in ghee and sprinkled over the rasam every time it is made. Copra can be stored in the refrigerator.

MANGALORE RASAM POWDER

Makes: Approx. 250 gm
Serving size: 5 gms
Calories per serving: 40

INGREDIENTS

Coconut oil ½ cup
Fenugreek seeds 2½ tbsp
Dried red chillies 100 gm
Dhania/Coriander seeds 75 gm
Jeera/Cumin seeds 3 tbsp
Bengal gram dal/Chana dal 3 tbsp
Curry leaves 4 sprigs

METHOD

1. Heat coconut oil in a vānali/wok. Add fenugreek seeds, red chillies, coriander seeds and fry over medium heat for 2 minutes.
2. Add cumin seeds, chana dal and and fry till dal turns golden. Remove.
3. Add curry leaves to pan and fry till crisp.
4. Cool. Grind slightly coarsely.
5. Store in a clean, dry and airtight container.

MILAGĀI PODI FOR IDLI AND DOSAI

Spicy Red Chilli Powder for Idli and Dosai

Makes: Approx. 300 gm
Serving size: 5 gms
Calories per serving: 21

INGREDIENTS

Bengal gram dal/Chana dal ½ cup
Black gram dal/Urad dal ½ cup
Oil 1¼ tbsp
Asafoetida powder 1 tsp
Dried red chillies 50 gm
Salt 2 tsp

METHOD

1. Roast chana dal and urad dal separately in a dry vānali/wok over medium heat, till golden. Remove.
2. Add oil to vānali/wok and fry asafoetida powder. Remove stalks from red chillies, then add to vānali/wok. Fry till colour changes to deep red, not black.
3. Grind red chillies and salt first. Halfway through add dals and grind coarsely.
4. Store in a clean, dry and airtight container.

Variations:

- *Tengāi/Coconut Milagāi Podi: Grate ½ a coconut and fry in a little ghee or oil.*
- *Grind with remaining ingredients to make a coarse powder. Store in an airtight container for up to a week.*
- *Ellu/Sesame Milagāi Podi: Roast about 70 gm of sesame seeds over medium heat, till aromatic. Grind with other ingredients.*

UDUPI RASAM POWDER

Makes: Approx. 215 gm
Serving size: 5 gms
Calories per serving: 15

INGREDIENTS

Byadagi red chillies/Kashmiri red chillies 20–25
Dhania/Coriander seeds 1½ cups
Jeera/Cumin seeds ½ cup
Fenugreek/Methi seeds ¼ cup
Asafoetida powder 1½ tsp
Coconut oil 5 tbsp

METHOD

1. All ingredients have to be roasted separately.
2. Place a vānali on medium heat. Add the 5 tbsp of coconut oil.
3. Add the coriander seeds to the oil. Fry, stirring constantly till they turn dark brown, for 1½ minutes.
4. Strain oil completely and pour the coriander seeds on to a blotting paper or kitchen tissue.
5. Take strained oil in the vānali, add ½ cup cumin seeds and fry for 40 seconds.
6. Strain oil and pour cumin seeds over the coriander.
7. Repeat process with fenugreek seeds.
8. Fry the byadagi chillies in the strained oil over a low flame. Chillies have to be stirred constantly or else the rasam colour will be black.
9. Fry chillies for 1½ minutes, strain oil completely and add to the rest of the fried ingredients.
10. Take 15 to 20 curry leaves and fry in the oil left in the pan.
11. Add 1½ tsp asafoetida to the curry leaves and sauté for a minute.
12. Add to the other ingredients.
13. Cool to room temperature and grind to a medium coarseness in a mixer-grinder.
14. Transfer it to an airtight container.

Note: This powder can be used in various poriyals and sambar.

PARUPPU PODI Red Gram Dal Powder

Makes: Approx. 100 gm
Serving size: 5 gms
Calories per serving: 17

INGREDIENTS

Red gram dal/Tuvar dal 100 gm
Dried red chillies 1
Whole black pepper 2
Salt ½ tsp

METHOD

1. Dry roast tuvar dal in a vānali/wok till aromatic. Cool.
2. Grind tuvar dal, red chilli, salt and peppercorns together to a fine powder.

DHANIA–JEERA POWDER Coriander and Cumin Powder

Makes: Approx. 175 gm
Serving size: 5 gms
Calories per serving: 14

INGREDIENTS

Dhania/Coriander seeds 100 gm
Jeera/Cumin seeds 50 gm
Dried red chillies 25 gm

METHOD

1. Dry all ingredients well in the sun and grind coarsely.
2. Store in a clean, dry and airtight container.

GARAM MASALA POWDER Zesty Spice Powder

Makes: Approx. 350 gm
Serving size: 5 gms
Calories per serving: 7

INGREDIENTS

Black cardamom 30 gm
Cloves 50 gm
Pepper 50 gm
Jeera/Cumin seeds 40 gm
Mace 20 gm
Cinnamon 25 gm
Dried ginger 50 gm
Nutmeg 20 gm
Shah jeera 25 gm
Small cardamom 40 gm
Bay leaves 4

METHOD

1. Toast all spices lightly in a dry vānali/wok and grind to a fine powder.
2. Store in a clean, dry airtight container.

Variation: Omitting cumin seeds and mace, add 15 gm of pippli (Piper longinum) to this recipe; keep all spices in the sun for 15 minutes and grind to a powder. This powder can also be made without black cardamom and pippli.

COSMOPOLITAN CURRENTS

COSMOPOLITAN CURRENTS

Times are truly a-changing. As we look around us, we see changes in fashion, style and behaviour. These transformations are reflected in our homes, in the food that we eat, in the way we cook, and in the way we serve our meals.

These changes are not merely happenstance. They are linked to the rapid globalization of India, new forms of social interaction and the cosmopolitan attitudes generated by travel and the intermingling of cultures. Students who go overseas to pursue their education tend to eat out a lot and get used to new cuisines. Indians of even moderate means are now exposed to multi-regional and international foods.

Socioeconomic changes brought about other alterations in lifestyles. More Indian women started working outside the home and no longer had the time, or the inclination, to engage in preparing long and complex menus. Convenience foods such as two-minute noodles or readymade sevai (rice vermicelli) found a keen market, especially when families had to deal with children coming home hungry from school.

Many other convenience foods followed, almost in proportion to the number of women who started working outside the home year upon year. Readymade frozen chappatis; refrigerated idli and dosai batter; and ready-to-eat north Indian sabzis—ālu matar, sarson ka sag, paneer dishes.

The entry of American pizza chains were an immediate hit with children and the youth, becoming the favourite takeaway dinner even for adults who were usually very conservative eaters.

Convenience is the catchword of contemporary times. However, the older way of cooking on firewood added flavour to the simplest dishes. It also gave more time to attend to other household chores while the spices gently nurtured the vegetables and gravies. Gas stoves, on the other hand, give out too much heat and one has to hover constantly over them till the cooking is completed. Other innovations like the induction stove are leading to a different style of cooking.

The changes in cooking fuel have had their effect on the vessels used in the kitchen. Earthen pots once used for cooking sambar and rasam gave way to vessels made of brass, bell metal, tin—each with its own special place in the kitchen. These, in turn, were made obsolete by what can only be called the stainless-steel revolution. The availability and affordability of stainless steel has helped it dominate the Indian kitchen completely. Large stores display tier upon tier of vessels hanging from the ceiling, enticing shoppers and passersby.

Not everything old was perfect. Brass vessels meant the trouble of constant coating with tin. They were also difficult to clean, requiring tamarind, time and effort. In the last decade, pans with aluminum-clad bases, stainless steel cooking vessels of all kinds and non-stick kitchenware in many sizes and shapes have taken over the kitchen. Though there are questions about the possible toxicity of Teflon-coated and microwave cookware, it has now been accepted (though arguably), as contributing to good health because non-stick pans require less oil.

Though the vessels for cooking changed in a gradual way, the method of serving remained traditional, even orthodox, one might say. The banana leaf, the supremely hygienic way of serving food, remained popular for a long time. As the banana leaf was bio-degradable, this natural 'plate' became more expensive till it is now used only for weddings and on ritual occasions, and also as a lining for buffet plates. The use of china and glass used to be looked down upon once, but now are taken out with pride for dinner parties. We also see cheap porcelain from China flooding the Indian market. As new and easily disposable materials are available and used without the thought of their non-degradability, the urban Indian landscape presents a picture of ecological and aesthetic devastation, strewing the once pristine countryside with unimaginable numbers of plastic bags, cups and bottles.

Indian recipes which depend a great deal on grinding and powdering lose something of their flavour with the use of new kitchen gadgets. Idli batter ground in a stone grinder in the old-fashioned way is matchless in taste. Toasted and fried spices take on a different flavour when ground in the new food processors as the heat produced by the new equipment changes the fine nuances of the spices ground.

If the aroma of roasting coffee seeds on a coal fire in the backyard made one nostalgic for another time, a more leisurely time, those times have come to an end because many other fundamental changes have occurred in Indian society, from the modular kitchen to the lack of domestic help.

Maybe once there was time enough and more for long conversations with friends and relatives over Madras 'degree' coffee, the thick decoction of freshly roasted, powdered and filtered coffee. Maybe once there was time enough and more for vegetables and lentils to cook gently over a wood fire, but we now realize that this nostalgia may come from not taking into account the many reasons why these changes have occurred.

The Growth of 'Hotels'

As part of these changes in society, we find that Indians who rarely ate outside except at weddings or in friends' homes are now to be seen 'trying out' the enormous array of cafés and restaurants that have changed the landscape of our cities. From 1800 onwards, these orthodoxies started to slacken to some extent.

Some of the first cafes that sprang up all over the South in the 1920s were called Brahmin Coffee Hotels that were mostly run by Brahmin families. These catered largely to a vegetarian clientele taking into account the orthodox requirements of their customers. The food in these 'tiffin rooms' was completely vegetarian and cooked without onion and garlic. 'Hotel' or 'café' was also the favoured rubric of the later restaurants ('hotel' in south India often means just restaurant and not necessarily sleeping facilities, although both terms now exist in parallel). Many of the most famous hotels were in George Town where many government offices and the law courts were situated.

Ramakrishna Lunch Home was a pioneer. Komala Vilas and Ambi's Café followed soon after. Rāyar's Hotel held sway in Mylapore and continues to do so until now. Modern Café opened in 1934 and was the flagbearer of the Udupi chain. It was this same hotel that brought in the unique Indian concept of the 'family room', or rooms available upstairs in privacy and comfort for families and the upper classes, while the hoi polloi ate on the ground floor in an open area. The two areas were humorously referred to as the House of Lords and the House of Commons! Modern Café also initiated moonlight dinners in order to popularize the restaurant and its cuisine. Every month on the day of the full moon, an eminent speaker would address an invited audience. This would be followed by a music recital, and then the guests were treated to a special dinner with soups and cutlets, a menu borrowed from the British but strictly vegetarian!

These 'hotels' that specialized in Udupi cuisine also introduced the murugal dosai (crispy dosai) to south Indian homes, which until then had only prepared kal dosai (soft dosai) at home. Another of their innovations is the immensely popular masala dosai, a dosai with the spicy filling of potato and onion. This in turn inspired the Mysore masala dosai which augmented the original filling with peas and tomatoes. Recent additions include cheese fillings, fruit fillings, and spicy options.

With the advent of the 1990s and its foreign clientele, Chennai saw a proliferation of restaurants serving Korean, Japanese, Thai, Malaysian, Mexican, Mediterranean and especially Italian cuisine. It was no longer the 5-star restaurants alone that dabbled in exotic cuisines. 'Multi-cuisine' has become the order of the day. Even ordinary restaurants sport the 'multi-cuisine' brand, offering Udupi, Tandoori, Mughlai, Italian, Chinese, all under one roof.

The luxury hotels, in their turn, have brought in other influences. With their emphasis on appearance, they offer food that is coloured and glazed and glamourized for the eye. Fusion food, some of which attempt to pair incompatbile elements like sandesh with wasabi dressing, green chilli with ice cream, or gulab jamun with wafers are sought after, while small courses and small portions are the order of the day. Nouvelle cuisine has reached Indian shores.

The trendsetters display this same love for the exceptional in the matter of wedding feasts. Street food carts and regional menus from Gujarat, Bengal or Lucknow or Hyderabad are considered passé. Italian, Chinese and even Mongolian food is served up at Indian weddings today and some families even fly in foreign chefs along with their entourage of assistants.

All these international cuisines have now found their way into Indian homes. Increasingly, it is these foreign dishes that are popular, and which are no longer confined to being tasted in restaurants. A niece, for her birthday dinner, cooked Italian pasta, Thai salad, and a lemon cake at home!

Whither Food?

All these changes of lifestyles, restaurant culture, and urban attitudes suggest that Indian culinary traditions are in profound transition along with the rest of Indian society. From being food-centered and community-oriented during traditional eras and even all the way till the departure of the British, the sociological changes that India is undergoing has led to individualistic attitudes to food and a simplified lifestyle that cannot accommodate too much fuss or time spent around the pursuit of traditional foods and recipes.

And for many modern Indian women, education, career, supporting the family business, and various forms of self-improvement seem more appealing than managing the kitchen.

Will India go the way of many countries in the West, more specifically the US where fast food, obesity, and poor eating habits dominate? Some studies tell us that Indians are healthier and living longer but are also subject to greater ill health with the spread of diabetes, heart disease and hypertension. Some of this is certainly on the increase because of the greater consumption of high-calorie, low-nutrient foods.

However, there are potentially optimistic scenarios as well. Will India rediscover and retain its culinary pride in the way that some parts of Europe continue to do, where 'slow food', family meals, and enlightened conversation around the dining table are indicative of the quality of life that cannot be compromised?

The point is to fuse tradition with innovation, and connect communal tastes and individual tastes and preferences. Under such circumstances, we do not have to look at changes in eating habits or cuisine as a narrative of loss or decline. Rather, the new arises in the place of the old, maintaining strong ties to it, creating something that is fresh but still draws from tradition. As the Hindu scriptures have averred in multiple ways, the gift of food is the greatest gift of all, something that fuses matter and meaning into one interconnected process.

GREEN PAPAYA SALAD

I was introduced to the Thai green papaya salad in Bangkok when I visited the chief of the Radhasaomi group there, a venerated guru with over a thousand disciples. The guru's wife personally supervised the making of this salad. I am yet to taste a more delicious version.

Makes: 4 servings
Serving size: 100 gms
Calories per serving: 68

INGREDIENTS

Green papaya 120 gm
Runner or French beans 3–4
Tomato (medium) 1
Fresh red or green chillies 3
Roasted peanuts 1 tbsp
Lime juice 2 tbsp
Light soy sauce 3 tbsp
Sugar 1 tsp

METHOD

1. Peel and grate papaya into fine, long shreds.
2. Trim beans and cut into 1-inch pieces.
3. Chop tomato and pound slightly in a mortar.
4. Pound chillies and roasted peanuts coarsely in a mortar. Stir occasionally while pounding to ensure that mixture does not get sticky.
5. Add shredded papaya, pound lightly and mix well.
6. Add pounded tomato and pound again.
7. Add beans and bruise lightly.
8. Stir in lime juice, soy sauce and sugar.
9. Serve in an attractive way.

CUCUMBER SLICES WITH WASABI

Makes: 4 servings
Serving size: 100 gms
Calories per serving: 22

INGREDIENTS

Cucumber 1
Wasabi powder 1
Salt ¼ tsp
Water ½ tsp

METHOD

1. Slice cucumber.
2. Mix a pinch of wasabi with water and salt.
3. Dot wasabi mixture on cucumber slices.

GREEN SOUP WITH YUBA SLIVERS

Makes: 4 servings
Serving size: 100 gms
Calories per serving: 117

INGREDIENTS

Yuba sheets 1 cup
Finely chopped French beans 2 cups
Pālak 4–5 leaves
Chopped green bell pepper 1 cup
Chopped celery ¼ cup
Broccoli florets 2 tbsp
Water 4 cups
Ginger ½-inch piece
Salt ½ tsp
Black pepper powder 1 pinch
Soy sauce 1 tsp
Shredded ginger ½ tsp
Black sesame oil 3 drops
Lime juice 2–3 drops

METHOD

1. Sprinkle some water over the yuba sheets to soften them. Roll sheets into cylinders. Slice into ½-inch rings.
2. Parboil each vegetable separately in 4 cups of water. Drain vegetables and set aside. Reserve the stock.
3. Grind parboiled vegetables coarsely in a grinder and press through a strainer into a bowl.
4. Heat a vessel and strain in the reserved vegetable stock. Bring to a boil. Remove from heat.
5. Add salt and pepper.
6. Sprinkle soy sauce, ginger, black sesame oil and 1 tbsp of water on the yuba rolls.
7. Steam yuba for about a minute.
8. Put 4–5 yuba rolls in a soup bowl and pour the hot vegetable stock over it.
9. Serve immediately with a drop of lime juice.

Note: When soy milk is boiled, a thin sheet is formed on top. This is skimmed off and dried into paper-thin circular sheets called yuba sheets or tofu skin.

GRATED TOFU SOUP

Makes: 3 servings
Serving size: 100 gms
Calories per serving: 12

INGREDIENTS

Thai chutney
Coriander powder ¼ tsp
Lemon grass, inner tender portion ¼ tsp
Lemon zest 1 pinch
Tender kaffir leaf 1
Red chilli powder 1 pinch
Thai ginger ¼ tsp

Stock
Green chilli 1
Lemon grass stalk 6-inch piece
Vinegar 1 tbsp
Salt to taste
Tomatoes (medium) 2, peeled and juiced
Water 5 cups

Soup
Chinese cabbage, leaf and ribs ½ cup, cut fine
Carrot 1 tbsp, cut fine
Tiny cauliflower or broccoli florets 2 tbsp
Silken tofu 3 tbsp, diced
Cornflour 1½ tsp
Water 1 tsp
Kaffir leaves 4
Lime juice, a few drops (optional)

METHOD

1. Grind all chutney ingredients to a fine consistency.
2. Combine all ingredients for stock with chutney and 5 cups of water in a wok over high heat. Boil for about 10 minutes. Remove, strain stock and set aside.
3. Blanch Chinese cabbage, carrot and cauliflower or broccoli (see page xxxiii) and set aside.
4. Place strained stock over high heat and bring to a boil. Add vegetables and tofu and continue to boil for 4–5 minutes.
5. Mix cornflour with 1 tsp of water. Lower heat and add to pan. Stir, till well blended. Simmer over medium heat, till it starts boiling. Remove from heat.
6. Add kaffir leaves and cover pan for about 5 minutes.
7. Stir in lime juice (if you wish) and serve hot.

BEPPE BELLINI, INSPIRED CHEF

Great cooks are akin to musicians. Like inspired public performers, they add notes, sprinkle divine variations and wave magic wands that transform the most ordinary dish into royalty.

So, I must remember my good friend Signor Beppe Bellini, an art and antiques expert and a connoisseur of fine dining who lived in Florence. He researched deeply into ancient recipes from the Medici library and was himself an extraordinary cook. Beppe was cherished by the community and was often called upon to cook for important public dinners where he would present the menus of the Medicis.

Beppe Bellini introduced me to several delicious Italian dishes. His minestrone soup was unparalleled. He made a radiccio dish where the tender whole plant was grilled and dipped in virgin olive oil. He also showed me a delightful dish—batter-fried whole olives. And his strawberry puddings were divine. Each of his preparations enchanted with its special Tuscan nuances.

Beppe asked me once if we had an Indian pasta dish. I said 'yes' and transformed the traditional dal dhokli of Gujarat, which is somewhat akin to the Tamilian paruppu rasam, into a soup.

Beppe was a frequent visitor to India and he always made it a point to visit Chennai. We even made nebulous plans to write a cookbook together, but it was not to be.

DAL DHOKLI SOUP Indian Pasta Minestrone

Makes: 4 servings
Serving size: 100 gms
Calories per serving: 64

INGREDIENTS

Dal

Tomatoes (medium) 2
Red gram dal/Tuvar dal 1 cup
Water 4 cups + 1½ cups
Tamarind juice 1 tbsp (see page xxxv)
Grated jaggery ½ tsp
Shelled, cooked green peas 1 tbsp
Finely shredded cabbage ½ tbsp
Finely shredded carrots ½ tbsp
Roasted peanuts ½ tbsp
Chopped coriander leaves with stems 1 tbsp
Lime juice ½ tbsp
Ghee 1 tbsp (if required)

Seasoning

Oil 1 tsp
Mustard seeds ½ tsp
Jeera/Cumin seeds ¼ tsp
Asafoetida powder 1 pinch
Rasam powder ¾ tbsp (see page 309)
Cloves 3
Dried red chillies with stem 2
Green chillies 2, each slit into 2 pieces
Ginger 1-inch piece, sliced into a fine julienne

Dhokli

Wholewheat flour ½ cup + extra for rolling
Cumin seeds or ajwain 1 pinch
Turmeric powder 2 pinches
Oil ¾ tbsp

METHOD

1. Remove and discard seeds from tomatoes. Cut tomato into long, thin strips.
2. Wash tuvar dal and pressure-cook with 4 cups of water for 5 minutes after the cooker reaches full pressure. When cool, churn with a beater with 1½ cups of water. Strain and set aside.
3. Heat oil in a vānali/wok. Splutter mustard seeds over medium heat. Add remaining seasoning and fry for about a minute.
4. Stir in tamarind juice and simmer for about 5 minutes.
5. Add reserved dal water and jaggery. Stir well and simmer for 2–3 minutes.
6. Add vegetables and peanuts to soup and transfer to a deep vessel.
7. Combine all ingredients for dhokli and make soft dough. Knead. Divide dough into 20 equal portions.
8. Roll each portion of dough into a 2-inch thick chappati. This is dhokli.
9. Place vessel with soup over high heat. Bring to a boil and reduce heat to medium.
10. Drop dhokli one by one gently into the boiling soup and stir to separate them so that they do not stick to each other.
11. Cook for about 8 minutes.
12. Add coriander leaves, reserving some for garnishing, and lime juice.
13. Taste to see if it is too spicy. Add 1 tbsp of good ghee if it is too spicy.
14. Serve soup in individual bowls, ladling out all the ingredients equally for each.
15. Garnish with reserved coriander leaves and serve hot.

KALI CONGEE DOSAI

Here is a case of orthodoxy making inroads into modernity! Āppam was invented to replace bread during colonial times, by adding toddy to raise the dough. The orthodox replaced this with kali congee (gooey rice dough) and fermented it overnight.

Makes: 10 servings
Serving size: 100 gms
Calories per serving: 221

INGREDIENTS

Raw rice 1 cup
Black gram dal/Urad dal 10 tsp
Water ⅓ cup + ¼ cup
Ghee ½ tsp
Cooking oil to wipe griddle 1 tsp
Salt to taste
Water to mix with the dough

METHOD

1. Soak both rice and dal together for 2 hours.
2. Drain and grind to a fine paste with ⅓ cup water.
3. Mix this 1 tbsp of dough with ¼ cup water, place on fire and make a congee. Cool.
4. Mix congee with the rest of the dough and salt, and keep overnight.
5. The next day, add ¼ cup water to the dough. Mix well.
6. Heat griddle over medium heat, wipe with oil and spread dough to 5-inch size, then cover with lid. After 2 minutes, remove and spread 1 tsp ghee all around. Keep for 30 seconds. Do not turn over. Remove.
7. Make the rest of the dough in the same way.

PASTA UPPUMA

Makes: 4 servings
Serving size: 100 gms
Calories per serving: 276

INGREDIENTS

Pasta 200 gm
Salt 1 tsp. Water for boiling

Seasoning
Oil 3 tbsp. Mustard seeds 1 tsp
Black gram dal/Urad dal 1 tsp
Dried red chillies 2
Green chillies 2, chopped fine
Ginger, ¼-inch piece, crushed
Asafoetida powder ½ tsp
Curry leaves 1 sprig

METHOD

1. Cook pasta in plenty of boiling salted water, till al dente.
2. Heat oil in a vānali/wok. Splutter mustard seeds over medium heat. Add remaining seasoning and sauté for about a minute.
3. Drain pasta and add to vānali/wok.
4. Stir well, till all the liquid from the pasta is absorbed. Cook over low heat for another minute.
5. Remove from heat and serve.

TOFU-LAYERED VEGETABLES

Makes: 4 servings
Serving size: 100 gms
Calories per serving: 51

INGREDIENTS

Cotton tofu 2
Zucchini 1
Red capsicum 1
Green capsicum 1
Carrot 1
Ginger 2 tsp
Black sesame oil 2 tsp
Soy sauce 1½ tbsp
Water 3 tbsp

METHOD

1. Wash ginger, peel and cut into juliennes.
2. Reserve 1½ tsp of black sesame oil and 1 tsp of soy sauce.
3. Mix 1 tsp of ginger, remaining black sesame oil, soy sauce and water to make a sauce.
4. Cut zucchini, red capsicum, green capsicum, and carrot into 3-inch long juliennes.
5. Cut tofu into 24 thin slices.
6. Blanch all vegetables.
7. Heat 1 tsp of sesame oil in pan. Add 1 tsp of chopped ginger and blanched vegetables. Sauté for a minute. Remove from heat.
8. Add 1 tsp of soy sauce and 3–4 drops of black sesame oil.
9. Take a slice of tofu in a plate. Place a layer of cooked vegetable mixture on top. Sprinkle prepared sauce. Repeat for 5–6 layers. Add sauce to the top layer.
10. Prepare 4 more sets of layered tofu and vegetables.
11. Place layered tofu on a plate and steam-cook in a steamer for 2 minutes.
12. Remove from steamer. Sprinkle prepared sauce on tofu layers and serve hot.

ROSE PETAL PĀYASAM

Makes: 6 servings
Serving size: 100 gms
Calories per serving: 263

INGREDIENTS

Rose petals 50 gm
Milk 2 litres
Sugar 250 gm
Cardamoms 6–8, powdered

METHOD

1. Pluck rose petals and chop them finely, reserving a few petals whole for decoration.
2. Boil milk in a large pan over high heat. Lower heat to medium and simmer, stirring periodically, till it is reduced to a third of its original volume.
3. Add sugar, powdered cardamoms and rose petals.
4. Simmer over medium heat, till mixture thickens further.
5. Remove from heat, cool and refrigerate.
6. Serve cold, sprinkled with reserved rose petals.

SPINACH AL MIGNON

Makes: 4–5 servings
Serving size: 100 gms
Calories per serving: 286

INGREDIENTS

Spinach
Spinach 450 gm
Grated Parmesan cheese 1 cup
Butter 1 tsp + extra for greasing
Breadcrumbs 1 cup

Béchamel sauce
Butter 2 tbsp
White flour 1½ tbsp
Cold milk 1 cup
Salt 1 tsp
Black pepper powder ½ tsp

METHOD

1. Pluck leaves of spinach and discard stems. Wash leaves.
2. Cook spinach over low heat without adding any water, till it wilts. Set aside.
3. Melt butter for sauce in a pan over low heat.
4. Add flour and blend for 3–5 minutes, without letting it brown. (This is called a roux.)
5. When it starts to sizzle, remove pan from heat and allow it to cool slightly. Add milk. Stir vigorously, till sauce is smooth and silky.
6. Return pan to medium heat and stir continuously, till it thickens.
7. Add salt, pepper, spinach and cheese.
8. Lightly grease a shallow baking dish with butter. Dust some of the breadcrumbs over the base.
9. Pour in spinach. Spread with a spatula. It should be about ½-inch thick.
10. Sprinkle with remaining breadcrumbs. Lightly score the surface with a knife to form squares. Dot with butter.
11. Bake in an oven preheated to 190°C/275°F, till the surface is golden brown.

GREEN CHILLI WITH CHEESE AND OLIVE STUFFING

Makes: 4–6 servings
Serving size: 100 gms
Calories per serving: 117

INGREDIENTS

Long green chillies 12
Feta cheese 5 tbsp
Pitted olive chopped 2 tbsp
Chopped green chilli 1 tsp
Salt ½ tsp
Olive oil 2 tbsp

METHOD

1. Slit the green chillies without splitting them into two and remove the seeds.
2. Blanch chillies.
3. Mix feta cheese, olive, chopped green chillies and salt together.
4. Stuff chillies with this mixture.
5. After stuffing, sauté the chillies with olive oil in a vānali/wok, turning them a few times.
6. Remove from heat and serve.

KAHWA TEA

Makes: 4 servings
Serving size: 100 ml
Calories per serving: 62

INGREDIENTS

Water 4 cups
Cardamom 2
Cinnamon powder 1 pinch
Kahwa tea leaves ½ tsp
Almonds 3–4, peeled and finely slivered
Saffron 6-8 strands
Sugar to taste

METHOD

1. Bring 4 cups of water to a boil in a pan with cardamoms and cinnamon powder.
2. Lightly crush the kahwa leaves and add to pan when water starts to boil.
3. Let it boil till water turns golden.
4. Place slivered almonds and 2 saffron strands in each teacup.
5. Pour in hot kahwa.
6. Serve and allow each person to add sugar to taste.

Note: Kahwa tea leaves are fresh tea leaves that are wilted and rolled. They are available in speciality tea shops.

ARABIC COFFEE

Makes: 4–6 servings
Serving size: 100 ml
Calories per serving: 70

INGREDIENTS

Water 3 cups
South Indian strong filter coffee 1½ tbsp
Cardamoms 3
Rose water 1½–2 tbsp
Saffron 10 strands
Sugar to taste

METHOD

1. Powder cardamoms finely.
2. Boil 3 cups of water.
3. When water is boiling, remove from heat and add strong filter coffee. Stir.
4. Add powdered cardamoms. Stir.
5. Add rose water. Stir and transfer to a warm coffee pot.
6. Add the saffron strands into the coffee pot and serve.

COFFEE–NECTAR OF THE GODS

The title of this piece will bring on an appreciative nod of acknowledgement from south Indians, so dear is coffee to them. While British colonials introduced the plant for cultivation in India, they were tea drinkers and had no feeling for this bitter brew.

In the South, the earlier morning drink, milk kanji mixed with jaggery with a dash of cardamom, was slowly replaced by coffee with the same accompaniments of jaggery (known as karupatti coffee) and cardamom. The nature of coffee brewing changed slightly with time. Sugar began to replace jaggery and the strength of the coffee decoction extracted from the roasted beans became the benchmark for good coffee. The word 'degree' as in degrees marked on a thermometer came to be associated with 'best', 'excellent', 'first', etc. When used with coffee—first-degree coffee became over time 'degree' coffee, to mean unsurpassed.

The original coffee filters made of brass and coated with tin came in all sizes. From the smallest 4-ounce filter the size extended to 50-person or 100-person filters. No south Indian home was without a coffee filter. Each home had its own preference for the type and quality of the coffee beans and the strength of the first 'degree' coffee.

Serving good coffee at weddings was as important as bridal jewellery! Many a wedding had ground to a halt because the uncle of the groom had not been served coffee of the right strength!

In every home, the first cup of coffee was the most important and went with the morning newspaper. To this day, that first coffee does not taste the same for many without the newspaper in hand. It is a common belief down south that it is this golden brew that makes the south Indian brain tick!

This coffee song is from the end of the nineteenth century. A man returns home tired from work and asks his wife for a cup of hot coffee. The wife, like most of the women of that time, was orthodox and conscious of home remedies, and suggests some alternatives and the man bluntly refuses all of them, wanting only the coffee.

Husband: 'Talaiya valikudu talaiya valikudu ta oru tumbler coffee.'
Wife: 'Adhu vendam. Moolaiyile pudu panaiyile mondu kudipadu oru lotta
Husband: 'Adhu vendam.'
Wife: 'Tayirudan neerum, kadaindu kudippadu oru lotta.'
Husband: 'Adhu vendam.'
Wife: 'Gama gama enru vasanai veesum cocoa umakku oru lotta.'
Husband: 'Chee chee adhu vendam.'
Wife: 'Kasindidum coffee kaduttidum coffee kudiyai kedutthidum coffee aduvva vendum.'
Husband: 'Hahaha adhudan vendum adhudan vendum adhudan vendum ...'

This translates to the following:

> Husband: My head is splitting/Coffee please!/ The ache is blinding/ Put me at ease!
> Wife: Drink some water; drink a lot/ Drawn from the new water pot.
> Husband: Not that rot!
> Wife: Now, drink it away./Some curds with whey.
> Husband: Not that rot!
> Wife: Fragrant cocoa, piping hot!/ Surely, that will hit the spot?
> Husband: Hot chocolate? Oh no, not that rot!/ What I want is a coffeepot!
> Wife: Coffee of dregs? Coffee that's bitter?/That evil drink that drowns its better?/Surely you don't need that!
> Husband: No, no, that is what I want!/ That is what I want!/If that is indeed what you've got/I am sure that it will hit the spot!

Therefore the coffee wins!

To make 'degree' coffee

Take 3 tablespoons of coffee in a 4-ounce filter. Tamp it lightly and add 2 ounces of boiling water to it. Put back water to boil when 2 ounces have been filtered, then add another 3 ounces of water. This thick brew is first-degree coffee and beloved of all serious coffee drinkers in the South!

SOUTH INDIAN COFFEE

Makes: 4–6 cups
Serving size: 180 ml
Calories per serving: 127

INGREDIENTS

Water 3 cups
South Indian strong filter coffee 1½ tbsp
Cardamoms 4
Rose water 1½-2 tbsp
Saffron 10 strands
Sugar to taste

METHOD

1. Powder cardamoms finely.
2. Boil 3 cups of water.
3. When water is boiling, remove it from the heat and add strong filter coffee. Stir.
4. Add powdered cardamoms. Stir.
5. Add rose water. Stir and transfer to a warm coffee pot.
6. Serve. Offer sugar separately.

MISCELLANEOUS COOKING TIPS

Frying

- Heat the oil well before adding seasoning or vegetables.
- Fry seasoning ingredients until they change colour to get their full flavour.
- If spices stick to the pan, it shows that the quantity of oil included is insufficient.
- While making potato patties or tikki, ensure that the potatoes are boiled well in advance and cooled before you use them. It would be better if they are refrigerated for a while. This helps the starch in the potatoes to settle down and they do not become gooey.
- Puri can be rolled and placed between well-rinsed wet muslin cloth at least an hour ahead of frying and serving.

Making Kūtu/Gravies

- Fry ground spices over low to medium heat to retain colour and flavour.
- A little plain sugar or caramelized sugar added to the gravy imparts a special flavour.
- To attain a good colour, always use ripe red tomatoes.
- Good variety chillies and chilli powder also impart colour to the gravy. As far as possible, use long red chillies. Dry in the sun for a few days and powder coarsely at home. A coarse powder provides a better flavour to gravies and pickles.
- If the gravy is too salty, it can be corrected by cutting and adding a potato to it. Cook for a while and remove and discard the potato.
- Always add hot water to a gravy to enhance the flavour.

Miscellaneous Tips

- If you forget to soak pulses overnight, just soak them in boiling water for about an hour before cooking.
- Use leftover dal water to make rasam or sambar.
- Whenever curd is added to a masala, it should be beaten well and added gradually.
- While boiling milk, add a little water to the pan before pouring in the milk. This prevents the milk from sticking to the bottom (you can also leave a spoon in the pan while boiling milk over low heat, to prevent it burning).
- Always use heavy-bottomed pans to make desserts to prevent milk from burning.
- Soak overripe tomatoes in salted water for about 8 hours. They will turn firm and fresh.

Vegetables and Fruits

- Wash vegetables before peeling or cutting to preserve water-soluble vitamins.
- Peel vegetables as thinly as possible to preserve minerals and vitamins.
- Soak potatoes, brinjals and raw plantain after cutting, to avoid discolouration.

- If you boil vegetables in water, do not discard the water, use it to make gravies.
- Keep coriander leaves in a muslin (cheese) cloth bag or in a brown paper bag in the refrigerator. They will remain fresh for a longer time.
- Remove the stems of green chillies while storing them as they stay fresh for a longer time.
- Use a sharp knife and a wooden chopping board to cut vegetables.
- Remove the outer leaves and husks from corncobs.
- Wrap fruits and vegetables in newspaper before refrigerating to keep them fresh for longer.

For Measures and Temperature

- This book has metric cup and spoon measurements.
- All spoon measurements are level unless mentioned otherwise.
- Time given for cooking is an approximate guide. At times, preparation and cooking time differ with the techniques used, quality of grain, season and water of the place one lives in.
- Serving sizes are also approximate. Quantity will vary according to other dishes served.
- Learn to estimate small measurements to save time.

KITCHEN HYGIENE

Kitchen Upkeep

- Proper lighting and cross-ventilation are very important in a kitchen.
- Work area must be kept neat, clean and orderly.

Work Methods in the Kitchen

- Wash hands before handling ingredients and utensils. Nails should be kept clean. Keep a towel for wiping hands near you.
- Keep all provisions and equipment required for the recipe handy before starting to cook.
- At all times, food should be covered, especially on counters and in the refrigerator. Place fruits under a net in order to avoid flies.
- For uniform results, use accurate weighing and measuring cups and spoons.
- Always use heavy-bottomed pans for cooking.
- Plastic or melamine articles must be kept away from fire.
- Buy knives that are sturdy with very sharp edges.
- Keep a first-aid box with burnol and band-aids handy.

Cleanliness of the Kitchen

- Clean shelves and kitchen cupboards frequently. Wipe containers as you return them to the shelves.
- Sprinkle flour on oil spills. This will help to clean the spill faster.
- Always rinse utensils, chopping board and other surfaces with hot water (preferably) before use.
- For burnt utensils, make a paste of baking soda and water. Leave it on the burnt portion for an hour. Rub and wash off.
- To quick-dry metal strainers and sieves, place them in a warm oven for 2 minutes. Remove them with an oven mitt. It also clears the mesh of particles.
- To prevent odours and mildew in the refrigerator, wipe the inside with vinegar.
- Charcoal keeps food odours out of the fridge.
- Outside footwear should not be worn in the kitchen.

GLOSSARY

Spices

English	Tamil	Hindi	Botanical
Aniseed/Anise	Sombu	Saunf	pimpinella anisum
Asafoetida	Perunkāyam	Hing	ferula asafoetida
Black Cumin Seeds	Karunjeerakam	Shajeera	lagacia cuminoids
Cardamom	Elakkai	Elaichi	elettaria cardamomum
Carum copticum	Omam	Ajwain	trachyspermum ammi
Chinese pepper	Timru	Timru	zanthoxylum simulans syn z.
Cinnamon	Ilavanga pattai	Dālchini	cinnamomum zeylanicum
Cinnamon leaf	Ilavanga Pattai Mara Ilai/ Brinji Ilai	Tej patta	cinnamomum zeylanicum
Cloves	Krāmbu/Lavangam	Lavang	caruphyllus aromaticus
Coconut	Tengāi	Nariyal	cocos nucifera
Copra	Copparai	Sukha nariyal	cocos nucifera
Coriander seeds	Kottumalli vidai	Dhania	coriandrum sativum
Cumin seeds	Jeerakam	Jeera	cuminum cyminum
Dry ginger	Sukku	Sonth	zingiber officinale
Edible camphor (highly refined)	Pacchai karpuram	Kapur	cinnamomum camphora
Fennel seeds	Perunjeerakam	Bada saunf	foeniculum vulgare
Fenugreek seeds	Mentiyam/Ventiyam	Methi	trigonella foenum-graecum
Garcinia Indica	Kokum	Kokum	garcinia indica
Ginger	Inji	Adrak	zingiber officinale
Gourd, dried and powdered, available in desert regions in India	Sukkān kāi	Kachri powder	cucurbita species
Indian caper	Maratti moggu	Pamar/Chakunda	1. cassia tora or 2. coiba bombaxya
Long pepper	Arisi tippili	Pipli	piper longinum
Mace	Jātipatri	Jāvithri	myristica fragrans
Mango powder	Māngāi Podi	Amchur	mangifera indica linn
Mustard seeds	Kadugu	Rai/Sarson	brassica juncea
Nigella	Kalonji	Kalonji	nigella sativa
Nutmeg	Jatikai	Jaiphal	myristica fragrans
Pepper	Milagu	Kalimirch	piper nigrum
Poppy seeds	Khus khusa	Khus khus	papaver somniferum
Raisins seedless	Dry drakshai	Kishmish	vitis vinifera
Red chilli	Milakai vatral	Lal mirch	capsicum annum l.

English	Tamil	Hindi	Botanical
Saffron	Kumkumappū	Kesar	crocus sativus linn.
Salt	Uppu	Namak	
Salt—Black	Black salt	Kala namak	
Sesame seeds	Ellu	Til	sesamum indicum
Turmeric	Manjal	Haldi	curcuma longa

Cereals/Pulses

English	Tamil	Hindi	Botanical
Bengal gram dal (split)	Kadalai paruppu	Chana Dal	cicer aritinum
Bengal gram red whole	Kondai kadalai	Lal Chana	cicer arietinum l.
Bengal gram—Toasted	Pottukadalai	Bunna hua chana dal	cicer arietinum
Bengal gram white whole	Kabuli Chana	Kabuli Chana	cicer aritinum l.
Black-eyed beans	Tattam Payaru (both black & red)	Lobia/Chowlai	vigna aconitifolia catjung
Black gram dal	Uluttam paruppu	Urad Dal Dhuli	phasleolus mungo
Dolichos	Mochai	Sém	dolichos lablab
Green gram dal	Payattam paruppu	Mung Dal	phasleolus aureus
Horse gram	Kollu	Kulti	dolicas biflores
Moth beans	Kalpayaru	Moth	phaseolus trilobatus
Red beans	Rajma	Rajma	phaseolus vulgaris
Red gram dal	Tuvaram paruppu	Tuvar Dal	cajanus cajan
Coracana	Rāgi	Rāgi	eleusine coracana
Corn flour	Chola māvu	Makki ka atta	zea mays
Bengal gram flour	Kadalai māvu	Besan	cicer arietinum
Rice	Arisi	Chaval	oryza sativa
Rice—Parboiled	Puḷungal arisi	Sela chaval	
Rice—Raw	Pachai arisi	Kacha chaval	
Rice—Black (Burma rice)	Puttarisi		
Rice flakes /Beaten rice	Aval	Poha	
Rice flour	Arisi āvu	Chaval ka atta	
Sago	Javvarisi	Sabudana	manihot esculenta crantz syn. utilissima
Semolina	Ravā	Sooji	durum wheat
Vermicelli	Semia	Seviyan	
Wheat–broken	Bulgur wheat	Dalia	triticum spp.
Wheat flour	Godumai māvu	Gehun ka atta	
White flour	Maida māvu	Maida	

Oil

English	Tamil	Hindi	Botanical
Castor oil	Vilakku ennai	Erandi ka tel	ricinus communis
Coconut oil	Tengāi ennai	Nariyal ka tel	cocos nucifera
Mustard oil	Kadugu ennai	Sarson ka tel	brassica juncea
Sesame oil	Nalla ennai	Til ka tel	sesamum indicum

Nuts

English	Tamil	Hindi	Botanical
Almonds	Badam	Badam	amygdalus communis.
Cashewnuts	Muntiri paruppu	Kaju	anacardium occidentale
Groundnuts /Peanuts	Ver kadalai	Mungfali	arachis hypogea
Pine nuts	Chilkosa	Chilgoja	pinus
Pistachio	Pista	Pista	pistacia vera
Walnut	Akrot	Akrod	juglans regia

Vegetables

English	Tamil	Hindi	Botanical
Amaranth	Mulaikeerai (tender) Thandukeerai (matured)	Chaulai ka Sag	amaranthus gangeticus
Ash gourd	Kalyāna pūshanikāi	Bhopla/Kaddu	cucurbitte benin/ benincasa hispida /casa cerphea
Bitter gourd	Pāvakkāi	Karela	momordica charantia
Black solanum berries	Manatakkali kai		solanum nigrum
Bottle gourd	Suraikai	Doodhi/Lauki	lagenaria siceraria
Brinjal	Katrikāi	Baingan	solanum melongena
Cabbage	Kôsu	Bandh gobi	brassica oleracea capitata
Capsicum	Kuda Milakai	Shimla mirch	capsicum annuum
Carrot	Carrot	Gajar	daucus carota
Cauliflower	Cauliflower	Phool gobi	brassica oleracea botrytis
Citron	Nārtankāi	Baranimbu/Bijaira	citrus jambhiri
Cluster Beans	Kothavaran kai	Gaur ki Phali	cyamopsis tetragonoloba
Colocasia/Taro	Seppankiḷangu /sembu	Arabi	colocasia esculenta
Corn	Cholam	Makka	zea mays
Cucumber	Vellarikāi	Kakdi	cucumis sativus
Custard gourd/Chow-chow	Chow-chow	Chow-chow	sechium edule/cucurbitta dacus

English	Tamil	Hindi	Botanical
Dolichos beans	Avaraikai	Papadi	dolichos lablab
Drumstick	Murungaikai	Saijan ki phal	moringa oleifera
Green Chilli	Pachai milakai	Hari mirchi	capsicum annum l
Green peas	Pattāni	Mattar	pisum sativum
Indian Gooseberry	Nellikai	Amla	emblica officinalis
Indian round gourd	Tinda	Tinda	praecitrullus fistulosus
Ivy Gourd	Kovaikai	Tindli	coccinia indica
Jackfruit—Raw	Palā kāi	Kathhal	artocarpus heterophyllus
Ladies' finger	Vendaikai	Bhindi/Okra	abelmoschus esculentus
Lime	Elumichai palam	Nimbu	citrus aurantifolia
Lotus stem	Tāmarai tandu	Nadru/Kamal kakdi	nelumbo nucifera
Mango—Raw	Māngāi	Kacha aam	mangifera indica
Mango ginger	Māngāi inji	Aam haldi	
Neem flowers	Vèppam pū	Neem phūl	azardica indica
Onion	Venkayam	Pyaz	allium cepa
Plantain—Green (Raw banana)	Vaḷaikai	Kacha kela	musa acuminata
Plantain flower	Vaḷaipū	Kela ka phul	
Plantain stem	Valaitandu	Kela ka tara	
Pointed gourd	Parwal	Parwal	trichosanthes dioica
Potato	Urulai kiḷangu	Ālu	solanum tuberosum
Pumpkin—Red	Parangikāi/Chakkarai pūshani	Kaddu	Cucurbitte p.pepo
Radish	Mullangi	Mooli	raphanus sativus
Ridge gourd	Peerkankāi	Turai	luffa aegyptica
Runner beans/String beans	Payatankai/Karamani	Lobia/Chowlai	vigna aconitifolia
Snake gourd	Pudalankai	Chachindra	trichosanthes cerphea
Solanum forum	Chundaikāi	Bhankatiya	solanum torvum
Sweet Potato	Śarkaraivalli kiḷangu	Shakarkandi	ipomoea batatas
Tomato	Takkāli	Tamatar	lycopersicon esculentum
Yam/Elephant yam	Śenai	Suran/Zamin khand	dioscorea cayenensis

Greens

English	Tamil	Hindi	Botanical
Banana leaf	Vāḷai ilai	Kela ka patta	musa acuminata
Betel leaves	Vetrilai	Pan ka patta	piper betle
Colocasia leaves	Sembu ilai	Arabi ka sag	colocasia esculenta
Coriander leaves	Pachai kothumalli	Hara dhania	coriandrum sativum
Curry leaves	Kariveppilai	Curry patta	murraya koenigii (l.)
Fenugreek leaves	Venthiyakeerai	Methi leaves	trigonella foenum
Jackfruit leaves	Palā ilai	Kathhal leaves	artocarpus heterophyllus
Mint leaves	Pudina ilai	Pudina patta	mentha sativa
Spinach	Pālak	Pālak	spinacia oleracea
Tender stems of amaranth	Keerai tandu		amaranthus gangeticus

Fruits

English	Tamil	Hindi	Botanical
Banana	Vāḷai palam	Kela	musa acuminata
Jackfruit	Palāpaḷam	Kathal	artocarpus heterophyllus
Orange	Kamala orange	Santra	citrus reticulata
Mango	Māmpalam	Aam	mangifera indica
Pineapple	Pineapple	Ananas	ananas sativus
Pomegranate	Mādulai Paḷam	Anar	punica granatum

Miscellaneous

English	Tamil	Hindi	Botanical
Butter	Vennai	Makkhan	
Buttermilk	Móru	Chaas/Matta	
Clarified butter/ Ghee	Nei	Ghee	
Cottage cheese	Pālādai katti	Paneer	
Curd	Tayir	Dahi	
Jaggery	Vellam	Gud	
Milk	Pāl	Doodh	
Pickle	Urukāi	Achar	
Rose water	Pannir	Gulab jal	
Tamarind	Puli	Imli	tamarindus indica

DIACRITICAL MARKS USED IN THIS BOOK

ā—as in ball
e—as in prey
é—as in been
u—as in full
ū—as in boot
ai—as in mail
ś—as in shankar
ḷ—as in Tamil letter 'ழ'

ACKNOWLEDGEMENTS

This book is the work of many hearts and hands. At the outset, I wish to acknowledge the unstinted support that I received from all my children—Sheela, Venu, Malini and Gopal—while writing this book.

My grandchildren, Priyamvada and Lakshmi, were the initial inspiration for me to write down all the recipes that have been part of my kitchen and, which, they said, they had enjoyed for so many years.

This edition of the book is special to me in that my granddaughters, Samiha and Surabhi, spontaneously insisted on wanting to oversee this impression through its publishing. I thank them both.

My interest in cooking can be traced back to my aunt and my mother who sowed the initial seeds in me. I cannot forget my grandfather from whom I learnt the meticulous ways of the kitchen.

Deepest thanks are to my nephew, Srinivas Aravamudan, who supported my venture and offered valuable editing counsel. I would like to thank my niece, Maya Narasimhan, immensely, who worked with me on the book at every stage of its writing and correcting. Her efforts have truly made the impossible possible.

I must remember my good friends, with whom I shared a whole lifetime of friendship, and who were all good cooks and who shared their recipes with me. Thank you, Prem Punja, Radha Panikar and Komu Vaidyanathan. I wish you were here now.

Deep gratitude to H.H. Marthānda Verma, Maharaja of Travancore, who, in spite of his commitments and health, took the trouble of writing out, in his own hand, authentic information about the sacred offerings for the deity at Sri Padmānabhaswamy temple at Thiruvananthapuram.

K.S Balakrishna Rao's contribution has been invaluable. A well-known restaurateur, hailing from the family of pioneer hoteliers from Udupi, he shared with some of the authentic Udupi recipes that were part of his family legacy, besides giving me the background details concerning Udupi *samārādhana* and the list of the offerings at Udupi Sri Krishna temple.

Translating these recipes to reality was no mean task. I cannot forget my cook, Karuppiah, who, day after day, experimented with all the recipes, noting them down carefully, all with a smile on his face and cooked many of the dishes for photography. My thanks to cook Thyagarajan of Madurai, whom I have known for a long time, and who helped me with valuable tips on many recipes. My thanks also to cooks Padmanabhan and Shankar.

I thank my dear friend, Sucharita Reddy, an incredibly gracious hostess whose presentation of food is always a delight. She has supported me in many of my endeavours, and this book is no exception.

Sincere appreciation for my good friends—Manju Jhaver, Pari Sadhwani, Vijaya Shivpuri and Nisha Sood ,Usha Amla, Sangeet Chopra,

Daksha Singh, Uravi Khasliwal, Banashree Baruah and Rahul Krishnan who refined some of the recipes and added nuances to them. Barbara Radice, who gave me encouragement that never ceased.

Kamala Sivasubramaniaman, a great patron of traditional decorative art and crafts—the floral arts, garland-making, kolam designs and pandal designs—helped greatly with the Kongunādu recipes. Sudarshana RamsubramaniaRaja, who represents the quintessence of Rājapālayam hospitality and culture, provided me with recipes from that region. Bhuvaneswari Swayambhunathan, VanithaRamani and Uma Muthukumaraswamy who contributed the Tondaimandalam recipes and to them my heartfelt thanks.

Chef Praveen Anand and Latha Praveen, principal of a catering college in Navi Mumbai, helped with miscellaneous cooking tips. Dr Satyavati Jhaveri, Rachana Group of Women, for her tips on kitchen hygiene. Abha Dalmia and Avantika, for the information on the daily offerings at the Puri Jagannath temple, and the photographs.

I thank S.R. Jagannathan of Srirangam who sent me valuable notes about Srirangam Thatayyan. My gratitude to Sri K.R. Desikan, who patiently provided the requisite botanical names of the ingredients.

Sri Muniratnam Reddy of the ASI procured the details of epigraphic inscriptions of the temples of Tirumala and Tirupati. He travelled tirelessly to get these and the translations of the offerings given to the Lord Venkatanatha in Tirumala. My thanks are also to Sri Channa Reddy of ASI, Hyderabad, Professor K.V. Raman and T.V. Ramanan.

My heartfelt thanks to Dr M. Menaka, associate professor, Department of Clinical Nutrition and Dietetics, Ethiraj College for Women, Chennai, for her meticulous calculations of calorie counts for all the recipes in the book.

The delight I experienced in the simple but effective design will surely be felt by the readers. I have to thank the accomplished designer, Haitenlo Semy, for this. The photographs for this edition have all been shot anew and have been brilliantly composed by Sumanth Kumar and his team.

My thanks to Sreevidya Ravichandran and Sreevidya Chengalvarayan who assisted me in collating the recipes for this edition. My thanks to Sri Jagannathan and Ms Sucharita of Crystal who helped in the early stages of the book. I appreciate the efforts and assistance offered by Mr Jayendhiran, Ms Sharmila and Ms Meenakshi of TVS Educational Society who helped me in many different ways.

This book has been a long-cherished dream but would not have become a reality without Hemu Ramiah who saw the value in the idea behind the book, and my principal thanks go to Rakesh Chander and Hina Khajuria of HarperCollins whose unceasing efforts have given the book its final form and completeness.

ABOUT THE AUTHOR

Prema Srinivasan (1932–2022) grew up in Chennai, in the heart of Mylapore, in the shadow of the gopuram of the Kapaleeswarar Temple. She belonged to an orthodox middle-class Tamil household that believed in simplicity. Food was always an integral part of her life, and growing up, she learned important lessons about it—food as nutrition, food as an indulgence, food as worship and food as medicine. It was in Mylapore that her interest in food, art, music and textiles took root. She continued to expand her knowledge about food post-marriage in Madurai, being part of a home that welcomed people from different cultural backgrounds. Her foreign travels gave her the opportunity to explore how food in India and the world is bound together by common threads of spices, herbs, vegetables and cereals.